DOES   הַעוֹד

DAVID   דָּוִד

STILL PLAY   מְנַגֵּן

BEFORE YOU?   לְפָנֶיךָ?

DOES DAVID STILL PLAY BEFORE YOU?

הַעוֹד
דָּוִד
מְנַגֵּן
לְפָנֶיךָ?

ISRAELI POETRY AND THE BIBLE

שִׁירָה
יִשְׂרְאֵלִית
וְהַתַּנַ"ךְ

David C. Jacobson

Wayne State University Press   Detroit

LIBRARY OF CONGRESS

CATALOGING-IN-PUBLICATION DATA

Jacobson, David C., 1947–

Does David still play before you? : Israeli poetry and

the Bible / David C. Jacobson. p. cm.

Includes bibliographical references and index.

ISBN 0-8143-2623-4 (alk. paper)

1. Israeli poetry—History and criticism. 2. Bible—In

literature. I. Title.

PJ5024.J33 1996

892.4' 1609—dc20

Designer: S. R. Tenebaum

FOR JUDAH, MIRIAM, AND DANIEL

CONTENTS

ACKNOWLEDGMENTS

During the period that I wrote this book I joined the faculty of the Program in Judaic Studies at Brown University. My colleagues in the program have provided a warm, supportive, and intellectually stimulating atmosphere, which contributed greatly to my ability to bring this study to a successful conclusion.

I am grateful to Arnold Band, Warren Bargad, and Max Ticktin, who each read the manuscript and made invaluable suggestions for its improvement. I want to thank in particular my colleague at Brown, David Hirsch, who not only read and commented on the manuscript but also provided much encouragement during the final stages of my writing. I also thank David Hirsch, who, as editor of *Modern Language Studies,* granted me permission to reprint my article "The Holocaust and the Bible in Israeli Poetry" from *Modern Language Studies* 24, no. 4 (1994): 63–77, which appears in revised form as part of chapter 3. I also am grateful to the two anonymous readers who evaluated the manuscript for Wayne State University Press. Both readers considered the manuscript in a careful manner, and I benefited greatly from their detailed critiques as I prepared the final version of the manuscript. Since moving to Providence I have had the opportunity to teach a number of the poems in this study to not only students at Brown but also adult learners in the community. My discussions of these poems in these settings provided me with important insights. Although I do not acknowledge specific insights gained from comments by my professional colleagues or my students, they have played an important role in my formulation of interpretations of poems and in my thinking about the relationship between Israeli poetry and the Bible in general. In addition, Yehudit Kafri, Aryeh Sivan, and Meir Wieseltier made helpful suggestions to improve my translations of their poetry.

I thank Arthur Evans, director of Wayne State University Press, with whom it has been a pleasure to work during the process of acceptance and publication of the book. I also wish to thank Brown University for providing me with a sabbatical leave in Spring 1995, during which I was able to revise the manuscript and prepare it for publication.

I dedicate this book to my children, Judah, Miriam, and Daniel, with much love.

Acknowledgment is made to the following sources for permission to reprint materials for this book:

ACUM, Ltd. for the original Hebrew versions of the poems reprinted in the book. All rights for the original Hebrew versions are reserved by the authors.

HarperCollins Publishers, Inc. for the translations by Benjamin and Barbara Harshav of "The Real Hero of the Sacrifice," "I Want to Confuse the Bible," and "29," by Yehuda Amichai, from Yehuda Amichai, *A Life of Poetry* (New York: HarperCollins, 1994), copyright 1994 by HarperCollins Publishers, Inc. and Yehuda Amichai.

Indiana University Press for the translations by Warren Bargad and Stanley F. Chyet of "My Samsons" and "Jericho" by Haim Gouri; "Testimony," "Another Testimony," and "Autobiography," by Dan Pagis; "Like Sand," by Nathan Zach; and "Like Rachel," by Dalia Ravikovitch, from Warren Bargad and Stanley F. Chyet, eds. and trans., *Israeli Poetry: A Contemporary Anthology* (Bloomington: Indiana University Press, 1986), copyright 1986 by Indiana University Press.

The Institute for the Translation of Hebrew Literature for the translation by Gabriel Levin of "This Idiot Isaac (Late Version)," by

Yitzhak Laor, from *Modern Hebrew Literature* 11 (1993), copyright 1993 by The Institute for the Translation of Hebrew Literature.

The Jewish Publication Society for passages from *Tanakh: A New Translation of the Holy Scriptures According to the Traditional Hebrew Text* (Philadelphia: Jewish Publication Society, 1985), copyright 1985 by The Jewish Publication Society; the translations by Stephen Mitchell of "Written in Pencil in the Sealed Railway-Car" and "Homily," by Dan Pagis, from Dan Pagis, *Points of Departure* (Philadelphia: Jewish Publication Society of America, 1981), copyright 1981 by The Jewish Publication Society of America; and the translation by Grace Shulman of "Eve Knew," by T. Carmi, from T. Carmi, *At the Stone of Losses* (Philadelphia: Jewish Publication Society of America, 1983), copyright 1983 by The Jewish Publication Society of America.

Shirley Kaufman for her translation of "Joshua's Face," by Amir Gilboa, from Howard Schwartz and Anthony Rudolf, eds., *Voices Within the Ark: The Modern Jewish Poets* (New York: Avon, 1980), copyright 1979 by Shirley Kaufman.

Gabriel Levin for his translation of "Sometimes He Longs For," by Nathan Zach, from *The Literary Review* 26, no. 2 (1983), copyright 1983 by Gabriel Levin.

Stephen Mitchell for his translation of "Under Siege," by Amir Gilboa, from *Ariel* 33–34 (1973), copyright 1973 by Stephen Mitchell.

Mosaic Press for the translation by Denis Johnson of "Does David Still Play Before You," by Moshe Dor, from Moshe Dor, *Crossing the River: Selected Poems* (Oakville, Ontario: Mosaic Press, 1989), copyright 1989 by Mosaic Press.

Scribner, a division of Simon and Schuster, Inc., for the translation by Peter Everwine and Shulamit Yasny-Starkman of "When God First Said," by Nathan Zach, from Nathan Zach, *The Static Element: Selected Poems of Nathan Zach* (New York: Atheneum, 1982), copyright 1977, 1982 by Peter Everwine.

The Sheep Meadow Press for the translation by Chana Bloch and Ariel Bloch of "Blood Heifer," by Dalia Ravikovitch from Dalia Ravikovitch, *The Window: New and Selected Poems* (Riverdale-on-Hudson, New York: Sheep Meadow Press, 1989), copyright 1989 by The Sheep Meadow Press.

Sifriat Poalim for the translation by Richard Flantz of "Another Poem on Absalom," by Nathan Yonathan, from Nathan Yonathan,

Stones in the Darkness (Tel Aviv: Sifriat Poalim, 1975), copyright 1975 by Sifriat Poalim.

Aryeh Sivan for his translation of "On the Sex Life of the Man Moses," by Aryeh Sivan, copyright 1995 by Aryeh Sivan.

Three Continents Press for the translation by Barbara Goldberg of "Jericho," by Moshe Dor, from Moshe Dor, *Khamsin: Memoirs and Poetry by a Native Israeli* (Colorado Springs: Three Continents Press, 1994), copyright 1994 by Moshe Dor.

University of California Press for the translations by Ruth Finer Mintz of "Isaac," by Amir Gilboa, and "His Mother," by Haim Gouri, from Ruth Finer Mintz, ed. and trans., *Modern Hebrew Poetry: A Bilingual Anthology* (Berkeley: University of California Press, 1966), copyright 1966 by The Regents of the University of California.

Linda Zisquit for her translation of "Akedah," by Aliza Shenhar, from Howard Schwartz and Anthony Rudolf, eds., *Voices Within the Ark: The Modern Jewish Poets* (New York: Avon, 1980), copyright 1979 by Linda Zisquit.

AUTHOR'S NOTE

The assassination of Israeli Prime Minister Yitzhak Rabin on November 4, 1995 occurred after I completed writing the manuscript of this book. The assassin, Yigal Amir, was associated with religious Jewish Israelis whose opposition to territorial compromise with the Arabs is based on the Bible and its later rabbinic interpretations. Amir assassinated Rabin in the hope of halting the gradual withdrawal of the Israel Defense Forces from the West Bank and Gaza that had begun under the auspices of the Rabin government. A central theme of this book is the critique by Jewish Israeli secular humanists of the assumption of many religious Jewish Israelis that territorial compromise with the Arabs is in violation of biblical teachings. If I had not completed the manuscript before the assassination, I would have referred to it in parts of the book that deal with this theme, particularly in the introduction and in chapters 1, 2, and 5.

Amir's decision to assassinate Rabin was based on an extreme interpretation of his fellow Jewish religious Israelis' ideology. Few of them would ever seriously contemplate such an act. Furthermore,

Amir's claim shortly after the assassination that he received "a heavenly command" to do so (*Ha'arets,* November 5, 1995) and his assertion upon being convicted of the murder of Rabin that he acted "for the God of Israel, the Torah of Israel, the people of Israel and the Land of Israel" (*New York Times,* March 28, 1996) place him very much on the fringe of the religious Jewish population of Israel. This assassination must therefore not be seen as representative of mainstream trends in religious Jewish thinking in Israel. Nevertheless, as I argue in chapter 2 in reference to the massacre of Arab worshipers in the Tomb of the Patriarchs by Baruch Goldstein in 1994, extreme acts of violence in the name of biblical teachings are significant examples of the powerful role of the Bible in developing the discourse in Israel on the Arab-Israeli conflict. Such acts also serve to remind us of the potential danger in allowing the Bible to influence contemporary perceptions of this conflict.

A NOTE ON TRANSLATION AND TRANSLITERATION

English translations of poetry and prose passages cited in this work are by me unless otherwise indicated in the endnotes. Approximately one half of the Hebrew poems analyzed in this book were translated by me, and approximately one half were translated by others. When I was able to locate a translation of a poem that I considered to be a faithful rendering of the original Hebrew text, I chose it as the English translation to be included in the book. In the cases of a poem for which I could not locate a translation and a poem for which I could not locate a translation that, in my opinion, was sufficiently close to the original Hebrew text, I composed my own translation for the book. Readers who know Hebrew will note that my translations tend to be more literal than those of the other translators. It is my hope that this mixture of translation styles will present to those who do not know Hebrew an illuminating view of the original Hebrew texts of the poems.

Translations from the Bible are primarily from *Tanakh: A New Translation of the Holy Scriptures According to the Traditional Hebrew Text* (Philadelphia: Jewish Publication Society, 1985). The transliteration of Hebrew is based on the "general" transliteration style for Hebrew of the *Encyclopaedia Judaica* (Jerusalem: Keter, 1972), 1:90–91, with some modifications. Proper names and other well-known terms are often spelled according to common usage in English, even when this differs from the *Encyclopaedia Judaica* transliteration style.

THE TORAH OF MOSES, NOT THE TORAH OF DAVID | **BIBLICAL ALLUSION POETRY IN ITS CULTURAL CONTEXT**

In December 1994, an argument broke out in the Knesset, the Israeli parliament, between Foreign Minister Shimon Peres and members of Knesset from religious and right-wing parties. It occurred during a parliamentary debate on the decision of Prime Minister Yitzhak Rabin and Peres to accept the Nobel Prize for Peace that year together with the chairman of the Palestine Liberation Organization, Yasser Arafat. Some Israelis were opposed to that decision because they were convinced that Arafat, whose organization had participated so frequently in terrorist attacks against Jewish and Israeli civilian targets in the past, did not deserve the prize. They believed that by joining Arafat in the award ceremony, the leaders of Israel would be endorsing the erroneous decision of the Nobel Prize Committee to award the Peace Prize to a man with Jewish and Israeli blood on his hands. The controversy, however, was not only about Rabin and Peres accepting a prize. It also served as a focal point for those who opposed the recent peace agreement between Israel and the PLO because they either did not want to yield any territory to the Palestinians or they deeply distrusted Arafat's intentions.

In defense of the peace process that his government was pursuing, Peres attacked the biblical basis for his opponents' position. He condemned their appropriation of the aggressive trend in the Bible represented by King David's military conquests. To Knesset Member Shaul Gutman of the right-wing *Moledet* party Peres declared his support for what he saw as the more morally sensitive trend in the Bible represented by Mosaic law:

> Your Judaism is not acceptable to me. Judaism is "for you were strangers in the land of Egypt [Exodus 22:20; 23:9; Leviticus 19:34; Deuteronomy 10:19]." Judaism is for "love your neighbor as yourself [Leviticus 19:18]." What kind of Judaism are you preaching to me? Of hatred, of domination, of racism. This is Judaism? It's not mine. Take it. . . . I recognize the Torah of Moses our teacher and not the Torah of David our patriarch.[1]

Not only did Peres criticize David for excessive militarism; but he also sarcastically referred to David's affair with Bathsheba, which began when the ancient king spied his attractive neighbor bathing on her roof. "I want to tell the great Torah scholar, Mr. Gutman," declared Peres, "that not everything that King David did, on land, on the roofs, appears to me to be Judaism, or finds favor in my eyes."[2] When Knesset Member Rabbi Yosef BaGad of *Moledet* declared that Peres should be ashamed of what he said about King David, Peres retorted, "I am happy to hear that you are also proud of Bathsheba, no?"[3]

At this point right-wing and religious Knesset members reacted strongly to Peres's criticism of King David. They defended the ancient Israelite king's honor, referring to him, for example, as "the sweet singer of Israel" (*neʿim zemirot yisraʾel*), a biblical expression (II Samuel 23:1) that the Jewish tradition has understood to refer to David's poetic abilities as the author of the book of Psalms. *Moledet* and two religious parties, *Mafdal* and *Yahadut Hatorah,* even went so far as to file a motion of no confidence in the government because of Peres's remarks.

The fact that the Israeli Knesset held such a heated debate about a biblical character tells much about the relationship of Israeli culture to the Bible. The central goal of pre-State Zionism had been to return the Jewish people to the glories of its ancient biblical past. The fact that the ancient forebears of the Jews inhabited the Land of

Israel in biblical times had provided Zionism with a moral and political defense for the resettlement of the Land by Jews. Furthermore, the traditional Jewish faith in the ultimate restoration of Zion in the messianic era had provided an inspiring mythic basis for Jews to attempt to solve the political, economic, social, and cultural crises of the late nineteenth and twentieth centuries by establishing a modern nation-state in their ancient homeland. Even after the Zionist movement succeeded in establishing the State of Israel in 1948, Israelis continued to see events of contemporary Israeli history as analogous to those of biblical history.

Those who participated in the parliamentary debate on King David knew what was at stake in this debate; given the persistence of the assumption that contemporary Israeli events are analogous to biblical events, one of the most powerful ways to justify a position taken on a social, cultural, or political issue in Israel has been to draw on the Bible as an authoritative source. To do this effectively, it has been necessary to present a plausible interpretation of the Hebrew Bible that would support one's position. The opposing readings of the biblical accounts of David's life presented in the Knesset debate clearly reflected this relationship between positions on contemporary issues and biblical interpretation. Peres, the "dove," saw David (at least partially) as an aggressive conqueror and adulterer, whose way of life should be rejected by Israelis. His right-wing "hawkish" opponents, in contrast, were not as repulsed as Peres by David's military achievements. For both sides, their reading of the Bible was influenced by their vision of how the contemporary State of Israel should act in the present, while at the same time their reading of the Bible reinforced that vision. Meanwhile, in opposing Peres's references to David the religious members of Knesset, allied with the right-wing "hawks," sought to maintain the traditional Jewish reverence for David and to register their dissent from the tendency of secular Israelis of the entire political spectrum to appropriate biblical imagery to support mundane political positions.[4]

In this book I explore how Israeli poets relate to this central trend in Israeli culture to connect the present with the ancient biblical past. The tendency to connect the present with the ancient past is, of course, not unique to Israeli culture. One of the most widespread expressions of this tendency is the pervasive presence of allusions to the Bible (as well as to other ancient literary classics) in a wide range of modern national literatures throughout the Western world. Milton's "Paradise Lost" and "Samson Agonistes," Thomas Mann's *Joseph and His Brothers,* André Gide's *Saul,* Archibald MacLeish's *JB* are only a few of the many examples throughout the history of Western literature of works drawing substantially on the Hebrew Bible. Even outside the realm of belles lettres the trend to connect the present with the Bible is found in Western culture as a whole. Phyllis Trible cites a number of twentieth-century examples of areas in which "readers understand scripture from the perspective of contemporary issues; or conversely they view present interests in light of the Bible."[5] Her examples include the political and cultural agendas of Marxists, African-Americans, feminists, and homosexuals, as well as the exploration of the Bible in works by the two most influential thinkers in the field of modern psychology: Sigmund Freud's *Moses and Monotheism* and C. G. Jung's *Answer to Job.*

Nevertheless, there is a unique quality to the role of the Bible in Israeli culture and to the ways that Israeli poets make use of the Bible. Not only is Israel's national identity permeated by the sense that it is reconnecting the Jewish people to its biblical past, but Israel is also the country in which most biblical events took place. As Ruth Kartun-Blum puts it, "one cannot escape the feeling that here [in Israel biblical] reality is repeating itself."[6] Israeli literature, Kartun-Blum observes, is "an actual witness to events which are so visibly mimicking ancient historical events and even taking place in the same physical and geographical settings [as those events]."[7]

Furthermore, there is no country in the world where as widespread a familiarity with the Bible may be found. It does a writer no good to allude to a literary text that the readers of the work cannot identify. The Israeli writer can allude to the Bible with the assurance that, because of the central role of the Bible in Israeli culture, in most cases the readers of the work will immediately identify the text alluded to without consulting the Bible, and in the worst case they will not have much difficulty finding the allusion in the Bible. Indeed, we can see how central the Bible is to Israeli consciousness when we realize that Peres's audience in the Knesset was well aware that when he referred to what David did "on land," he meant David's expansion of the territory of ancient Israel by military conquest, and when he referred to what David did "on the roofs," he was alluding to the beginning of the David and Bathsheba story when David first spied

Bathsheba taking a bath on her roof. Furthermore, both sides in the Knesset debate traded barbs rich in biblical allusions with a spontaneous ease that conveyed their conviction that Israel's relationship to its biblical past was of crucial importance to them.

In this exploration of the relationship of Israeli poets to the role of the Bible in their culture I focus on short lyric poems whose "governing technique is allusion," to use Carmela Perri's term.[8] Such poems, to which I refer following Perri's terminology as "biblical allusion poems," must be distinguished from poems that make occasional allusions to the Bible. In comparison to the latter, biblical allusion poems have more to teach us about poetic responses to the trend in Israel to make connections between the present and the ancient past, for in such poems inevitably a central element of the meaning of the poem is the relationship between contemporary Israel and the Bible.

Although many Israeli writers have produced works of fiction and drama, as well as longer poetic works, with sustained biblical allusions, I have chosen to focus on short lyric poems of this nature for two reasons. The relative shortness of the lyric poems provides the opportunity to quote and interpret each poem in its entirety and thereby to cover a larger number of poems and present a more comprehensive picture of the role of the Bible in one genre of Israeli literature. Furthermore, in general I find these shorter lyric poems to be of greater literary value. To my mind, in many cases longer works of poetry, fiction, and drama with sustained biblical allusions give the impression of competing with biblical narrative, even as they often fall short of achieving the aesthetic heights of the original, and therefore they are less effective as works of art. Short lyric biblical allusion poetry does something else: it conveys a concentrated response to the biblical text that can be of impressive aesthetic value and thereby have a powerful effect on readers.

As Israeli poets have explored the relationship of the Bible to issues of contemporary existence, they have drawn on a rich legacy of allusions to the Bible in Hebrew poetry of the late nineteenth and early twentieth centuries. This earlier poetry spanned a period of two generations during which the center of modern Hebrew literature moved from Eastern Europe to the Land of Israel. Poets of the first generation, represented most prominently by Hayyim Nahman Bialik (1873–1934) and Shaul Tchernichowsky (1875–1943), generally established themselves as poets in Europe before emigrating to the Land of Israel. They were either at the end of their life or had already died when the State of Israel was established in 1948. Members of the second generation of poets, including Uri Zvi Greenberg (1894–1981), Avraham Shlonsky (1900–1973), Yonatan Ratosh (1909–1981), Nathan Alterman (1910–1970), and Leah Goldberg (1911–1970), generally began writing poetry in Europe, continued to publish poetry after their emigration to the Land of Israel, and remained active as poets even after the establishment of the State.

I have chosen not to include in this study any poets from these first two generations of twentieth-century Hebrew poets, even though central members of the second generation continued to publish poetry during the first two decades or so after the establishment of the State. Instead, I focus on the third and fourth generations of twentieth-century Hebrew poets, who were born in the 1920s or later and who began their poetic careers at the earliest in the decade or so before the establishment of the State.[9] These third and fourth generations of poets were the first to write most or all of their poetry during the years of the State; they therefore provide a unique perspective on how poets have responded to the central role of the Bible in Israeli cultural discourse since 1948. The ideological context in which the third and fourth generations wrote differed from that of the first and second generations. Poets in the first and second generations wrote primarily during a period when the ideological focus among Jewish intellectuals was on issues of national and cultural revival and Zionist ideologies played a central role in the life of Hebrew writers. Poets in the third and fourth generations, however, wrote for the most part after the Zionist program to establish a Jewish state gradually gave way to the realities of the State; Israeli intellectuals had to adjust their ideologies in accordance with these new realities.

The sheer quantity of Israeli biblical allusion poetry is beyond the scope of a study of any reasonable length. In this study I discuss fifty poems by twenty Israeli poets that were published throughout the period of Israeli statehood, from the 1950s through the early 1990s. The poems provide a wide sample that conveys a comprehensive view of the genre of biblical allusion poetry as it has developed in the history of Israeli literature. The trend of Israeli poets writing biblical allusion poetry persists to this day. Given the continued role of the Bible in cultural discourse in Israel, it is reasonable to assume that in the foreseeable future Israeli writers will continue to publish such poetry. It will therefore be important for scholars to keep monitoring this trend in future years to see what new directions it may take.

From a biographical and historical perspective members of the third generation of twentieth-century Hebrew poets whose works are included in this study may be divided into two groups. In one group, the poets were born in Europe (with the exception of one poet born in America to immigrants from Europe). They came to the Land of Israel either as children, as adolescents, or as young adults. These include Amir Gilboa (1917–1984), who emigrated to Israel from Poland at the age of twenty, and T. Carmi (1925–1994), who emigrated from America at the age of twenty-two. They also include poets who came to the Land of Israel as children when their parents decided to emigrate: Nathan Yonathan (1923–) was born in the Ukraine and emigrated at the age of two; Matti Megged (1923–) was born in Poland and emigrated at the age of three; Yehuda Amichai (1924–) was born in Germany and emigrated at the age of twelve; Anadad Eldan (1924–) was born in Poland and emigrated at the age of six; Nathan Zach (1930–) was born in Germany and emigrated at the age of five. One poet, the Holocaust survivor Dan Pagis (1930–1986), was born in Bukovina, spent his early adolescence in Europe in the Holocaust, and emigrated after the war at the age of seventeen.

The second group of poets in the third generation include Haim Gouri (1923–), Aryeh Sivan (1929–), Moshe Dor (1932–), Yehudit Kafri (1935–), Dalia Ravikovitch (1936–), and Asher Reich (1937–). They are the contemporaries of the first group, but their biographical background is distinguished by the fact that they were born in the Land of Israel. Unlike members of the first group, these poets were born into an emerging Hebrew-speaking culture and held a special status in the eyes of Zionists as the first native-born Jews in the Land of Israel (*tsabbarim,* or sabras, as the term is usually rendered in English), whose birth signified the fulfillment of the Zionist dream in their generation. In addition, with the exception of Carmi, the members of the first group emigrated from areas that were eventually conquered by the Nazis in World War II. In some cases, their close relatives were killed by the Nazis. The members of the second group may have lost distant relatives in the Holocaust, and the Holocaust may have had a great emotional impact on them; but, unlike the members of the first group, the world of their childhood was not destroyed by the Nazis.

The members of both groups of this third generation of poets were old enough in 1948 to remember the period before the establishment of the State of Israel. The older members fought in the War of Independence, while the younger members witnessed the events of 1948 in their early teens. In contrast, the members of the fourth generation of twentieth-century Hebrew poets (all sabras, with one exception) were young children or not yet born when the State was founded. For them the State has not been the fulfillment of a Zionist dream, but rather a fact. The members of this generation include Meir Wieseltier (who was born in Moscow in 1941 and emigrated to Israel in 1949), Aliza Shenhar (1943-), Edna Aphek (1943-), Rachel Chalfi (194?-), Yitzhak Laor (1948-), and Maya Bejerano (1949-).

In terms of the relationship of these poets to the Jewish tradition, they all may be identified as secular Jewish Israelis. Most grew up in secular families. Some received a religious Jewish upbringing, but those who did had ceased to maintain a religious Jewish life style by the time they began publishing poetry: Amir Gilboa was raised in a traditional Eastern European Jewish family, although in his youth he received a secular as well as a traditional Jewish education; Yehuda Amichai's parents were traditionally observant Jews; T. Carmi's father was an Orthodox rabbi, and Carmi studied at Yeshiva University in New York before emigrating to Israel; and Asher Reich grew up in an ultra-Orthodox Jewish family in Jerusalem. Although some religiously observant Jewish Israelis have published works of belles lettres, I focus in this study on those poets who, regardless of upbringing, have had a secular world view that has provided them with a distinct type of relationship to the Bible that may not be shared by religiously observant Jews.

It is clear that the rabbinic tradition of classical midrash has influenced each of these poets' compositions of biblical allusion poems.[10] Along with other Israelis, the poets whose works we are considering were exposed, whether in the context of a religious or a secular education, to the wide-ranging transformations of the text of the Bible that permeate postbiblical midrashic Jewish texts. Their knowledge of this midrashic tradition legitimated for them the option of submitting biblical texts to such transformations and undoubtedly inspired their own attempts to recast the Bible in a contemporary spirit. In the Fall 1994 issue of *Heliqon: sidrah 'antologit leshirah 'akhshavit (Helicon: Anthological Journal of Contemporary Poetry)*, dedicated to the theme of midrash, the Israeli poet Amir Or, co-editor of the journal, makes the case that contemporary poetry based on ancient texts has an affinity for classical midrash in that in both genres authors present readings of earlier texts that sometimes depart from the earlier texts and sometimes reveal insightful interpretations of those texts. On the one hand, Or states, "the earlier source is . . . a hook on which to hang matters that are new and sometimes foreign to the literal meaning of the text."[11] On the other hand, he argues, classical midrash and contemporary poetry based on ancient texts do not always engage in violations of the earlier sources. "Midrashic allegory [in its classical or contemporary forms] is not always a reduction that conforms to preconceived principles, and the flight of fantasy may serve as a narrative means to discover insight that is imbedded in the original text."[12]

This comparison between classical midrash and contemporary poetry based on ancient texts, however, should not be overstated. Classical midrash emerged in the framework of the rabbinic Jewish ideological consensus, while conemporary poetry has been written in a less clearly defined intellectual context. As Or states, "the interpretive course of [contemporary] poetic midrash is not under obligation to any ideology—religious or other—and therefore again and again it is surprising, personal, and daring, both in its interpretation and in the connections it makes of distant sets of texts to the primary focus, which is the poem."[13]

Biblical allusion poetry can also be seen as a response to the ways that Zionism and Israeli culture both before and after the establishment of the State have relied on the Bible as a source of identity. This reliance on the Bible has continued to be a strength as well as a weakness. As the Israeli novelist Amos Oz notes, the ability to draw on the past has driven the Zionist enterprise: "Zionism had to relate unceasingly to the collective memory of the Jews in order to draw from it inspiration, justification, and ardor."[14] At the same time, Oz maintains, it has always been the challenge of the Zionist enterprise not to allow that collective memory to obscure its vision: "Zionism had to destroy without mercy what the [Hebrew] writer Yosef Haim Brenner called 'the hypnosis of the past.' "[15] Again and again, therefore, pre-State Zionists and Israeli citizens have had to come to terms with the question of how constructive or destructive is their reliance on the Bible as a model for the present. Biblical allusion poetry affirms the value of making analogous connections between modern and ancient Israel. Indeed, it extensively uses biblical images available to it as a means of defining and clarifying the nature of contemporary Israeli existence. Nevertheless, much of this poetry critiques the ways that Israeli culture obscures the understanding of its current reality when it adheres to inappropriate analogous connections between Israel's present and its ancient past.

To the extent that Israeli poets sense they can identify with the human experiences recorded in the Bible, they find in the Bible images, characters, and plots that can serve as powerful vehicles to express their understanding of their contemporary situation. They make creative use of the many associations that accompany well-known biblical texts to express in a compact and emotionally effective manner the human experiences central to the poem's meaning. Allusions to biblical stories often serve the aesthetic purposes of the poet. As David H. Hirsch and Eli Pfefferkorn note, references to the Bible can help the Israeli poet "to avoid excessive emotionalism in his poetry"[16] by providing "an objective correlative which allows him to give poetic utterance to what is otherwise unutterable, and describe what is beyond the scope of human imagination."[17] This is particularly true in the case of poetry that deals with painful losses of friends and loved-ones in both the Holocaust and Israel's wars. As Sidra Dekoven Ezrahi notes, modern Jewish writers responding to catastrophe "have appropriated the classical forms [of traditional Jewish texts], as if these provided access to an otherwise unintelligible and inarticulate experience."[18] Thus, when Amir Gilboa writes poetry about his inability to save his immediate family from being slaughtered in the Holocaust, he alludes to the image of the slaying of the Judean King Zedekiah's sons in front of him by the Babylonian conqueror of Jerusalem, Nebuchadnezzar (Jeremiah 39). When Yehuda Amichai seeks to capture the pain of Israelis confronting the deaths of youthful soldiers in the unpopular Lebanon War, he portrays these soldiers as victims by using the ram that is sacrificed at the end of the story of the binding of Isaac (Genesis 22) to represent them. In this way, as Yair Mazor observes, "an esthetic distance is achieved and the poem is redeemed from potential sentimentality."[19]

Yehuda Amichai makes the point that in poetry a poet can convey a great deal by means of a concrete image. For example, he observes, in a poem "you don't need to videotape the whole love affair between two young people which went on for two months, but sometimes it can be concentrated in just a pair of shoes or a book with torn pages or a broken glass or something like this."[20] In the case of biblical allusion poetry, given the readers' knowledge of the biblical story and the range of associations with the story in the mind of the readers, a biblical allusion can provide just the right concrete image to convey human experience in a concentrated way. Thus, when Anadad Eldan writes a poem about Israel's occupation of Gaza following the Six-Day War, he makes use of the image of Samson to represent the Palestinian residents of that area. In so doing he needs few details to conjure in the minds of his readers the story of Samson's fall from invincible power to humiliating defeat and thereby to convey his view of the fate of the Palestinians of Gaza.

Another factor that makes the Bible so useful for Israeli poets is the way that its archetypal structure resonates with the archetypal ways that human minds work. Colin Falck asserts that "the successful literary text . . . is . . . a capturing of some part of the essential nature of human life, and an insight into the nature of . . . reality itself."[21] Literary works, he argues, can most effectively provide such insight into reality by drawing on myths of the past because just as in ancient times, "the most important structures of our fully-articulated linguistic awareness will continue to fall within the outlines of myth and will be most satisfyingly open to 'explanation' through an assimilation to mythic patterns."[22] Indeed, according to Falck, the "imaginative archetypes"[23] that form the basis of mythic patterns are the best sources for authors to explain our world to us, for "the myths of our culture—which include those myths of other cultures which are imaginatively accessible to us—contain, and can therefore reveal, the fullest possible meaning of the world in which we live."[24] Thus, when Israeli poets have sought to make sense of the painful and frustratingly long state of war between Israel and her Arab neighbors, the archetypal struggle of the ancient Israelites with the residents of Canaan conveyed in such stories as Joshua's toppling of the walls of Jericho or David's slaying of the Philistine giant Goliath are powerful means that serve these poets' purposes because they tap into the natural tendency of Israelis to see their struggle with the Arabs in archetypal mythic terms.

As effective as biblical images, characters, and plots are as vehicles to express a poet's understanding of the present, authors of biblical allusion poems must struggle with the problematic aspects of the cultural assumption that what happens in Israel is a recurrence of events from the ancient past. Israelis do not always feel comfortable with this assumption, and these poets convey their full awareness of how threatening such an assumption can be. If your culture is telling you that what you are and do is modeled after what people were and did in the past, then you might come to resent the implication that the past can dictate your understanding of the present. In particular, you will resent it if it becomes clear to you that your values, your world view, and your perception of reality are in fact significantly different from those represented by past discourse.

Semiotic theorists recognize the role that literature can play in challenging the limited perspectives of people too wedded to the simplified definition of reality that is central to their cultural identity. Yuri Lotman has noted that semiotic systems tend to define themselves for the purpose of imposing norms on the complexity of points of view reflected in what he calls the "semiosphere" of the society. The tendency in Israeli culture to associate present events with the Bible is an important part of the Israeli semiotic system that imposes norms on the complexity of points of view in the culture. Although the self-definition inherent in creating a semiotic system is an essential cultural activity it involves, Lotman maintains, leaving out many aspects of the semiosphere that could be valuable to the culture: "whole layers of cultural phenomena, which from the point of view of the given metalanguage are marginal, will have no relation to the idealized portrait of that culture."[25] By indicating the ways that the cultural impulse to connect the present with the ancient past may prevent Israelis from being aware of some aspects of their culture, Israeli biblical allusion poems play the role that, as Jonathan Culler notes, literature often plays, of raising serious questions about the rules and conventions that constitute the semiotic systems of cultures by presenting "a critique of the codes and interpretive processes manifested in our languages and in previous literature."[26]

Often Israeli poets go so far as to suggest a new semiotic system as an alternative to the semiotic system of the Bible or the contemporary semiotic systems influenced by the Bible. These poets play an important role in forcing the culture to undergo a constructive self-critique. In so doing, they continue a Hebrew poetic tradition that began to develop at the turn of the century. As Benjamin Harshav notes, many members of the first two generations of twentieth-century Hebrew poets engaged in "an important activity of de-automatization of the use of sources."[27] In this period, Harshav notes, "de-automatization of 'dead' idioms and ready-made collocations [in the Bible and other traditional sources] was accomplished through the unraveling of their images and unexpected meanings in the new fictional situation created in the poem and absent in the source."[28] Based on this literary tradition authors of Israeli biblical allusion poems engage in a process characterized by Robert Alter as "stand[ing] the [biblical] sources on their heads, borrowing images, symbols, and situations for the expressive needs of a very different kind of poetic voice."[29]

Some of the most powerful examples of this process in Israeli biblical allusion poetry may be found in poems that make use of biblical accounts of the ancient Israelite conquest of the Land to raise questions about the prevailing cultural understanding of the Arab-Israeli conflict. In these poems the authors critique what they consider to be the Bible's morally insensitive approach to enemies that they believe has reinforced in contemporary Israeli culture a morally insensitive attitude toward the Arab enemy. In one poem, for example, Haim Gouri transforms Deborah's song celebrating the ancient Israelite victory over the Canaanite general Sisera into a meditation on the loss of life on both sides in the Israeli-Arab wars. He seems to be saying that if Israelis relate to their enemies with the more "primitive" hatred and disdain that ancient Israelites did, they will not realize what war is doing to their souls.

A number of poems present versions of biblical stories of relations between male and female characters in the Bible with the purpose of questioning the tendency of men in contemporary times to distance themselves from women for the sake of other goals. For example, in one poem Aryeh Sivan portrays the suffering of Moses' Ethiopian wife whose sexual needs are not fulfilled by her husband. In the poem Sivan makes use of expressions from Mosaic law that regulate sexuality to suggest that the reluctance of some men to relate freely to the erotic has been transmitted by the Bible to Israeli culture and must be overcome for the sake of women as well as of men.

The meaning of Israeli biblical allusion poetry is based largely on what the poet does to the biblical sign system in the process of alluding to the Bible. This, in general, is characteristic of the literary phenomenon of intertextuality, which involves, as Julia Kristeva notes, "transposition of one (or several) sign system(s) into another."[30] Michael Riffaterre refers to this process as the literary work "producing a sign system equivalent to [that of the text to which it alludes] but couched in a different code."[31] Israeli poets exploit the linguistic connection between modern and biblical Hebrew to present what on one level looks like the biblical sign system but which a deeper reading reveals to be a transformation of that sign system into one that reflects a contemporary perspective. In some cases the poets radically reverse the biblical sign system. The speaker in a poem by Nathan Yonathan, for example, systematically rejects the more aggressively successful biblical characters Moses, Abimelech, Barak, and David, in favor of the more vulernable characters Joseph, Jotham, Sisera, and Jonathan, thereby celebrating the greater value of those who undertake the less aggressive pursuits of love and art.

Sometimes, the transformation of the biblical sign system is more subtle. Careful attention, therefore, must be paid to the interplay between biblical and modern Hebrew in this poetry. For example, when Aliza Shenhar makes use of the binding of Isaac story to write a poem about the bitter feelings of mothers who are forced by the State to send their sons to their deaths in war, she includes the word *maʿarakhah,* which in modern Hebrew means "battle," but which has the same root (ʿ-r-kh) as the verb that refers to Abraham's orderly arranging of the wood as he prepares to sacrifice his son Isaac to God (*vayaʿarokh ʾet haʿetsim*). This one word reinforces the tension Shenhar discerns between the assertion of meaning in the human relationship with God that lies at the heart of the biblical semiotic system and the sense of absurd meaninglessness fostered by modern warfare.

When Israeli poets incorporate biblical language into their contemporary Israeli poetry, sometimes in modified form, they in effect comment on the adequacy of both the biblical semiotic system and the biblically influenced contemporary semiotic system. In this sense such poems engage in what Ziva Ben-Porat has characterized as central to all literary allusion: "the simultaneous activation of two texts."[32] Both the text of the contemporary poem that alludes to the Bible, which Ben-Porat calls the "alluding text,"[33] and the text of the Bible evoked by the poem, which Ben-Porat calls the "evoked text,"[34] are activated in that the reader's understanding of the meaning and significance of both contemporary Israeli existence as reflected in the poem and ancient Israelite existence as reflected in the Bible are affected by the process of reading the poem. This poetry both responds to biblical texts and comments on contemporary issues by means of what Chana Kronfeld describes as "iconoclastic intertextual patternings of secular, mudane alluding texts with biblical or other religious evoked texts."[35] For example, in a poem about Eve T. Carmi includes allusions to not only Genesis but also modern, bourgeois family life, thereby commenting on both the role of Eve in the Garden of Eden and the role of women in contemporary Israeli society.

The relationship between an alluding text and an evoked text can be quite complex. The elements from an evoked text that are incorporated in an alluding text can be, as Ben-Porat points out, "secondary . . . with regard to the element which can best represent a given text, but they are primary in terms of the actualized allusion."[36] The story of David's son Absalom would best be represented with the central image of his rebellion against his father. Rachel Chalfi, however, exploits the more secondary sensual associations of Absalom's long hair and physical beauty and his act of sleeping with his father's concubines to write a poem that represents sexual intimacy between a man and a woman by means of the image of Absalom's fatal entanglement in a tree.

At the same time, a poet may exploit a whole range of associations with the evoked text without explicitly referring to them in the poem. As Perri notes, "[Alluding's] great power of signification resides in the additional inter- and intra-textual patterns of associated attributes it can evoke once the primary sense is comprehended."[37] For example, in one poem Amir Gilboa is able to exploit his readers' familiarity with events in the life of Joshua in the Bible to draw a painful contrast between that life and the life of his brother Joshua who died in the Holocaust, with very few references to the Bible. In so doing he comments on not only the book of Joshua but also the tension in Israeli society between the value of heroic Israeli warfare in the spirit of Joshua and the reality of the deaths of the defeated Holocaust victims.

In a discussion of allusions (or "intertexts," to use her term) in the poetry of Yehuda Amichai, Nili Scharf Gold notes how the meaning of a poem can derive in part from the relationship among the various allusions. "The meaning [of the poem]," she observes, "is created by means of the weaving of the threads of the intertexts in the poem while approaching the original meaning [of each evoked text] and departing from it at the same time. The new situation [in the poem] both includes the conventional associations that derive from the intertexts and induces tensions among the interexts . . . and between them and the poem."[38] In a poem about Abraham by Meir Wieseltier, for example, the speaker critically assesses the patriarch by viewing expressions spoken by Abraham in the Bible in a negative light. At the same time, he presents Isaac and Jacob in ways that resemble the portraits of these patriarchs in the Bible but that depart from those portraits with the purpose of disparaging Abraham by comparison with the other two patriarchs. The meaning of the poem, thus, is based largely on the tension the poet creates between the biblical portraits of Israel's three patriarchs and the speaker's assessments of them, as well as on the tension among the allusions to these three patriarchs as they appear in the poem.

Biblical allusion poetry shares many features of any poem that makes an occasional allusion to the Bible. It is important, however, to note that biblical allusion poetry has a relationship to the Bible that differs significantly from that of a poem based only partly on biblical allusions. Although any biblical allusion connects the alluding text to the evoked text of the Bible, works of biblical allusion poetry are largely about the relationship between the the text of the poem and the text of the Bible.

The poems in this study can be divided into four categories in terms of their relationship to the biblical text. Not all poems fit neatly into one category, but these four categories provide a good sense of the range of relationships in this genre between the poem and the Bible. In the first category poems retell (usually a portion of) a biblical story. In these poems the speaker plays the role of a relatively objective third-person narrator. Stories that speakers in these poems retell include the creation of the universe, Adam and Eve in the Garden of Eden, the flood in Noah's time, the life of Sarah, the binding of Isaac, the death of Rachel, Judah and Tamar, the Joseph story, Moses and his Cushite wife, David and Goliath, David and

Michal, Jonah, Daniel in the lions' den, and Job. Although the speaker in each of these poems plays the role of narrator, the way that he or she tells the story reflects how the poet defines the relationship between the present and the ancient past. For example, in a poem by Yehuda Amichai instead of triumphantly presenting Goliath's head to King Saul, as he does in the Bible, an antiheroic David stands holding the head, uncertain exactly what to do with it.

In the second category the speaker explicitly offers reflections on a biblical story. The distinction between the first and second categories, it should be noted, is not always clear. In poems in the first category the speaker's perspective may be sufficiently subjective to convey his or her attitude toward the story. In poems belonging more purely in the second category, the focus is on the speaker offering a personal reaction to a biblical story. In a poem by Yehuda Amichai, for example, the speaker offers the opinion that the real hero of the binding of Isaac story was the ram. In a poem by Yehudit Kafri the speaker expresses her dismay at the fact that Sarah did not try to prevent Abraham from taking his son to be sacrificed, and in another poem by Kafri the speaker insists that Joseph must have seduced Potiphar's wife before she called out to him to lie with her.

In the third category the speaker either observes or actually attempts to interact with a biblical character. In one poem by Anadad Eldan the speaker tells of seeing the defeated Samson in Gaza. In poems by Haim Gouri the speaker witnesses multiple incarnations of a victorious Samson and multiple incarnations of a defeated Absalom. In one poem by Yehudit Kafri the speaker calls out to Joseph as he is about to descend into the pit, while in another poem by Kafri the speaker recounts seeing Joseph suffering in the pit. In a poem by Amir Gilboa the speaker tries to convince the prophet Jeremiah to take a pistol from him and assassinate King Nebuchadnezzar.

In the fourth category the speaker *is* a biblical character. In these poems either the speaker tells his or her own story, or the poem consists of words spoken or written by the biblical character when he or she was still alive. Isaac tells the story of his binding in poems by Matti Megged and Amir Gilboa. Abel tells the story of his death and its impact on human history in a poem by Dan Pagis. Other poems by Pagis consist of a note written by Eve in an attempt to communicate with Cain and a prayer by Saul just before his death by suicide. In a poem by Asher Reich, Lot's wife addresses Lot after the destruction of Sodom when she is about to be turned into a pillar of salt. In a poem by Nathan Yonathan, David calls out to his son Absalom after he is killed in the course of his rebellion.

The third and fourth categories, in a sense, test the credulity of the reader more than do the first and second categories. In poems of the first two categories it is plausible that a contemporary speaker would either seek to tell his or her own version of a biblical story (as Jews have continued to do since ancient times) or offer a personal reaction to a story. In the third and fourth categories, however, it is less plausible that a speaker could travel back to biblical times or that a biblical character could write a contemporary poem. The plausibility of poems in these categories rests largely on the fact that the poets live in the land of the Bible and have been educated to see Israel as a reenactment of the Bible. If an Israeli can actually go to Gaza, then it is not too far-fetched for him to see Samson, at least in his imagination. If these biblical characters once walked this same land speaking Hebrew, then they could be seen as returning to tell their story to a contemporary Israeli audience.

Significant linguistic factors have reinforced the connection of Israelis to the Bible and allowed Israeli writers to convey meaning by means of biblical allusions. One factor is the large degree of continuity between biblical Hebrew and contemporary Hebrew. For many centuries following biblical times Hebrew functioned primarily as a written and occasionally as a spoken language; only relatively recently, in the first half of the twentieth century, has Hebrew emerged as the everyday spoken language of a society. Without the effect that spoken language has of increasing the speed of linguistic change, Hebrew has developed relatively slowly on the lexical and syntactic levels. Much of the lexicon of biblical Hebrew is in usage in contemporary Hebrew, although modern Hebrew has a much larger lexicon. On a morphological level, nouns and verbs are formed in essentially the same way today as they were in ancient times. On the level of basic syntax biblical and modern Hebrew bear a great deal of resemblance. As Robert Alter notes, "Though much of the biblical vocabulary, idiom, and grammar has disappeared from modern [Israeli] speech, the language of the Bible remains perfectly familiar in a way not easily imaginable for the average speaker of English, to whom the much more recent past of his own literature—Chaucer, say, or even Spenser—is barely intelligible."[39]

Biblical allusion does not seem artificial in the context of Israeli literature because modern Hebrew is really a fusion of all periods of Hebrew, what Benjamin Harshav calls "the all-embracing receptacle and crucible of materials from all the layers that preceded it, turning the diachronic and 'multilingual' library into a synchronic, fused text."[40] Literary works, Harshav observes, can easily exploit this fused nature of Hebrew: "From this fused base language of society, a writer can take off for particular purposes toward a Biblical or some other historical Hebrew style, thereby achieving a special stylistic effect."[41]

Despite the relatively close connection between biblical and modern Hebrew, and the persistently central role of the Bible in Israeli culture, we must take into account the ways that modern Hebrew has distanced itself from biblical Hebrew. As Harshav notes, rather than faithfully follow the syntactic style of the Bible, "the structure of the complex sentence and the paragraph [in modern Hebrew] follow the constraints and licenses developed in the logical writing, political commentary, and belles lettres of Europe and America."[42] Furthermore, spoken and written Hebrew makes less use of biblical expressions than it did a generation ago, and Israelis' knowledge of the Bible, while still impressive by contemporary standards in the West, has declined over time. In an article on the language of the communications media over the course of the first forty years of the State, the Israeli novelist Shulamith Hareven points out how extensively such language has refrained from making use of idioms from the Bible or other classical Jewish sources. She cites a passage from an article in the popular Hebrew newspaper *Ma'ariv* in 1948, in which an accompanying picture bears the caption: *k'an nilhamim bemar hamavet* (literally: "here they fight against death"), which refers to death with a biblical idiom used by Agag the King of Amalek when he knows he is about to be killed by the prophet Samuel (I Samuel 15:32). As Hareven notes, "this [current] generation sees itself as free to say 'death' without depending on Agag the king of Amalek, and it is possible to see in this an improvement in the cleanliness of expression and in the freedom from excessive awkwardness."[43] Furthermore, she suggests that one reason for this trend is that neither the journalists nor the readers are as well versed in classical sources as those of the previous generation in the early days of the State.

The process of breaking from the confines of what Hareven terms "the flowery expression from the sources,"[44] has been a trend in the development of modern Hebrew poetry since the turn of the century. T. Carmi describes this process as an outgrowth of Hayyim Nahman Bialik's attempts to create a poetic language in which "not every word carried the label of the sources,"[45] and it was continued by Avraham Shlonsky and poets of his time, who attempted "to liberate the language of poetry from enslavement to the sources."[46] It persisted, according to Carmi, as a trend among "poets in Israel who had a declared ideology of writing in the language of the street or of speech that does not arouse 'literary' echoes."[47] This process of liberating the Hebrew language from its classical sources did not, however, involve the wholesale rejection of biblical allusion by writers. In fact, even as they sought to forge a modern poetic language not overly dependent on classical sources, Bialik, Shlonsky, and their respective contemporaries continued to allude to the Bible quite extensively in their works.

In a paradoxical way, this very distancing of modern Hebrew from the biblical sources has facilitated the continuing effective poetic use of biblical allusion by Israeli writers. As modern Hebrew has freed itself from the excessive and not particularly meaningful use of flowery biblical phrases it has allowed contemporary Israeli writers to return to the Bible with a fresh perspective. Biblical language, therefore, is not seen by the reader as an obsolete classical expression, but rather as a vehicle for literary allusion that stands out and bears meaning far more significant than that provided by a mere linguistic ornament. Indeed, many contemporary Israeli poets have effectively used the contrasting languages of contemporary colloquial Hebrew and biblical Hebrew. Zvia Ginor, for example, describes how in his poetry Aryeh Sivan juxtaposes high classical literary language with everyday language: "Amidst the prosaic pose, as it were, elevated words are woven infrequently, which endow the poem with magic and almost never sound flowery in the context."[48] Zvi Luz makes a similar observation regarding poetry on biblical themes by Nathan Yonathan. He calls attention to the flexible way in which Yonathan moves between biblical and contemporary Hebrew in one of his poems. "On the basis of this new flexibility," Luz writes, "elevated language permeated by allusions and low, prosaic language can live together and in absolute accord, as the interweaving of the levels serves in an artistic manner a thematics of many meanings."[49]

At the same time, there is the potential danger that the further that modern Hebrew gets from the classical sources, the less available will biblical allusions be to poets who wish to communicate with the public. Although Carmi affirms the value of poets keeping some distance from the clichés of biblical Hebrew, he warns of the impoverishment of the language of poetry that can accompany the trend to avoid allusions to classical sources. Israeli poetry, he maintains, must appreciate anew the value of classical sources that had been called into question by the poetic "reformers" since the days of Bialik. "The joy [for a poet]," Carmi declares, "is in the weaving together of periods, when you discover the great vitality that is in the ancient levels of the language."[50]

The body of Israeli biblical allusion poetry that I explore in this book provides a wide range of poetic responses to the central themes of Israeli existence during the period in which Israel underwent the transition from a newly established developing nation whose very existence provoked international controversy to a well-developed country tempered by war and increasingly recognized as a legitimate and valuable member of the family of nations. I have identified four themes that recur with great frequency in the Israeli biblical allusion poems of this period: the Arab-Israeli conflict, the Holocaust, relations between men and women, and relations between God and humanity. As one explores each theme one gains a greater understanding of what may have driven these poets to resort to biblical imagery in their writing. One also discovers what at times is a surprising range of biblical texts to which poets allude as they write on the same theme. At times, the responses of these poets to themes of Israeli existence appear to reflect changes in the development of Israeli history and at other times one sees similar responses to themes over the past five decades. Obviously, the gender and the biographical and historical background of each poet influence his or her perspective. To the extent possible, I attempt in this study to account for the influence of the historical period in which the poem was written and the biography of the poet on his or her response to a particular theme, even as I seek to establish the extent to which there is a similarity of response to a theme among Israeli poets.

This poetry must be read in the context of prevailing discourse on the Bible in Israeli culture. To convey some sense of this context, I have devoted the first chapter to analyzing both specific examples of the use of the Bible in Israeli public cultural discourse from 1948 to the present and poems in which Israeli poets express their relationship to the Bible. Each of the next four chapters is devoted to one of the four central themes of biblical allusion poetry mentioned above. In each chapter I explore the role of the Bible and of biblical Hebrew in public cultural discourse on the theme discussed in that chapter, and I then proceed to analyze biblical allusion poems that I understand to be addressing that theme. In the conclusion, I address the question of how to account for the fact that these four themes figure so prominently in this genre of biblical allusion poetry, and I consider what makes biblical allusion such a powerful literary technique for expressing poetic responses to these themes.

The title of this book, *Does David Still Play Before You?*, is taken from a poem by Moshe Dor, which I analyze in chapter 1. This title signifies the way that Israeli biblical allusion poetry is caught between the worlds of ancient and modern Israel. Even as the speaker wonders in the poem about the relevance of the Bible to his fellow Israelis, he makes clear how central to him this question is. Like this poem, Israeli biblical allusion poetry in general attempts to create new versions of the biblical text that more clearly take into account that which distances the modern world view from the biblical world view, while it also affirms the common humanity of the modern and ancient residents of the Land of Israel.

CHAPTER ONE

THE PILOT
AND THE MAN
UNDER
THE FIG TREE   **ISRAELIS**
AND THE
BIBLE

The significance of Israeli biblical allusion poetry can be appreciated only by examining the central role of the Bible in public discourse on the issues most central to the definition of Israeli identity. This important role of the Bible in public discourse accounts for much of what motivates Israelis to write biblical allusion poetry. Again and again, the Bible is cited to support positions taken on such fundamental issues of Israeli identity as the right of Israel to exist, its relationship to the Jewish Diaspora, the cultural and political values of Israel as a modern nation-state, and the controversy since 1967 over the relationship of Israel to the territories occupied in the Six-Day War. In recent decades, moreover, there has been increasing public debate in Israel between those who take a secular humanistic approach to the Bible and those who insist on reading the Bible in the spirit of traditional religious and/or right-wing nationalist values. To have a clearer understanding of this cultural context in which Israeli biblical allusion poetry has been written, I begin this chapter with examples of how the Bible has been used to address these issues of Israeli identity since the founding of the State.

Justifying Israel's Right to Exist

As Myron J. Aronoff points out, because so many people have challenged the Jews' right to statehood in the Land of Israel, "perhaps the primary goal of Israeli political culture has been to make the continuity of the ancient past with the contemporary context a taken-for-granted reality."[1] By establishing the reality of that continuity Israel could separate itself from association with European colonialism and establish that it is, instead, the product of a movement of national self-determination seeking independence for the Jewish nation in its homeland.

On May 14, 1948, the day before Israel was to become an independent state, the Zionist leadership of the Jewish residents in the Land of Israel issued a Declaration of Independence. This document had three purposes: to argue in support of the right to existence of the new State of Israel; to declare the principles on which the new State would be founded; and to appeal to the nations of the world in general, the Arab world, and Jews in the Diaspora to support the establishment of the State.[2]

The Bible plays a central role in the rhetoric of the document, particularly when it attempts to justify Israel's right to exist. The Hebrew term that came to be adopted for the document, *Megillat ha'atsma'ut* (The Scroll of Independence) grants it a quasi-sacred character, for it suggests that the Declaration of Independence is analogous to one of the biblical scrolls (*megillot*) read on Jewish holidays in the synagogue. The argument presented in this document to support the right of the Jewish people to establish a sovereign state in the Land of Israel is based on the assumption that in restoring ancient Israelite sovereignty the Jews were transforming their national past into a contemporary present, which in many ways resembled the past but expressed it in a more contemporary idiom. The Israeli Declaration of Independence reflects the tendency of Zionist thought and of Israeli political discourse from 1948 to the present to perceive the struggle to establish and maintain a Jewish state in the Land of Israel as analogous to a range of biblical and postbiblical events: the Exodus from Egypt, the entrance of the ancient Israelites into the land of Canaan, the recurrent military conflicts between the ancient Israelites and the residents of Canaan from the days of Joshua to the periods of the Judges and Kings, the return to Zion following the

Babylonian Exile, the struggle for religious freedom in the days of the Maccabees, and the challenges to Roman rule over the Land of Israel culminating in the siege of Masada and in the Bar-Kokhba revolt.[3]

A significant example of this intertextual process that links current reality to the Bible is the way that the authors of the Declaration of Independence make use of two terms to refer to the Zionist settlers who contributed to the effort to establish a Jewish state in the Land of Israel: *halutsim* and *ma'pilim*. The term *halutsim* refers to the Jewish settlers who came from abroad in the late nineteenth and early twentieth centuries to establish agricultural settlements in the Land of Israel, and the term *ma'pilim* refers to Jews who secretly entered the Land of Israel in the 1940s in illegal defiance of the immigration quotas set by the British Mandate. These terms connect modern Zionism with the ancient Israelites' contact with the Land in Moses' time. *Ma'pilim* derives from the description of the abortive battle by some Israelites with the Amalekites and Canaanites shortly after the return of the twelve spies Moses had sent to scout the Land: *vaya'pilu la'alot 'el rosh hahar* ("yet defiantly they marched to the crest of the hill country," Numbers 14:44). *Halutsim* was used in the agreement between God and Moses on the one hand and the tribes of Reuben and Gad on the other hand that the latter would lead the other tribes in the conquest of the Land: *nahnu na'avor halutsim lifnei 'adonay 'erets kena'an* ("We ourselves will cross over as shock-troops, at the instance of the Lord, into the land of Canaan," Numbers 32:32).[4]

The authors of the Declaration of Independence state that in ancient times the Jews lived a life of *qomemiyyut mamlakhtit* ("sovereign independence") in the Land of Israel and that they have strongly desired to achieve *'atsma'ut mamlakhtit* ("independent sovereignty") in that land. The term *qomemiyyut* alludes to God's description of the Exodus from Egypt as a time of freedom and dignity: *va'olekh 'etkhem qomemiyyut* ("and [I] made you walk erect," Leviticus 26:13). The term *mamlakhtit* derives from the biblical term for king, *melekh,* and thereby associates contemporary Israeli sovereignty with the period of the kings of Israel that began in the days of Saul and concluded with the destruction of the First Temple.

Other expressions in the Declaration of Independence suggest historical parallels between the establishment of the State of Israel in 1948 and the return to Zion in the days of Ezra and Nehemiah, a few decades after the destruction of the First Temple and the Babylonian Exile. The authors of the declaration write of the many Jews who "returned to their land" (*shavu 'el 'artsam*), and later in the document they declare that the new State will be open "to Jewish immigration and to the ingathering of the exiles" (*le'aliyyah yehudit uleqibbuts galuyyot*). The roots of *shavu* (*sh-v-b*, "return"), *'aliyyah* (*'-l-y*, "immigration," "ascent"), and *galuyyot* (*g-l-y*, "exiles") are central to the narratives of the books of Ezra and Nehemiah, which refer to the return and ascent of the Jewish people to Judea in the days of King Cyrus of Persia after their exile from their land by King Nebuchadnezzar of Babylonia.

The conviction generally held by Israelis that the right to an independent Jewish state in the Land of Israel is based on a natural continuity with the ancient past is reinforced by the fact that they indeed live in the land of the Bible. Many place names in contemporary Israel are of biblical origin; thus, the perception prevails that present Israeli existence continues that of ancient Israel. It makes perfect sense to many Israelis that the descendants of King David, who in biblical times established Jerusalem as his capital, would establish and maintain a Jewish state in modern times with that same city as its capital. Indeed, the belief among Israelis that their State provides a natural continuity with ancient Israel was expressed in the plans made by the Israeli government to hold a celebration in 1954 of what was purported to be the three thousandth anniversary of the establishment of Jerusalem as the capital of Israel by King David. When some scholars questioned the accuracy of the dating of the anniversary, the plans for the celebration were postponed.[5] The idea resurfaced in the series of cultural events presented in Israel to mark that anniversary in 1996.

The extensive archeological exploration of Israel has also made a significant contribution to the effort to use the Bible to justify Israel's right to exist. As Amos Elon notes, the passion of Israelis for archeological exploration has been motivated largely by the need to affirm to themselves and their enemies the national right of the Jews to establish a state in their ancient homeland. "Israeli archeologists professionals and amateurs," Elon writes, "are not merely digging for knowledge and *objects,* but for the reassurance of roots, which they find in the ancient Israelite remains scattered throughout the country."[6]

On viewing the archeological remains of an ancient city mentioned in the Bible, modern Israelis easily experience a sense of close connection between their modern country and the ancient Land of Israel. In explaining his fascination with archeology Moshe Dayan, who served as chief of staff of the Israeli army and later as defense minister of Israel, described the sense that by visiting an archeological site a person can feel as if he were passing in time from modern to ancient Israel:

> You sometimes feel that you can literally enter [the] presence [of those who lived here in the ancient Land of Israel]. They are dead to be sure. But you can enter the homes of silenced people and sometimes feel more than when you enter homes of the living. I like to stick my head into a hole in which the people of Bnei Brak lived 6,000 years ago ... to have a look at their kitchen, to finger the ashes left there from long ago, to feel the fingerprints which that ancient potter left on the vessel.[7]

The Primacy of Israel over the Diaspora

Since Zionist ideology envisioned the creation of a Jewish state in the Land of Israel as a viable alternative to Jewish existence in the Diaspora, Israel has had to come to terms with its relationship to the Diaspora Jewish communities that continued to exist after the establishment of the State. Jews in the Diaspora have been reluctant to accept the assertion of Zionist ideologues that Israel is the primary, and perhaps the only legitimate, place to develop Jewish existence in the latter part of the twentieth century. The persistence of a thriving Diaspora, particularly as it has continued to develop in America, has sometimes driven Israelis to reaffirm the classical Zionist "negation of the Diaspora" (shelilat hagolah) as a means to justify their commitment to Israel.

The most extreme expression of the negation of the Diaspora was found in the short-lived minor cultural movement popularly known as the Canaanites, active mainly in the early years of the State. This movement, whose most important leader was the poet Yonatan Ratosh, advocated the notion that by settling in the Land of Israel Jews were essentially returning to their prebiblical and biblical roots in the Middle East. Therefore, the Canaanites argued, they should reject any identification with the religious civilization that developed in the Diaspora in postbiblical times in favor of a reconstituted Hebrew nation that would blend with other ethnic groups of the contemporary Middle East.[8] While the ideology of the Canaanites was not embraced in its pure form by many Israelis, this movement took other Israelis' inclination to negate the Diaspora to its most logical conclusion.

Israel's first prime minister, David Ben-Gurion, while not an adherent of the Canaanite movement, was a vociferous proponent of the Israeli trend to negate the significance of the Diaspora. Shortly after the debate in the Knesset over King David to which I referred in the introduction, the Israeli newspaper *Ha'arets* published a statement that Ben-Gurion made in 1953 to a gathering of writers and artists in which he rejected rabbinic legendary adaptations of the portrait of David in the Bible that asserted "that he sat all day and engaged in exegetical study."[9] Ben-Gurion could not accept the way that rabbinic tradition recast the Bible because he saw it as a product of an exilic (*galut*) mentality of "a persecuted people, a people cut off from the land, from free creativity, both spiritual and material."[10] And the prime minister was particularly repelled by the ways that the rabbinic tradition views those in the Bible who exercised physical power. When an Orthodox rabbi told Ben-Gurion that "Joshua the son of Nun was the head of a yeshiva," the secular prime minister found it "a bit hard to imagine," but he understood that only by viewing Joshua this way could the rabbi understand the biblical notion of Joshua as "the servant of Moses."[11] From Ben-Gurion's point of view, the rabbi, too wedded to the exilic mentality, unfortunately ignored not only the role of Joshua as a military leader but also the fact that even "Moses began his career by killing an Egyptian."[12]

In 1960, Ben-Gurion called a press conference to present his theory of the historical reality behind the biblical account of the Exodus from Egypt.[13] As one newspaper commented, such a press conference was unique in the annals of politics throughout the world: "We tried to recall when it had happened that the prime minister of any country, big or small, would take a few hours' leave to appear before a large crowd of journalists and dignitaries to present not a political statement of importance, but a chapter in the history of his nation, the product of research and deep thought."[14] Although it is clear from the content of the press conference that Ben-Gurion had put much thought into developing his theory, his political message of the primacy of Israel over the Diaspora is not difficult to discern.[15]

According to Ben-Gurion's theory, most ancient Israelites who descended from Jacob never left the land of Canaan for Egypt, and in fact the Exodus story is based on a relatively small number who had settled in Egypt and were reunited with their brethren in Canaan. The relationship of this theory to the struggle for primacy between Israel and the Diaspora becomes clear, as Michael Keren notes, when at one point Ben-Gurion justifies his theory by using the growing assimilation of American Jews as proof that it was impossible that the Israelites as an entire nation could have preserved their national identity in Egypt. "We have witnessed in our day," Ben-Gurion declares, "how a Jewish community of 5,000,000 arose in the United States, and behold, not even fifty years have passed, and they have not preserved the language which they brought with them from overseas, and have almost all switched to the use of the English language."[16] In effect, Ben-Gurion sought to justify his conviction that Jewish national identity could never flourish in the Diaspora by writing out of biblical history the notion that the Jewish nation was founded in a country other than Israel, namely Egypt. The logic of his Zionist ideology led him to the conclusion that, as Keren puts it, "the origins of Jewish culture can be found [only] in 'normal,' historical surroundings,"[17] that is in the Land of Israel.

In recent decades, when the Israeli writers Shulamith Hareven and A. B. Yehoshua addressed the relationship of Jews to the Diaspora and to Israel, they both alluded to the earliest biblical residents of the Land—the patriarchs and matriarchs. For both writers, the movement by biblical patriarchs and matriarchs in and out of the Land serves as a paradigm of the unstable relationship of modern Jews to the State of Israel. Because both writers assume that the greatest potential for Jewish national development is in Israel, they view this unstable relationship as detrimental to the Jewish people.

Hareven connects the tendency of the patriarchs to stray from the true monotheistic path with the moments in their lives when they were in exile (*bagolah*). In effect, she understands the Bible to be saying that there can be no fulfillment of the national purpose of the people of Israel outside the Land of Israel. She sees Joseph as "the first exilic Jew" (*hayehudi hagaluti hari'shon*),[18] who like the Jews living outside of Israel in her day, rose to political power in a foreign land and lived there the paradigmatic Diaspora existence. "The cleverness, the diligence, the charm [of Joseph] that captures the heart of strangers," Hareven argues, "all these together with the material compensation are signs of exile (*hagalut*)."[19] Even with the many rewards of the Diaspora, Joseph's descendants, like Jews throughout the history of the Diaspora, Hareven believes, ultimately paid the price of slavery and powerlessness. "Afterward comes the hard work and the enslavement. . . . And the result is being left out of the great divine 'master plan' and on its periphery."[20] As far as Hareven is concerned, only the Land of Israel can save the Jew from this abject state.

Yehoshua associates biblical references to Abraham and Jacob leaving the Land with what he sees as the ambivalent attitude of modern Jews to living in Israel. He refers to Abraham, as "the first Jew . . . [and] the first ʿoleh, the first immigrant to [the Land of] Israel," but also as "the first *yored,* the first emigrant from the country."[21] As soon as the economic situation in the Land of Israel became difficult, Yehoshua observes, "Abraham immediately set out for Egypt."[22] Two generations later, Abraham's grandson Jacob emigrated to Egypt to be reunited with his beloved son Joseph. "Let us take note," Yehoshua writes, "[in the period of] the patriarchs a new nation [is] being born, and the attitude to the land, which in a certain sense should have served as a model for the nation as a whole, [is] already ambivalent."[23] Yehoshua sees the stories of the patriarchs as warnings of how problematic the ambivalent attitude toward the Land was in their day and continues to be in modern times. For Yehoshua, the patriarchs represent a model of how *not* to build a nation. He wants Jews in his day to learn from that negative model and reject the attraction of the Diaspora, so that they can give all their energy to the nation-building taking place in the modern State of Israel.

Developing a Culture for the Modern Nation-State

In defining its national identity, Israel has had to develop a culture that not only drew on Jewish tradition but also fit the secular orientation of the majority of its citizens. No single source has contributed more to the development of this Israeli national identity than has the Bible. Since the establishment of the State, the Bible has been central to Israeli popular culture and to Israel's educational system. During the first years of the State, Bible study groups became popular features of Israeli society. Even Prime Minister David Ben-Gurion held a Bible study group in his house every two weeks.[24] As Charles Liebman and Eliezer Don-Yehiya point out, the national "annual Bible quiz which received a great deal of publicity in the mass media" made a very important contribution to the awareness of the Bible and its relevancy to contemporary life, especially in the early days of the State.[25] The Bible continues to have a prominent place in the curriculum of Jewish Israeli religious and secular schools.

Biblical holidays have been reinterpreted in Israel to reflect contemporary Israeli experience and to serve the development of an Israeli civil religion that celebrates the national identity of the State of Israel. One of the most creative centers of the development of an Israeli civil religion has been on secular kibbutzim, where the secular Israeli reinterpretation of Passover has been ritualized.[26] The focus of this ritualized approach is the seder celebrated on the first night of Passover, for which secular kibbutzim have rewritten the traditional Haggadah. The degree of departure from the traditional text of the Haggadah has depended on how ideologically extreme the kibbutz has been. A Haggadah published in 1965 for use in the left-wing kibbutz movement *Haqibbuts Ha'artsi*,[27] for example, rewrites the story of the Exodus as told in the traditional Haggadah to emphasize the significance of the ancient Israelites' entrance into Canaan much more than does the traditional Haggadah. The traditional text introduces the section of the Haggadah that tells the story of Passover with the following declaration:

> We were slaves of Pharaoh in Egypt, and the Lord our God brought us out from there with a strong hand and an outstretched arm.

The kibbutz version reworks this text by eliminating part of the original and adding other expressions of biblical origin:

> We were slaves of Pharaoh in Egypt, and they caused us to work hard, and we built for him the storage cities of Pithom and

Raamses. And we were redeemed from there, and we crossed the sea on dry land, and we came to our Land.

The most obvious change introduced in this kibbutz Haggadah is the elimination of God's involvement in the story, which reflects the atheistic tendencies of members of this kibbutz movement. The addition of the reference to building the storage cities for Pharaoh may reflect the labor orientation of the movement. Of particular significance is the addition of the reference to entering the Land added in this new version. Implied in this retelling of the Passover story is the notion that Zionism has accomplished a mission parallel to what the ancient Israelites accomplished by freeing themselves from slavery in Egypt and settling in the Land of Israel.

The Exodus and the establishment of the State of Israel are even more explicitly linked in the way that this Haggadah approaches the traditional custom of drinking four cups of wine at the seder. Instead of the traditional blessing that accompanies each of these drinks praising God for creating "the fruit of the vine," this Haggadah substitutes a kind of secular toast to be recited before drinking each cup. One toast is: "We will raise the cup of salvation for the Exodus of Israel from enslavement to freedom, from exile to redemption to life and to salvation." This toast makes use of such terms as "freedom" (*herut*) and exile (*golah*), which may be found both in traditional discourse referring to premodern Jewish history and in modern Zionist discourse. Another toast explicitly refers to contemporary Israel: "A second cup we will raise to the welfare of the State of Israel, to its security, to the welfare of our sons and our daughters who stand guarding our borders, to life and to peace!"

Not only in kibbutz circles can we find ritualized connections between ancient and modern Israel. Another illuminating example can be found in a Haggadah published between the Six-Day War and the Yom Kippur War, edited by Eli Landau, who at the time was the military correspondent for the Israeli newspaper *Ma'ariv*.[28] This Haggadah preserves the traditional text, based on the official version used in the Israeli army, but in the editor's introduction Landau makes clear his understanding of the parallels between the Passover story and two major challenges facing Israel at the time: the struggle for the free immigration to Israel of Soviet Jews and the military efforts to defend Israel against its enemies:

Today [the Haggadah] has a sharply relevant meaning—a meaning related to the expectations for the Exodus of the Jews from the slavery of the land of the Soviets to freedom in their homeland, the Land of Israel. Today's Israel adds to the Haggadah a dimension of relevance—a dimension which contains a wondrous mixture of the story of redemption and its fulfillment, while those who tell about the freedom are the bearers of its banner.

The redeemers of Israel—the fighters of the Israel Defense Forces—recline at the seder night in their camps and tell of the Exodus from Egypt and the freedom of Israel and tell of the wonders of these days in addition to the miraculous acts of those days. The Haggadah for them is not a legend. It is the reality of life.

Landau's message is reinforced by the photographs and drawings that accompany the text. They consist of pictures of Israeli soldiers and military weaponry and Jews yearning to leave the Soviet Union. Particularly striking are two maps found in the Haggadah. One contains arrows that trace the main points of attack by the Israeli armed forces against the surrounding Arab states in the Six-Day War of 1967. The other is a map that includes Israel and all the occupied territories without any pre–Six-Day War boundaries as an illustration of the traditional Haggadah song, "For It is Pleasing to Him, For It is Fitting to Him" (*Ki lo na'eh ki lo ya'eh*), thereby suggesting divine sanction for the Six-Day War and for the continuation of Israeli rule over the territories Israel conquered in that war.

The Territorial Boundaries of Israel

The Bible has been used by both sides of the ongoing debate in Israel since 1967 over the future of the territories occupied by Israel in the Six-Day War. Prime Minister Menachem Begin, first elected in 1977, legitimized the practice of referring to the Jordanian territory conquered by Israel in the Six-Day War of 1967 not as *hagadah hama'aravit* (the West Bank) or *hashetahim hamuhzaqim* (the administered, or occupied territories), but rather with the biblical names of that area, *yehudah veshomron* (Judea and Samaria). As Myron J. Aronoff points out, the use of this terminology served the political goal of Begin and his Likud party to maintain Israeli control over this territory. "If the territories were perceived to be the biblical heartland of the Jewish people, rather than the 'occupied territories,' " observes Aronoff, "the legitimacy of the government and its settlement policies would be enhanced."[29]

The continuity with the biblical past inherent in the occupation and settlement of the West Bank has been further reinforced by the tendency in Israel to refer to the Jewish settlers of that area and of the Gaza Strip and the Golan Heights as *mitnahalim*. This term comes from the root *n-ḥ-l*, used in the Bible to refer to the taking by each tribe of its assigned portion upon entering the Land, as in the pledge by the tribes of Gad and Reuben that they will fight on the west side of the Jordan river to help the other tribes take possession of their assigned portions: "We will not return to our homes until every one of the Israelites is in possession of his portion (*'ad hitnaḥel benei yisra'el 'ish naḥalato,* Numbers 32:18).

A significant example of the way that a broad spectrum of Israeli positions on the occupied territories seek legitimacy in the biblical past is found in an account by the novelist Amos Oz of conversations he held with Jewish residents of the West Bank settlement of Tekoa. Oz's account of the differences between his position in favor of territorial compromise with the Palestinians and the position of the settlers that Israel should maintain control of the occupied territories contains allusions by Oz and by one of the religious settlers to the book of the prophet Amos, who according to the Bible was born in Tekoa. It is important for both the religious Jewish settler and the secular Jewish writer (whose name, coincidentally, is Amos) to believe that his political position represents the true continuation of the teachings of the biblical prophet. Nevertheless, each side sees a very different parallel between current events in Israel and the words of Amos. The settler, Amiel Unger, a religious Jewish immigrant from America who works as a university lecturer in political science, sees the settlement of the West Bank as a fulfillment of the prophecy of Amos that God would restore the people of Israel to their land after the destruction of the First Temple: "I will restore My people Israel. They shall rebuild ruined cities and inhabit them; they shall plant vineyards and drink their wine ... and I will plant them upon their soil, nevermore to be uprooted from the soil I have given them" (Amos 9:14–15). "You'd have to be completely blind, God forbid," Unger declares to Oz, "not to see that this is the beginning of the Final Redemption."[30] In contrast, Oz expresses his fear that what makes the settlement of the occupied territories parallel to the period of Amos is that it resembles the sins of social oppression by the ancient Israelites that the prophet warned would be punished by the destruction of the nation: "Thus said the Lord: For three transgressions of Judah, for four, I will not revoke it. . . . I will send down fire upon Judah, and it shall devour the fortresses of Jerusalem" (Amos 2:4–5).[31]

In an article she published in 1984, Shulamith Hareven, who like Oz has long favored territorial compromise with the Palestinians, tried to counter the claims of religious annexationists that the holiness of the land precluded such compromise by harking back to the biblical account of King Solomon ceding Israelite cities to Hiram, king of Tsur, in exchange for an economic deal (I Kings 9:11). Hareven calls attention to the fact that at the time "not one prophet arose to rebuke [Solomon] for giving away parts of the Land of Israel—and we are speaking of a period in which prophecy had not ceased in Israel, but rather was very widespread."[32] Hareven, like Oz, tries to beat the religious annexationists at their own game by citing Scripture to bolster her political position. It is not enough, as she states later in this passage, to assert that most Israelis reject the myth of "the whole Land of Israel" and therefore refuse to pay the heavy price that would accompany the annexationists' program. Moreover, it is important for her to establish that the biblical precedent of the annexationists' claim is in fact a distortion of the text. "From all this," she declares, "we can learn that our ancestors were not at all a party to the modern myth of the whole Land of Israel, or the automatic holiness of every place of settlement in it."[33]

Humanistic Israelis vs. Religious and Right-Wing Israelis

The responses in the 1980s of Oz and Hareven to biblical justifications for Israel's maintaining control of the occupied territories were part of a more general debate that intensified in that decade between secular humanistic Israelis on the one side and religious and right-wing Israelis on the other side regarding how Israelis are to approach the interpretation of the Bible. Not only Oz and Hareven, but other secular humanistic Israelis such as Arie Lova Eliav and

Yehoshafat Harkabi, publicly criticized religious and right-wing Is-
raelis for abandoning what these humanists saw as the original Zion-
ist understanding of the Bible.[34] It is not surprising that these writers
felt the need to make such criticism at this time. When the 1981
Knesset elections retained Menachem Begin's right-wing coalition in
power, left-leaning humanists saw that the rise of Begin to power in
the previous election in 1977 did not represent a passing phenome-
non: the influence of right-wing Israelis and their religious political
allies had made serious inroads in public opinion. The outbreak of
the Lebanon War in 1982, soon opposed by left-wing and many cen-
trist humanists, put these writers increasingly on the defensive and
drove them to fight back against ways of seeing Israeli existence that
they believed were in part based on a false understanding of the
Bible. They hoped that by deflecting the way Israelis read the Bible
from that of religious and right-wing Israelis they might be able to
shift the direction of public opinion in Israel to one closer to their
own dovish, secular humanistic orientation.

In 1986, the Israeli politician and writer Arie Lova Eliav published
the book *Lev hadash veruah hadashah* (*A New Heart and a New Spirit*),
in which he ardently defended a humanistic reading of the Bible. In
his preface Eliav explains that he wrote the book to challenge what he
saw as a dangerous new trend in Israel to weaken "the bonds of per-
sonal and national ethics that linked Zionism with the best of biblical
values."[35] He writes that this trend, embraced by many religious Zion-
ists and secular Jews opposed to territorial compromise with the
Arabs, seriously threatens to radically transform the Zionist relation-
ship to the Bible by embracing biblical values opposed to the tenets
of Western humanistic culture. Eliav and other secular humanistic Is-
raelis, he explains, have maintained the early Zionist attachment to
the Bible since the establishment of Israel because of the affinity that
they believe exists between the sovereign modern Jewish State and
the sovereign ancient Kingdom of Israel portrayed in the Bible. He
and his fellow secular humanistic Israelis, Eliav states, also value the
Bible as a text that struggles with issues of human existence as prob-
lematic now as they were in ancient times.

As a secular humanist, however, Eliav does not believe that bibli-
cal values are based on an eternally true divine revelation; rather he
believes that they are the product of human understanding. He
therefore feels free to reconsider all that is written in the Bible and to

choose from it only that which in his opinion does not violate his values. In particular, he is attracted to those biblical values that he sees as congruent with what he refers to as the "seven universal ethical values . . . [of] the sanctity of life, justice, freedom, equality, brotherhood, mercy, and peace."[36] There is, however, much in the Bible that repels Eliav. He cannot abide those values that represent for him evil tendencies within the ancient Israelites and evil influences on them from other peoples in ancient times: "evil and cruelty, slavery and oppression, hatred and war . . . rites, witchcraft, and human sacrifices."[37]

Eliav does not justify his position solely in terms of a modern critical approach to the Bible. He considers it important to justify his selectivity by claiming that this approach is in the spirit of the relative freedom with which rabbinic tradition creatively reinterpreted the Bible in the literature of Talmud and midrash and in medieval commentaries designed to free Judaism of that which was objectionable to later generations in their most sacred texts.[38]

Writing at about the same time as Eliav, Yehoshafat Harkabi, a former chief of Israeli military intelligence and director of the Leonard Davis Institute of International Relations at the Hebrew University, also asserted the need to confront the biblical support claimed by opponents of territorial compromise with the Arabs. He cites as an example the fact that the political extremist Rabbi Meir Kahane's call to expel the Arabs from the occupied territories is based primarily on the divine biblical commandment to Israel, "you shall dispossess all the inhabitants of the land" (Numbers 33:52) and later rabbinic interpretations of that commandment.[39] As a secular humanist like Eliav, Harkabi declares that Israelis must reject such biblical sources and rabbinic interpretations as "sediments of a negative nature"[40] and "embarrassing remnants"[41] of the Jewish past. Harkabi makes clear to his readers that he is not advocating a wholesale rejection of the Bible and later rabbinic tradition in the name of contemporary values: "I am not saying that Judaism has to be modernized to suit the contemporary world, and thus reformed," he declares. His main purpose, he maintains, is to be engaged in the process of "weeding out growths that have accumulated and have deformed and disfigured the religion."[42]

As was the case with Eliav, it is important for Harkabi to insist that the process of "weeding out" extreme trends in the Bible and later

Jewish tradition is not a modern invention. He insists that such relativism was often the approach of rabbinic interpretation throughout history. "The techniques of consigning ideas to oblivion are not new," he asserts. "Rabbis have always made halakhic rulings that contradicted the plain meaning of earlier halakhic literature. At times they have chosen to ignore certain texts, and their rulings were accepted."[43] Indeed, Harkabi points out, there were Orthodox "rabbis who signed Israel's Declaration of Independence, which advocates equal treatment of Arabs,"[44] even though traditional Jewish sources contain laws limiting the rights of non-Jews living in the Land of Israel.

Shulamith Hareven has also argued the secular humanistic position with the vehement insistence that this position is based on a more valuable and truer interpretation of the Bible than that of secular and religious Jews opposed to territorial compromise with the Arabs. Like Eliav and Harkabi, she maintains that ancient Israelite religion changed in an evolutionary way from biblical times on. Just as biblical religion replaced human sacrifice with animal sacrifice, so later rabbinic Judaism replaced animal sacrifice with prayer. The next stage of development, in Hareven's opinion, will be a secular Judaism not even based on prayer or other ritual observances but purely on moral obligations to humanity. She maintains that even religious Jews view the Bible in a selective manner. The problem for Hareven, however, is that they select the wrong values. In one passage she quotes a series of biblical verses that express her reaction to the group known as "The Faithful of the Temple Mount," who oppose Arab control of the site of Israel's ancient Temple in the old city of Jerusalem. Her biblical citations are from the first chapter of Isaiah, in which the prophet rebukes those Israelites who observe only the ritual of the sacrificial cult in the Temple but ignore their ethical obligations to their fellow human beings. For Hareven, when current political extremists go up to the disputed Temple Mount area they are involved in the same distortion of biblical values that Isaiah condemned when he berated his contemporaries with the words, "That you come to appear before Me—who asked that of you? Trample My courts no more. Bringing oblations is futile, incense is offensive to Me. . . . Though you pray at length, I will not listen. Your hands are stained with crime. . . . Cease to do evil; learn to do good. Devote yourselves to justice; aid the wronged. Uphold the rights of the orphan; defend the cause of the widow" (Isaiah 1:12–17).[45]

Hareven sees this group as part of a larger disturbing trend of viewing God and the Bible as exemplifying militarism and cruelty, a view diametrically opposed to her own conviction that the Bible is based on humane justice. From Hareven's point of view, one of the biggest mistakes of her ideological opponents is not realizing that modern humanistic values at times are superior to values to which the Israelites adhered in the time of the Bible. "According to my model," she argues, "human beings very frequently are better and possess a much better sense of justice than the image of God that they created for themselves in antiquity, when they were young and He was young and they all lacked experience."[46]

The secular humanistic approach to the Bible with which Oz, Eliav, Harkabi, and Hareven challenge religious and right-wing Jews in Israel draws on modern Western world views as well as traditional Jewish world views. In the name of modern Western culture these writers declare that some values their opponents draw from the Bible are so counter to the principles of secular humanism that they must be rejected. At the same time, it is important for these writers to argue that they have not radically departed from authentic Jewish culture. The biblical prophetic tradition, they argue, supports their opposition to their religious and right-wing opponents. Furthermore, they claim, the Jewish tradition has always been open to reinterpreting the Bible; in so doing at times it has rejected certain biblical values. What they are doing, these humanists believe, is very much in the spirit of Judaism as it has been understood by Jews since biblical times.

Although most biblical allusion poems focus mainly on one biblical text, some Israeli poets have written more general poems about the Bible, in which they allude to several biblical stories with the purpose of expressing their relationship to the Bible as a whole. The poems of this type that I examine in this chapter appeared in collections in the 1960s, 1970s, and 1980s. As we explore what these poets are saying about the Bible, we should keep in mind how central the question of one's relationship to the Bible is for an Israeli who has grown up with the constant use of the Bible in public discourse. Furthermore, given the fact that one's view of the Bible in Israel is so bound up with one's opinions on contemporary issues, it is inevitable that these poems on the Bible are more than just comments on Scripture. They also must be seen as comments on cultural values and world views in Israel that draw on the Bible. Like the secular humanistic writers whose positions we have examined, these poets insist on the freedom to understand the Bible on their own terms and selectively reject those aspects of the Bible that clash with their own understanding of reality and with secular humanistic values; they thereby critique the extent to which their culture has been influenced by the Bible. In some poems they assert their freedom to understand the Bible on their own terms by presenting new ways to read the Bible. In other poems they assert this freedom by the more radical suggestion that it might be necessary to rewrite the Bible.

Rereading the Bible

An Israeli whose relationship with the Bible develops in a secular context is relatively free beginning in childhood to read the Bible in a selective manner. Such selectivity can involve the reader's focus on certain aspects of the text, as well as an attempt to understand the events of the text in ways that depart from either the literal meaning of the Bible or traditional interpretations of the biblical text. In Meir Wieseltier's poem "*Tanakh bitemunot*" ("Illustrated Bible")[47] the speaker recalls changes in his reading of the Bible at various points in his personal development from his childish fascination with gory images of biblical stories to his adult secular humanistic understanding of the Bible. As a child, he was naturally drawn to the pictures, particularly those of violent conflict, he found in an illustrated Bible:

תַּנַ"ךְ בִּתְמוּנוֹת

לָרִאשׁוֹנָה נִקְלַעְתִּי אֶל הַתַּנַ"ךְ,
וַאֲנִי יֶלֶד רַךְ,
בַּתַּנַ"ךְ בִּתְמוּנוֹת דּוֹרֵה.
שָׁם רָאִיתִי חֶזְיוֹנוֹת, מַרְאוֹת נוֹרָאִיִּים:
מֶלֶךְ נוֹפֵל עַל חַרְבּוֹ, מֶלֶךְ
מֵטִיל חֲנִית בִּמְנַגֵּן. נַעַר
מֵנִיף רֹאשׁ נָפִיל כָּרוּת, בָּחוּר
מְשַׁסֵּעַ אַרְיֵה, עָרִים נוֹפְלוֹת.
נוֹדַע לִי כִּי הַתַּנַ"ךְ הוּא מָקוֹם מָלֵא מַרְאוֹת
זְוָעָה מַרְהִיבָה וּמְתוּחָה.

ILLUSTRATED BIBLE

At first I came upon the Bible,
at a tender age,
in the Bible illustrated by Doré.
There I saw visions, awesome images:
a king falling on his sword, a king
thrusting a spear at a musician. A youth
waving a severed giant's head, a young man
tearing apart a lion, cities falling.
I came to know the Bible as a place full of images
of horror spectacular and tense.

The speaker's focus as a child on violent images from such stories as the death of Saul (I Samuel 31), the conflict between Saul and David (I Samuel 18–31), David's victory over Goliath (I Samuel 17), Samson's struggle with the lion (Judges 14:5–6), and any number of stories of defeats of cities constituted a highly selective approach to these stories. The larger perspective of ancient Israelite history and the role of God in that history, both essential parts of the biblical text, were absent from this child's point of view. The experience of death and destruction, however, remained.

If as a child the speaker had received a traditional Jewish education, his knowledge of biblical stories would not have come primarily from illustrations; although not completely absent from the Jewish tradition, such illustrations have not played a major role in traditional Jewish culture. Instead, his sources would have been the Hebrew texts of biblical stories, as well as rabbinic commentaries and legendary adaptations of those stories. Indeed, the illustrations to which the speaker refers are not even from a Jewish source. They are from an edition of the Bible illustrated by the nineteenth-century French Christian artist Gustave Doré. It is significant that the speaker's memory of the Doré illustrations is highly selective: he does not remember the more peaceful images in several of these illustrations; rather he concentrates on Doré's more graphic portrayals of violence based on stories that took place during the period of the early settlement of the Israelites portrayed in Joshua, Judges, and Samuel, which had so attracted him as a child.[48]

As he grows older, the speaker's perspective is transformed from a focus on the spectacular and gory images of the Bible to its words.

This awareness of the centrality of words is undoubtedly linked to the emerging identity of the speaker as a poet:

אַחַר-כָּךְ הִכַּרְתִּי אֶת הַתַּנַ"ךְ בְּסִפּוּרֵי בְּרֵאשִׁית.
אָז גִּלִּיתִי בִּמְהֵרָה
כִּי הַתַּנַ"ךְ עָשׂוּי מִלִּים:
אוֹר, חֹשֶׁךְ, מַיִם,
כִּי הוּא מְסַפֵּר עַל אֲנָשִׁים רְפֵי-כֹּחַ
מוּל אֵיתָנִים וְאֵל מְדַבֵּר.

עַל זִרְמֵי מִלִּים רוֹעֲשִׁים, סוֹחֲפִים, שָׁטָה סִירַת הָאָדָם.

Afterwards I encountered the Bible in the Genesis stories.
Then I quickly discovered
that the Bible is made of words:
light, dark, water,
that it tells of people weakened
before the forces of Nature and a talking God.

On streams of words noisy, sweeping, floats the boat of humanity.

At this point not only have words replaced concrete images, but the speaker has become aware of the centrality of the relationship between human beings and God in the Bible. This awareness comes from a highly selective reading of the account of Creation in Genesis. In this reading God controls language: He makes use of words (light, dark, water) to create the world; His speech, accompanied by the forces of Nature, overwhelms human beings. In this section of the poem we hear echoes of the stories of the flood in Noah's time (Genesis 6–9), and of the Tower of Babel (Genesis 11:1–9), in which God controlled the excessive ambitions of humanity by causing them to speak in a variety of languages ("On streams of words noisy, sweeping floats the boat of humanity"). The speaker ignores the many initiatives taken by human beings in the first chapters of Genesis (for example, Eve's defiance of God's prohibition to eat of the fruit of the tree of knowledge in Genesis 3 and the various inventions of the descendants of Cain in Genesis 4) to emphasize his sense at the time that the power of God severely limits the power of human beings.

In the next stage the speaker moves away from his previous understanding that the Bible provides little room for human self-expression. He presents instead a more humanistic approach to the Bible. Here he focuses on the prophets, and his interpretation of their books reflects his changed understanding of the relationship between God and humanity. No longer does God speak, but rather the words that such prophets as Amos of Tekoa or Jeremiah of Anathoth claim to have come from God are in fact the creations of the prophets who are human beings not unlike the speaker. Here, human beings, more active than they were in the previous stage, attribute their own words to an inarticulate divine rumbling that they hear:

וּזְמַן רַב עָבַר עַד שֶׁהִגִּיעוּ הַנְּבִיאִים.
הֵם כְּבָר הָיוּ אֲנָשִׁים
לֹא בִּלְתִּי דּוֹמִים לִי, וֵאלֹהִים
נַעֲשָׂה הֲמִיָּה
מְסֻגְנֶנֶת עַל־יְדֵי בָּחוּר מִתְּקוֹעַ אוֹ מֵעֲנָתוֹת.

And much time passed until the prophets arrived.
They already were people
not unlike me, and God
became a rumbling
styled by a young man from Tekoa or from Anathoth.

The final stage involves the complete transformation of the speaker's reading of the Bible into one reflecting secular humanism. Here the focus is on the stories of the kings of ancient Israel. All events of the period of the kings are explained in sociopolitical terms that could equally be applied to contemporary realities. Kings honor prophets not because they were sent by God, but because they respect the personal courage of the prophets and because the prophets are supported by the will of the people. Furthermore, not God, but the political machinations of the royal court, determine the fate of the people:

מְלָכִים נָתְנוּ לָהֶם כָּבוֹד
מִכֵּיוָן שֶׁמְּלָכִים מִסּוּג מְסֻיָּם מְכַבְּדִים הֶעָזָה,
וּמַעֲמָד אֶכְּס-טֶרִיטוֹרְיָאלִי מְסֻיָּג
נִתַּן לָהֶם מִכֹּחַ הָרָצוֹן הָעֲמָמִי.

אַף-עַל-פִּי-כֵן כְּבָר חָלָה שָׁם
מוֹדֶרְנִיזַצְיָה מֻפְלֶגֶת שֶׁל הָאֱנוֹשִׁי.
תְּכָכִים מְדִינִיִּים מְפֻקָּחִים, עִוְרִים,
הִכְרִיעוּ אֶת גּוֹרַל הַהֲמוֹנִים. יַחַד עִמָּם
גָּלוּ אַחֲרוֹנֵי הַמְנַסְּחִים הָאֱלֹהִיִּים.

עַתָּה עָשׂוּ בַּתְּחוּם הָאֶפְשָׁרִי:
מָתְחוּ בִּקֹּרֶת, הִשְׁמִיעוּ קִינָה, הֵפִיחוּ תִּקְוָה.

Kings gave them honor
since kings of a certain type honor daring
and a limited extraterritorial status
was given them by virtue of the popular will.

Even so there already occurred there
an extensive modernization of the human.
Political designs, clever, blind,
determined the fate of the masses. Together with them
were exiled the last of the divine phrase makers.

Now they created in the realm of the possible:
they criticized, expressed lament, inspired hope.

By the end of the poem we realize that the speaker's final perspective reflects the generally accepted view of the Bible held by modern secular society. The "divine phrase makers," the prophets, who had been honored in the past were made increasingly irrelevant in their "extraterritorial status" and finally "exiled" from any meaningful role in human affairs. Their place was inherited by secular poets who, like the speaker, attempt to do with words what the Bible once did when it was considered a sacred text: challenge, mourn, and inspire the members of their society.

As we follow this account of the speaker's changing approaches to the Bible, we sense that much of the drama of the Bible has been lost

over time. The speaker is no longer interested in either violent con-
flicts between people or the confrontation between humanity and an
all-powerful God. He can no longer take literally the accounts of di-
vine revelation to the prophets. Whereas once the Bible played a
vital role in the speaker's youth and his people's past, the closest
equivalent to the Bible, modern poetry, can only partly and inade-
quately meet the needs that the Bible once met before its power and
authority were undermined by secular humanism.

When a secular Israeli adopts a humanistic approach to the Bible
as an adult, he or she must come to terms with the fact that while the
Bible is a rich source of imagery reflecting and illuminating human
experience, in order for it to function well as such a source its per-
spective and hierarchy of values often must be transformed to fit his
or her own world view. For Nathan Yonathan the Bible's viability is
called into question because he cannot accept the hierarchy of val-
ues found in the Bible and its subsequent interpretations. In his
poem "*Yonatan 'aviv*" ("*Jonathan Spring*"),[49] Yonathan challenges the
primary position of certain biblical heroes in favor of characters
whose position is secondary in the biblical text:

יוֹנָתָן אָבִיב

יוֹסֵף, לֹא מֹשֶׁה, טָרוֹף טֹרַף
חֲלוֹמוֹת נְחָשִׁים אַחִים אָב
חוֹטֵא וְשָׁב אוֹהֵב וּמַחֲשֶׂה
תּוֹעֶה בֵּין עוֹלָלוֹת אֶפְרַיִם לְחֶמְדַּת מְנַשֶּׁה
יוֹסֵף דַּעַת יוֹסֵף מַכְאוֹב
יוֹסֵף קַיִץ

לֹא אֲבִימֶלֶךְ, קָטֹן אֶחָיו יוֹתָם
בֵּין פֶּלֶךְ הָרֶכֶב לְחֶרֶב נָקָם
גִּבּוֹר בִּמְלִים
עַל פִּסְגַּת גְּרִזִּים שֶׁלּוֹ
אָדָם שֶׁלֹּא יִמְלֹךְ
לְעוֹלָם
בּוֹדֵד עַל בָּמוֹתָיו
יוֹתָם סְתָו

61

סִיסְרָא, לֹא בָּרָק, מוּבָס וְנָס
בַּבִּצּוֹת
כּוֹרֵעַ בֵּין רַגְלֵי אִשָּׁה
יְתֵדוֹ בִּשְׂמֹאלָהּ
פָּנָיו בִּנְחִילֵי חֲלָבָהּ וְדִבְשָׁהּ
גֶּבֶר תּוּגַת אִמּוֹ
סִיסְרָא חֹרֶף

יוֹנָתָן, לֹא דָוִד, שֶׁעֵינוֹ כְּיַעֲרַת עֶרֶב
וְלִבּוֹ דְּבַשׁ וְדִינוֹ חֶרֶב
חֲלוֹם שְׁפָחוֹת וּמְלָכִים
יוֹנָתָן אָחִי
מִלַּת אַהֲבָה אַחֲרוֹנָה בְּקִינַת דָּוִד
יוֹנָתָן אָבִיב

JONATHAN SPRING

Joseph, not Moses, torn apart
dreams snakes brothers father
sins and returns loves and is silent
wanders between the gleanings of Ephraim and the delight of
    Manasseh
Joseph knowledge Joseph pain
Joseph summer

Not Abimelech, his littlest brother Jotham
between the spindle of the chariot and the sword of revenge
a hero of words
at the summit of his Gerizim
a man who will not rule
ever
alone on his heights
Jotham autumn

Sisera, not Barak, defeated and in flight
in the swamps
kneeling between the legs of a woman
his peg in her left hand
his face in the swarm of her milk and honey

a man his mother's grief
Sisera winter

Jonathan, not David, whose eye is like an evening forest
his heart honey but his fate the sword
the dream of maidservants and kings
Jonathan my brother
final word of love in David's lament
Jonathan spring

The speaker rejects biblical characters who had outstanding successes in difficult political or military undertakings—Moses, Abimelech, Barak, and David—in favor of characters with whose sensitivity, sensuality, and vulnerability he identifies—Joseph, Jotham, Sisera, and Jonathan. As he raises the status of these relatively secondary characters, he adjusts some of the imagery associated with them to affirm the values of sensuality, love, and individual expression, which he embraces in opposition to such values as power, national survival, and military victory, which he believes contemporary Israeli culture derives from the Bible.

In rejecting Moses, the great prophet and leader of the Exodus, in favor of Joseph, the latter's experiences of rising from slavery to political power and his clever manipulation of his brothers are left out. Instead, his life is portrayed as one of confusion, sinful sensuality, and pain by means of words and expressions taken directly from the Joseph story: "torn apart" (*tarof toraf,* Genesis 37:33), "dreams" (*halomot,* Genesis 37, 40, 41), "wanders" (*to'eh,* Genesis 37:15), and the names of Joseph's sons Ephraim and Manasseh. In the next to last line of the first stanza the speaker plays on the similarity of the Hebrew name for Joseph (*Yosef*) and the imperfect form of the verb that means to increase (*yosef,* which also appears in the Bible as *yosif*). The line "Joseph knowledge Joseph pain" (*yosef da'at yosef makh'ov*) alludes thereby to the biblical expression *yosif da'at yosif makh'ov* ("to increase learning is to increase heartache," Ecclesiastes 1:18). The speaker affirms the image of Joseph that he has created—a hero whose path in life is fraught with confusion, pain, and change, one who continues seeking knowledge and exploring.

In rejecting Abimelech for his brother Jotham (Judges 9), the speaker does not challenge the biblical assessment of the worth of these two characters. Abimelech is not at all portrayed as a positive hero in the Bible, but the speaker rejects even his military and political successes, as if the speaker is saying he cannot abide the fact that the Bible tells of a period when Abimelech succeeded in his ruthless act of mass fratricide. The speaker instead pledges his loyalty to Jotham, the "hero of words" who, as the only brother to survive Abimelech's massacre, recited a parable from the summit of Mount Gerizim that eloquently protested what his brother had done. Although Jotham will never have military or political power, he stands proudly alone against a society controlled by Abimelech's immoral power.

When the speaker expresses his preference for the defeated Canaanite general Sisera over his Israelite victor Barak (Judges 4), not only does he choose the weaker character over the stronger one, but he even more subversively chooses the enemy of Israel over the Israelite. Furthermore, the scene of Sisera's defeat, the tent of Jael the Kenite, is transformed in the poem from a death scene to an erotic encounter. The tent peg with which Jael killed Sisera becomes Sisera's penis held in Jael's hand. The milk that Jael gave to Sisera before putting him to sleep and killing him is transformed into Sisera's sensual interaction with Jael's breasts associated with the nursing of an infant. Sisera's heroism consists of his abandoning war in favor of love. Although Sisera's mother grieves for him, Sisera has undergone the necessary process of maturing by detaching himself from his mother, as well as from his identity as a warrior, and finding fulfillment in his sexual relations with Jael. The speaker's reference to milk and honey in portraying the sensual pleasures that Sisera experiences reinforces the transformation of images of war into images of love. For the speaker the "land flowing with milk and honey" that the Israelites were commanded to conquer is not nearly as important as the milk-and-honey pleasure of the erotic.

In rejecting David for his close friend Jonathan, the speaker again chooses love and sensuality over military prowess. Here too love triumphs over power: although Jonathan fell in battle, the mighty warrior David made a point of mourning him as a beloved friend (II Samuel 1:17–27).

The association of each of these heroes with a season of the year suggests that the preference of the speaker for intellectual exploration, literary creativity, and love is closely connected with the world of nature, which he considers superior to the world of culture that produced the Bible. The association of heroes with seasons moves from the summer-like wildness of Joseph's confusing life to the heroic struggle against the fall-like and winter-like death and destruction of war in the Abimelech and Deborah stories and concludes with the spring-like love between David and Jonathan that triumphs over death. The truer natural values of human creativity and love, the speaker suggests, will ultimately triumph just as the world is gloriously reborn each year with the emergence of spring. It is not likely a coincidence that the poet, whose family name is Yonathan (the Hebrew pronunciation of Jonathan), ends the poem with that biblical hero, whom he associates with spring and human love.

In the poem "*Sippurei hamiqra*" ("Bible Stories")[50] Yonathan makes a different kind of attempt to reread the Bible. At the beginning of the poem the speaker attempts to freeze biblical characters at an early point in their lives, when they were still whole and uncorrupted:

סִפּוּרֵי הַמִּקְרָא

קַיִן לִפְנֵי שֶׁהָרַג אֶת הֶבֶל
שָׁאוּל כְּשֶׁהָיָה עוֹד אֶחָד מִנְּבִיאֵי הַחֶבֶל
דָּוִד כְּשֶׁהִתְחִיל לְנַגֵּן זְמִירוֹת יִשְׂרָאֵל עַל הַנֵּבֶל:

יַעֲקֹב שֶׁעָבַד בְּרָחֵל שֶׁבַע שָׁנִים תְּמִימוֹת
יוֹסֵף שֶׁהָיָה מֶלֶךְ בְּכָל הַחֲלוֹמוֹת
שִׁמְשׁוֹן לִפְנֵי שֶׁאָהַב נָשִׁים עֲרֻמּוֹת.

BIBLE STORIES

Cain before he killed Abel
Saul when he was still among the band of prophets
David when he began to play the songs of Israel on the lyre.

Jacob who worked for Rachel seven full years
Joseph who was king in all the dreams
Samson before he loved naked women.

In these first two stanzas we sense the desperate wish of the speaker to envision a happier series of stories than those found in the Bible. Nevertheless, the speaker allows himself to be swept along by the plot of each of these biblical stories and to tell of the failure and corruption that characterized these heroes' lives in later years. As this occurs, it becomes apparent that the speaker's inability to freeze these heroes in their earlier states of purity and naiveté is not so much because he feels a duty to submit to the authority of the biblical text, but rather because the ultimate corruption of each character reflects the inevitable corruption of human beings in the course of life. The speaker's reading of the Bible reflects a transition from naive optimism to sober pessimism that is not necessarily central to any of these stories. To emphasize the transition from optimism to pessimism the speaker downplays the positive in their characters and emphasizes the negative:

אַחַר הַדְּבָרִים הָאֵלֶּה אַחֲרֵי הַהַקְדָּמָה —
דְּמֵי-הֶבֶל צוֹעֲקִים אֵלַי מִן הָאֲדָמָה
שָׁאוּל מִתְגַּנֵּב אֶל הַזְּקֵנָה מֵעֵין-דֹּר לִשְׁאוֹל מִי וָמָה
דָּוִד שׁוֹלֵחַ אֶת אוּרִיָּה אֶל מוּל פְּנֵי הַמִּלְחָמָה.

יַעֲקֹב הָיָה כְּבָר עָשִׁיר וּבַדֶּרֶךְ בֵּית-לֶחֶם הִשְׁאִיר אֶת קֶבֶר רָחֵל
יוֹסֵף הַגָּדוֹל מֵת וְקָם בְּמִצְרַיִם מֶלֶךְ אַחֵר
שִׁמְשׁוֹן בִּזְרוֹעוֹת הַזּוֹנָה נִרְדָּם, עַכְשָׁו הוּא עִוֵּר בְּרֵחַיִם טוֹחֵן.

מִתְקָרְבִים לַסּוֹף. קַיִן נוֹדֵד בָּעוֹלָם וְאֵין לוֹ דָּמִים
שָׁאוּל עַל חַרְבּוֹ נוֹפֵל וּמִתְחַנֵּן אֶל הַנַּעַר שֶׁיְּמִית
וְדָוִד גַּם דָּוִד בָּא בַּיָּמִים וְלֹא יֵחַם לוֹ בְּלִי הַשּׁוּנַמִּית.

קַיִן מֵת וַדַּאי בְּאֶרֶץ נוֹד נְדוּדָיו. שָׁאוּל חַי כְּעַרְעָר בָּעֲרָבָה
דָּוִד כָּל יָמָיו פְּזֵר בֵּין מִלְחָמָה לְאַהֲבָה
מִיּוֹסֵף נִשְׁאֲרוּ חֲלוֹמוֹת בִּלְבַד
שִׁמְשׁוֹן שׁוֹכֵב בֵּין אוֹיְבָיו
וְכָל הַשְּׁאָר
וְכָל הַשְּׁאָר, אוֹמְרִים, כָּתוּב עַל סֵפֶר הַיָּשָׁר.

After these matters after the introduction—
The blood of Abel cries out to me from the ground

Saul steals away to the old woman at En Dor to ask who and
what
David sends Uriah to confront the face of war.

Jacob was already rich and on the way to Bethlehem left be-
hind Rachel's tomb
Joseph the great died and in Egypt arose a different king
Samson in the arms of the whore fell asleep, now he blindly
grinds the millstones.

We're getting near the end. Cain wanders the world his
murderer will bear no blood guilt
Saul on his sword falls and entreats the lad to kill
And David, even David, is old and can be warmed only by the
Shunammite.

Cain died certainly in the land of his wanderings. Saul lived as
a tamarisk in the wilderness
David wasted all his days between war and love
From Joseph remained only dreams
Samson lies among his enemies
And all the rest,
And all the rest, they say, is written in *Sefer hayashar.*

As their lives progressed these characters of great promise gained lit-
tle by their actions. None of them, according to the speaker, left the
world with anything of lasting significance. Cain ended up as a wan-
dering murderer; unlike Cain in the Bible, however, if someone kills
him the murder will not be avenged (Genesis 4). Saul engaged in
necromancy at En Dor (I Samuel 28) and committed suicide on Mount
Gilboa (I Samuel 31). David sent his lover's husband Uriah to die in
battle (II Samuel 11), and in old age he was pathetically dependent on
a maidservant to warm him (I Kings 1). Jacob's wealth could not pre-
vent his losing his wife Rachel to an untimely death (Genesis 35).
After Joseph's death a new king arose to reverse the fortunes of the Is-
raelites by enslaving them (Exodus 1). Samson let himself be tricked
by Delilah and eventually died a captive of his enemies (Judges 16).

This poem suggests both a discontinuous and a harmonious rela-
tionship between the biblical past and the present. From the anti-
heroic modern perspective it is difficult for the speaker to identify

with the great accomplishments of biblical heroes and more natural to assume that they were flawed. Nevertheless, because the Bible itself does not exempt its heroes from negative criticism, the speaker can feel connected to the Bible in his search for characters who fail in the world of action. In an effort to present biblical characters as unheroic, however, he ultimately creates a more negative portrait of them than does the Bible itself.

The speaker's reference to the book *Sefer hayashar* echoes allusions made in the Bible in connection with songs recited by Joshua and David. According to the Bible, the miracle of the standing sun that Joshua celebrates in his song and the dirge recited by David on the deaths of Saul and David (or a related song) were recorded in this *Sefer hayashar* (Joshua 10:13; II Samuel 1:18). These two texts reflect opposite ends of the spectrum of life's experiences: the great triumph and wonder reflected in a miraculous victory found in Joshua and the great despair reflected in death found in II Samuel. The speaker wishes to express a truth as ancient as *Sefer hayashar,* a text that apparently predated the Bible: just as life moves in a line that is straight (*yashar*) from birth to death, so it typically moves from hopefulness to a more sober view of reality, even though we wish we could preserve the naive world view of our early years.

Rewriting the Bible

For some poets the need to bridge the gap between the Bible and contemporary experience is met by not merely developing new readings of the Bible but also taking the more radical step of suggesting the need to rewrite the Bible. In Yehuda Amichai's poem, "*'Ani rotseh levalbel 'et hatanakh*" ("I Want to Confuse the Bible"),[51] the speaker begins with a need to synthesize the contradictory senses of his closeness to the Bible, represented by his identification as the man under the fig tree of the period of Solomon's reign (I Kings 5:5) and of Micah's messianic vision (Micah 4:4), and his distance from the Bible, represented by his identification as the pilot of a modern airplane. The dual identity of the speaker may also connote a state of being caught between the experience of tranquility represented by the prophetic messianic vision and the contemporary experience of being in a state of war represented by the airplane that threatens to attack.[52] A synthesis between these two sets of contradictory identities could perhaps be created if the speaker gets his wish to "confuse," to shake up, the Bible to produce a very different text that would better conform to the speaker's contemporary understanding of reality:

אֲנִי רוֹצֶה לְבַלְבֵּל אֶת הַתַּנַ"ךְ

מָטוֹס עוֹבֵר מֵעַל לַתְּאֵנָה
אֲשֶׁר מֵעַל לָאִישׁ אֲשֶׁר תַּחַת תְּאֵנָתוֹ.
הַטַּיָּס הוּא אֲנִי וְהָאִישׁ תַּחַת הַתְּאֵנָה הוּא אֲנִי.
אֲנִי רוֹצֶה לְבַלְבֵּל אֶת הַתַּנַ"ךְ.
אֲנִי כָּל כָּךְ רוֹצֶה לְבַלְבֵּל אֶת הַתַּנַ"ךְ.

I WANT TO CONFUSE THE BIBLE

An airplane passes over the fig tree
That is over the man under his fig tree.
The pilot is me and the man under the fig tree is me.
I want to confuse the Bible.
I want so much to confuse the Bible.

The speaker in Amichai's poem refers to a number of biblical terms that he finds impossible to apply in their original meanings to the period of the crisis of religious faith in which he lives:

אֲנִי מַאֲמִין בָּאִילָנוֹת, לֹא כְּמוֹ שֶׁפַּעַם הֶאֱמִינוּ,
אֱמוּנָתִי קְטוּעָה וְקִצְרַת מוֹעֵד
עַד הָאָבִיב הַבָּא, עַד הַחֹרֶף הַבָּא,
אֲנִי מַאֲמִין בְּבִיאַת הַגֶּשֶׁם וּבְבוֹא הַשֶּׁמֶשׁ.
הַסֵּדֶר וְהַצֶּדֶק מְבֻלְבָּלִים: טוֹב וָרָע
עַל הַשֻּׁלְחָן לְפָנַי כְּמֶלַח וּכְפִלְפֵּל
הַכֵּלִים כָּל כָּךְ דּוֹמִים. אֲנִי כָּל כָּךְ
רוֹצֶה לְבַלְבֵּל אֶת הַתַּנַ"ךְ. הָעוֹלָם
מָלֵא דַּעַת טוֹב וָרָע, הָעוֹלָם מָלֵא לִמּוּד:

צִפֳּרִים לוֹמְדוֹת מִן הָרוּחַ הַנּוֹשֶׁבֶת
וּמְטוֹסִים לוֹמְדִים מִן הַצִּפֳּרִים
וּבְנֵי אָדָם לוֹמְדִים מֵהֶם מְכֻלָּם וְשׁוֹכְחִים.
הָאֲדָמָה אֵינָהּ עֲצוּבָה מִשּׁוּם שֶׁמֵּתִים קְבוּרִים בָּהּ.
כְּשֵׁם שֶׁשִּׂמְלַת אֲהוּבָתִי אֵינָהּ שְׂמֵחָה
שֶׁהִיא חַיָּה בְּתוֹכָהּ.

I believe in trees, not as they once believed,
My belief is truncated and short-lived—
Till next spring, till next winter.
I believe in the coming of rain and in the coming of sun.
Order and justice are confused: good and evil
On the table before me like salt and pepper,
The shakers so alike. I want so much
To confuse the Bible. The world
Is filled with knowledge of good and evil, the world is filled
With learning: birds learn from the blowing wind,
Airplanes learn from the birds,
And people learn from all of them and forget.
The earth is not sad because the dead are buried in it.
As the dress of my beloved is not happy
That she lives in it.

The biblical *'emunah* (trust) in God's saving powers is not accessible to this modern speaker. Even a return to a pagan belief in the magical qualities of nature is impossible. *'Emunah* survives only as a tentative belief in the recurring cycles of nature. *Tsedeq* (justice) and *tov vara'* (good and evil) are defined as clearly distinct categories in the Bible. In modern society the distinctions between justice and injustice, good and evil, are no longer clear. Society is therefore incapable of constructing a clearly defined moral code. People are incapable of applying to their lives the lessons of what there is to learn about good and evil from the world. Furthermore, there is such a degree of alienation between human beings and nature that when people (*benei 'adam*) die they do not sense any connection between themselves and the earth (*'adamah*) out of which, according to the Bible, they were created.

The speaker sees this crisis of faith as most parallel to two stories of disaster in the Bible: the flood in the time of Noah and the suffering of Job. In each story disaster is followed by a renewal of trust between human beings and God: the flood in Noah's time subsides and God establishes the rainbow as a sign of a renewed covenant with humanity in which He promises not to bring another flood; Job is restored to his status as a healthy and wealthy husband and father. To shape the story of Noah to correspond to the contemporary crisis of faith, the speaker selects the image that introduces the part of the Noah story that leads to the affirmation of faith: the mountains of Ararat, on which Noah's ark found its resting place (Genesis 8:4), but he transforms those mountains into a valley, thereby suggesting not triumphant deliverance, but descent into despair. From the Job story the speaker selects only the image of the bad tidings of loss brought to Job (Job 1–2), not the restoration of Job's status (Job 42). Despair has triumphed over hope in modern times, the speaker believes, because we live in the post-Holocaust world with the knowledge that evil can so capture the world that adults are capable of turning children into cloudlike smoke. (The expression *yaldei benei 'adam,* which the translators render as "the sons of man," could also be translated as "the children of the sons of man" or "the children of human beings.")

יַלְדֵי בְּנֵי אָדָם הֵם עֲנָנִים
וַאֲרָרָט הוּא עֵמֶק עָמֹק.
וַאֲנִי לֹא רוֹצֶה לַחֲזֹר אֶל בֵּיתִי
כִּי אֶל הַבַּיִת מַגִּיעוֹת כָּל הַבְּשׂוֹרוֹת הָרָעוֹת,
כְּמוֹ בְּסֵפֶר אִיּוֹב.

The sons of man are clouds
And Ararat is a deep valley.
And I don't want to return home
Because all bad tidings come home
As in the Book of Job.

The speaker concludes the poem by doing what he has expressed his wish to do throughout the poem: he "confuses" the Bible. Despairing of the applicability of the original text of the Bible to the current crisis of faith, the speaker rewrites the Bible by turning its stories on their heads:

הֶבֶל הָרַג אֶת קַיִן וּמשֶׁה נִכְנַס
לָאָרֶץ הַמֻּבְטַחַת וּבְנֵי יִשְׂרָאֵל נִשְׁאֲרוּ בַּמִּדְבָּר.
אֲנִי נוֹסֵעַ בְּמַעֲשֵׂי הַמֶּרְכָּבָה שֶׁל יְחֶזְקֵאל
וִיחֶזְקֵאל עַצְמוֹ רוֹקֵד כְּמִרְיָם הַנְּבִיאָה
בְּגֵיא הָעֲצָמוֹת הַיְבֵשׁוֹת.
סְדֹם וַעֲמֹרָה מִתְפַּתְּחוֹת
וְאֵשֶׁת לוֹט הָיְתָה לִנְצִיב סֻכָּר וּדְבַשׁ
וְדָוִד מֶלֶךְ יִשְׂרָאֵל חַי וְקַיָּם.
אֲנִי כָּל כָּךְ
רוֹצֶה לְבַלְבֵּל אֶת הַתַּנַ"ךְ.

Abel killed Cain and Moses entered
The Promised Land and the Children of Israel stayed in the
    desert.
I travel in Ezekiel's divine chariot
And Ezekiel himself dances like Miriam
In the Valley of Dry Bones.
Sodom and Gomorrah are booming towns
And Lot's wife became a pillar of sugar and honey
And David King of Israel is alive.
I want so much
To confuse the Bible.

Common to many of these radically new versions of biblical stories is the painful experience of loss in each story, which is later transformed into triumph: the victim Abel defeats the aggressor Cain (Genesis 4); what could be perceived as the injustice of Moses, God's faithful servant, being prevented from entering the Promised Land is reversed (Numbers 20:12); Ezekiel transcends the despair of his vision of destruction in the valley of the dry bones (Ezekiel 37) by dancing as Miriam did in celebration of the miracle of the crossing of the Red Sea (Exodus 15:20–21); Sodom and Gomorrah are not destroyed, but rather flourish (Genesis 19); and Lot's wife is not turned into salt, but rather into sugar and honey (Genesis 19:26). What is important here is that for the most part it is not divine intervention, but rather the poet's imaginative transformation of the actions and fates of biblical characters that brings about deliverance in these new versions of biblical stories.

The poet's confusion of the Bible has a playful and down-to-earth quality to it.[53] It is delightful to think of the grim and tortured prophet Ezekiel dancing or Lot's wife becoming a pillar of sugar and honey. Nevertheless, in the midst of this playful imagining there is a sense of loss: in a world devoid of faith in the presence of God in human history, all that remains is the willful imagination of the poet who asserts the possibility of a better world in which human beings can escape the nightmares of the twentieth century.

On another level, these reversals of the Bible may be seen as not only an assertion of the poet's imagination but also the poet's affirmation of secular Zionism as a response to the theological gap between the Bible and modern experience. The reversals of each story to which the speaker alludes may represent the Zionist revolution in the consciousness of the Jewish people based on the assumption that Jews must bring about their own national redemption and not wait for the return to Zion in messianic times. Abel, the victim, may be seen to represent the Jewish people who now that they have a state are able to defeat their Cain-like enemies. Moses and Ezekiel, prophets to the Israelites outside the Land of Israel, are now allowed to participate in redemption—Moses enters the Promised Land, and Ezekiel experiences the equivalent of the crossing of the Red Sea— just as the impossible dream of Jews leaving the Diaspora for their own state has been achieved. The redevelopment of the Land of Israel by Zionist settlement occurred no more dramatically than in the wilderness of the Negev region, and the speaker captures that marvel of national rebirth by human effort in the images of Sodom and Gomorrah becoming "boom towns" and the pillar of salt of Lot's wife becoming "sugar and honey."

If we see the conclusion of the poem as the affirmation of the human efforts of Zionism, then it helps us to understand the allusion at the end of the poem to the expression *David melekh yisra'el ḥai ve-qayyam* ("David King of Israel is alive"), recited in the traditional Jewish ceremony of the Sanctification of the New Moon (*qiddush le-vanah*). This allusion is somewhat puzzling because here the speaker does not reverse the traditional wording that expresses the Jew's faith that a Messiah of the House of David will come to redeem the world. Instead, he preserves the traditional wording, thereby suggesting that he shares the traditional Jewish faith in the coming of the Messiah.

Nevertheless, in the context of all these other reversals of biblical stories, we are forced to consider the possibility that here too a reversal is made. What is reversed here, perhaps, is the death of David in the Bible. For the speaker, however, the reversal of David's death is not in the traditional sense that a descendant of his will one day appear as the Messiah to restore the sovereignty of the Davidic royal house, but more in the sense that generations of Zionist and Israeli youths have meant it when they sang these words as a folk song: the "King David" who lives is the secular transformation of the Davidic royal line into the modern State of Israel. The speaker thereby declares that the successful twentieth-century reestablishment of Jewish sovereignty in the Land of Israel may represent the primary source of hope for Jews in a faithless world. This sovereignty, the result of Jews pursuing the secular Zionist dream, falls short of the messianic vision of peace and tranquility represented by the image alluded to at the beginning of the poem of each man under his vine and his fig tree, but it does represent a positive human response to a world capable of turning children into smoke.[54]

Modern readers of the Bible may be tempted to reread or rewrite the Bible not only because of a clash between the biblical and modern world views but also because, like Arieh Lova Eliav, the very gutsy raw realities of life portrayed in the Bible that so attracted the speaker as a child in Meir Wieseltier's poem "*Tanakh bitemunot*" may offend their sensibilities. On the assumption that his culture's most sacred text should transcend raw reality, the speaker in poem number 29 of Yehuda Amichai's collection *Hazeman (Time)*[55] tells of his desire to purify the Bible of such base elements. In the course of this endeavor the speaker deletes the very powerful universal emotions and actions portrayed in the Bible; he thereby distances himself from the basic realities of human existence:

29

סִנַּנְתִּי מִתּוֹךְ מְגִלַּת אֶסְתֵּר אֶת מִשְׁקַע
הַשִּׂמְחָה הַגַּסָּה וּמִתּוֹךְ סֵפֶר יִרְמְיָהוּ
אֶת יְלֶלֶת הַכְּאֵב בַּמֵּעַיִם. וּמִתּוֹךְ
שִׁיר הַשִּׁירִים אֶת הַחִפּוּשׂ הָאֵין סוֹפִי
אַחַר הָאַהֲבָה וּמִסֵּפֶר בְּרֵאשִׁית אֶת
הַחֲלוֹמוֹת וְאֶת קַיִן וּמִתּוֹךְ קֹהֶלֶת אֶת

הַיֵּאוּשׁ וּמִתּוֹךְ סֵפֶר אִיּוֹב אֶת אִיּוֹב.
וְהִדְבַּקְתִּי לִי מִן הַשְּׁאֵרִיּוֹת סֵפֶר תַּנַ"ךְ חָדָשׁ.
אֲנִי חַי מְצֻנְזָר וּמֻדְבָּק וּמֻגְבָּל וּבְשַׁלְוָה.

29

From the Scroll of Esther, I filtered out the sediment
Of coarse joy, and from the book of Jeremiah
The wailing of pain in your guts. And from
The Song of Songs, the endless search
Of love, and from Genesis
The dreams and Cain, and from Ecclesiastes
The despair, and from the Book of Job, Job.
And from the leftovers, I pasted together a new Bible
              for myself.
I live censored, pasted, limited, in peace.

The speaker's approach to the Bible is most disturbing. It has al-
lowed him to arrive at a false sense of tranquility based on the desire
not to have to face the pain and passion of human existence so pow-
erfully portrayed in the Bible. He filters the impurities of powerful
emotions from the Bible and cuts and pastes the ancient text until a
Bible easier to handle on an emotional level emerges.

The price he pays for this false sense of tranquility is made clear
in the second stanza of the poem, in the conversation he has with a
woman about a mutual acquaintance:

אִשָּׁה אַחַת שָׁאֲלָה אוֹתִי אֶמֶשׁ בָּרְחוֹב
הֶחָשׁוּךְ עַל שְׁלוֹם אִשָּׁה אַחֶרֶת
שֶׁמֵּתָה לֹא בְּעִתָּהּ וְלֹא בְּעִתּוֹ שֶׁל אַף אֶחָד.
מִתּוֹךְ עֲיֵפוּת גְּדוֹלָה עָנִיתִי לָהּ:
שְׁלוֹמָהּ טוֹב, שְׁלוֹמָהּ טוֹב.

One woman asked me yesterday in a dark
Street about the health of another woman
Who died before her time, or anybody's time.
In great weariness I answered:
She's fine, she's fine.

The death of their mutual acquaintance at a young age is obviously very painful for the speaker. He refers to her death with the Hebrew expression *lo' be'ittah* ("before her time") and then plays on that expression with the words *velo' be'ittah shel 'af 'ehad* ("[not at] anybody's time") to suggest how unfair it is that the woman died at an age when no human being should die. When he is confronted with this painful reality, his perspective is so censored that he cannot come to terms with it. Instead, he pretends that nothing bad has happened to their acquaintance: *shelomah tov* ("she's fine"), he replies. The speaker's response suggests that he has so retreated from life that "in his tiredness" he has come to believe that death brings a much desired sense of peace and well-being.

Each time an Israeli reads the Bible its heroes, who speak Hebrew and live in the ancient Land of Israel, come alive and reinforce the assumption of Israeli culture that the Bible has been revived in Israel. In the poem by Moshe Dor, "*Ha'od David menagen lefanekha*" ("*Does David Still Play Before You*"),[56] which serves as the title of this book, the speaker questions this underlying cultural assumption by wondering whether in any sense the characters of David, Solomon, Elijah, and Ezekiel are truly alive for the contemporary Israeli:

הַעוֹד דָּוִד מְנַגֵּן לְפָנֶיךָ

הַעוֹד דָּוִד מְנַגֵּן לְפָנֶיךָ
בְּכִנּוֹר הַזָּהָב?
וּשְׁלֹמֹה,
הַעוֹדוֹ מְמַשֵּׁל בְּאָזְנֶיךָ
אֶת מְשָׁלֵי שׁוּעָלָיו?

וּבְאֵיזֶה שָׂדֶה מִתְנַשֵּׂא אֵלָיהוּ
בְּרֶכֶב אֵשׁ וְסוּסֵי אֵשׁ?
וִיחֶזְקֵאל,
אֵיזוֹ כָּנָף מַכָּה בּוֹ, עִם אֵיזוֹ חַיָּה הוּא
נִפְתָּל בַּחַשְׁמַל הַגּוֹעֵשׁ?

DOES DAVID STILL PLAY BEFORE YOU

Does David still play before you
on the golden harp?

And Solomon,
does he still invent, in your hearing,
his fox fables?

And from which field does Elijah take off
in a chariot of fire and with horses of fire?
And Ezekiel,
what being hammers him, with what creature
does he struggle in the stormy, shining substance?

In these first two stanzas the speaker focuses on creations of the human imagination in the Bible—David's music (I Samuel 16:23) and Solomon's fables (I Kings 5:12)—and on interactions between humanity and the divine—Elijah's ascent to heaven (II Kings 2:11) and Ezekiel's heavenly vision (Ezekiel 1). In raising the question of whether these experiences still exist the speaker suggests that they may not and that any attempt to bring them alive today by rereading the Bible may fail, for the reality of the Bible is too far removed from our own.

In the third stanza the speaker raises questions about the viability of the New Testament image of Jesus' crucifixion:

וּבֵין עַנְנֵי הַקְּטֹרֶת,
הַעוֹד לִסְלֹחַ וְלֶאֱהֹב
יְבַקְשׁוּ פָּנָיו הַחִוְּרוֹת מִכָּל תִּמֹּרֶת
שֶׁל יֵשׁוּעַ בְּכוֹכָב צָהֹב?

And among curls of incense,
does still to forgive and love
plead the face, paler than a cloud,
of Jesus, with the Yellow Star?

Wearing the yellow star of the Holocaust, Jesus represents the six million Jewish victims of the Nazis. In the New Testament and subsequent Church traditions Jesus' suffering was given theological and moral meaning. In particular, Jesus' willingness to forgive his enemies has been seen by Christian tradition as a model for humanity to follow. Because it is unusual for Jesus to appear in an Israeli poem, the image of his reacting to his suffering in such an extreme manner of forgiveness and love sharpens the question of whether there is any moral meaning to be discerned in the deaths of the victims of the Holocaust. The questions raised about the viability of Jesus' response to his suffering also represent questions directed at the Hebrew Bible and subsequent Jewish tradition that sought to find theological and moral meaning in the suffering of the Jews. The speaker connects these questions with the Bible by using such terms as *qetoret* (incense) and *timmoret* (here translated as "cloud," but actually more literally "pillar," suggesting the expression *timrot 'ashan*, "pillars of smoke," Joel 3:3). Both terms ironically connect the smoke of the crematoria in the death camps to biblical images of the relationship between God and humanity: the incense of the sacrificial cult of the Temple and the columns of smoke of the prophet Joel's vision of God's wonders at the time of the final redemption of Israel. This ironic juxtaposition of the Holocaust and biblical images of God interacting meaningfully with the people of Israel makes clear that for the speaker the deaths of the Holocaust victims have nothing to do with religiously meaningful acts of sacrifice and that the Holocaust mocks the traditional faith in ultimate redemption by the hand of God.

At this point in the poem we see from the speaker's rhetorical questions that he seriously doubts whether the Bible can work for the modern Israeli, for it is unclear whether a meaningful cultural context for aesthetic expressions and for interaction with the divine can be revived. Furthermore, as in Amichai's "*'Ani rotseh levalbel 'et hatanakh*," the challenge of the Holocaust to traditional faith, more than anything else, questions the viability of the Bible for the speaker. This speaker, however, is driven to "rewrite" the Bible in a way more radical and shocking than those of the speakers in Amichai's poems, who "confuse" or "filter" the Bible:

וּמֵאֵיזֶה תְּנַ"ךְ פָּרוּעַ
שֶׁל שְׁמָשׁוֹת נוֹלָדוֹת וְכָבוֹת
יָדֶיךָ קְשׁוּיוֹת-הָעוֹרְקִים תְּגַשֵּׁשְׁנָה בַּחֲרָטָה לִקְרֹעַ
אֶת הַהַבְטָחוֹת הַנִּכְזָבוֹת?

And from out which savage Bible
of erupting, extinguished suns

do your hands, hardened
in the arteries, grope regretfully to tear
up disappointed promises?

Jews in the post-Holocaust world have a very different relationship with God than did the writers of the Bible. Having let the Jews down by not protecting them in the Holocaust, God can no longer expect either the creative outpouring of human beings before Him or the intense interaction between people and Himself that characterized the biblical era. Furthermore, God must realize that humanity's disappointment with Him discourages people from living by the divine principles of love and forgiveness. In the post-Holocaust world the Bible looks very different than it did in the past. It is now a "savage Bible" (*tanakh parua͑*), with images of the meaningless outbreak and decline of violence, represented by the "erupting, extinguished suns." The only viable human response, the speaker suggests, is to complete the transformation of the biblical text by tearing out of it all of God's promises to save His people from harm, promises that are no longer trustworthy.

We would be mistaken to take literally the suggestion by these poets that in some sense we need a new Bible, whether it be Wieseltier's humanistic Bible, Yonathan's Bible with the primary heroes dethroned by secondary heroes or his Bible that emphasizes the inevitable corruption of human life, Amichai's "confused" or "filtered" Bible, or Dor's Bible with all God's promises torn out. I doubt that any of these poets believe that their poems can replace the Bible in Israeli culture, nor do I believe that they really wish them to do so.

Instead, the poets' call for a rereading or a rewriting of the Bible may be seen as a challenge to the ways the Bible is used in contemporary Israeli discourse, such as those we explored in the first part of this chapter. As they write their poems in modern Hebrew combined with allusive biblical language, the poets transform the original meaning of the language of the Bible and thereby express their serious reservations about much that is contained in this text and more importantly about the applicability of the Bible to current existence. Dor's repeated use of the question words *ha͑od* ("does [he] still") and *'ezeh* ("which") in "*Ha͑od David menagen lefanekha*" raises the questions: Is it possible that what once happened in the Bible can still happen today, and do we know where to find today what is described in the Bible? Yonathan's persistent use of the word *lo'* ("not") in *"Yonatan 'aviv"* clearly conveys his rejection of biblical heroes generally viewed by Israelis as successful in favor of other less successful biblical heroes he finds to be more relevant to his world view and values. Amichai's expression *levalbel 'et hatanakh* ("to confuse the Bible") suggests his very real discomfort with the Bible as it is both written and currently understood. As each poet writes of his problematic relationship to the Bible he suggests that the tendency in Israeli discourse to apply the Bible to the present is of dubious value.

While those who engage in discourse based on the Bible apply biblical texts primarily to political and cultural issues, these poets extend the use of biblical texts to the realm of personal existence. In their poems they reveal that the Bible can function as a repository of vital images serving as the means to express our deepest frustrations, longings, and elations as we confront the existential issues of the relationship between human beings and of the relationship of the individual to the cosmos. These poems remind their readers that the Bible can function in such a way only as long as one feels free to play with these images and to shape one's perception of them to fit one's own perspective and values.

Although Israeli humanistic critics of the Bible have been quick to dismiss aspects of the Bible that they considered primitively vulgar, at least two poets question the potential danger of a rationalistic humanistic approach to the Bible: it can become too detached from the vital complexities of human existence captured in a wide range of images in the Bible. We can discern in Wieseltier's poem *"Tanakh bitemunot"* a sense of loss once the vitality of violent conflict portrayed in the Bible that so excited the speaker as a child is replaced by a more mature, rational understanding of this ancient text. Amichai, recognizing the potential role of the Bible as a source of such images of vitality, warns in his poem number 29 of *Hazeman* that there is a price to be paid in repressing the variety of emotions expressed in the Bible.

Those who use the Bible in Israeli discourse generally do not explore as deeply as do these poets the implications of the difficulty of applying biblical notions of divine providence to Israel in the post-Holocaust world. God is largely absent from these poems—a significant transformation of the biblical semiotic system, to say the least. The only explicit reference to God among these poems is found in Wieseltier's poem "*Tanakh bitemunot*"; yet even in that poem belief in God gives way to a secular humanistic understanding of biblical events. Nevertheless, whether the poems explicitly refer to God or not, they are permeated with a strong sense of dismay at the wide gap between the way the Bible conceives of the role of God in the world and the way these poets do. In Yonathan's poems the absence of God is the starkest. His biblical characters live in a world bereft of God: the integrity of their souls is constantly challenged, and their lives are doomed to failure. Their only redemption is in willfully embracing in their lives the values of art and human love. For Wieseltier the triumph of secular humanistic thought over the sense of God's presence in the world is a mixed blessing. Amichai and Dor painfully conclude that the great unexplained evil of the Holocaust has questioned the covenantal relationship between God and the people of Israel.

More than in typical Israeli public discourse, we find in much of this poetry a convergence of issues of Jewish existence with general issues of human existence in Western culture. These poets confirm what David H. Hirsch and Eli Pfefferkorn assert is generally characteristic of the Israeli poet: the concern "with the living agony of the Jew as modern Western man caught in a world of escalating technology and destructiveness and declining faith and hope."[57] As the inheritors of the biblical tradition that gave the Western world so much faith and hope, Israeli poets use that tradition not only to reflect on the nature of their particular national identity but also to say something about whether reassuring meaning can be discerned by any person living through the tumultuous historical events of the twentieth century.

CHAPTER TWO

THERE WERE
NO MORE
DAVIDS | **RESPONDING**
TO THE
ARAB-ISRAELI
CONFLICT

In a report to the Provisional State Council of the State of Israel on July 22, 1948, Prime Minister David Ben-Gurion reviewed what he considered to be the three phases of the military conflict between the Jews and the Arabs that had raged since the United Nations decision of November 29, 1947, to partition Palestine into a Jewish and an Arab state. "All three phases," Ben-Gurion stated, "strangely resemble several chapters from Joshua and Judges that might have been written today."[1] The analogy that Ben-Gurion made between Israel's War of Independence and the period of the conquest of the land of Canaan portrayed in the books of Joshua and Judges was most likely accepted by his audience because it fit so well with the prevailing notion that Zionism reenacted the entrance of the ancient Israelites to the land of Canaan. Furthermore, there was in the analogy he drew between that war and the wars of Joshua and Judges a reassuring message that Israel's success so far on the battlefield would bring her to ultimate victory, just as the ancient Isaelites had so often been militarily successful against their enemies.

As he drew this analogy Ben-Gurion, in effect, cast himself as Joshua or as one of the judges and thereby asserted that like his ancient forebears he would by military means establish the sovereignty of the modern descendants of the ancient Israelites in their land. The association between Ben-Gurion and Joshua was not uncommon in his day. Myron J. Aronoff notes that "Ben-Gurion was frequently associated with one of his favorite biblical characters, Joshua, who led the Hebrews into the promised land."[2] Rabbi Haim Gevaryahu, head of the Bible study group that met every other week in Ben-Gurion's house, has stated that it was his impression that "Ben-Gurion saw himself as a second Joshua son of Nun."[3] Gevaryahu was convinced that "subconsciously [Ben-Gurion] believed that he was established by divine providence to assume this . . . role as Joshua son of Nun."[4]

By the end of its War of Independence, Israel had not only secured its existence as a state but had even expanded its borders beyond those originally granted it by the United Nations partition resolution of 1947. It paid a heavy price for these accomplishments: six thousand Jewish Israelis, representing 1 percent of the Jewish population and 10 percent of the Jewish youth in Israel at the time, died in the war.[5] Furthermore, the war left Israel in a continuously vulnerable position, for despite Israel's military success the Arab world was still unwilling to accept the existence of a Jewish state in Palestine. In addition, the thousands of Arab refugees who left the area controlled by Israel for Lebanon, the West Bank of the Jordan River, which came under Jordanian rule, and Gaza, which came under Egyptian rule, constituted a focal point for opposition to Israel.

Early in the history of the State the people of Israel had to deal as much with this feeling of vulnerability to Arab opposition as with the feeling of the heroic triumph of 1948–1949 that established Jewish political sovereignty in the Land of Israel. The Bible has played an important role in assuring Israelis that as in the past Israel would triumph over the challenges to its existence. As Nurith Gertz notes, through much of the history of pre-State Zionism and in the early years of the State, the Jewish community of the Land of Israel saw itself as reenacting the David and Goliath story.[6] Jews saw their relatively small size as a community to be analogous to the young, seemingly defenseless David taking on the more powerful Arab enemy, analogous to the giant Goliath. Gertz observes that the mythic nature of this biblical story has given it the power to convince Jews in

Israel that they need not see themselves as vulnerable, despite the relatively small size of their state in comparison with the Arab world. "The language is mythical," Gertz explains, "because it lends actual, specific struggles an aura of the cosmic, eternal confrontation of forces of light (the few) and darkness (the many). The actual, specific struggles in this case follow the pattern well known in Jewish history; thus it points to its authors' tendency to seek in the past the assurances and beliefs that will lead Jewish society toward the future."[7] The story of David and Goliath provided a reassuring myth of survival, not only because it told of the victory of the weak against the strong but also because the youthful victor of the battle with Goliath eventually emerged as the great ruler of ancient Israel, King David. By identifying with David, the Jews of both the pre-State and State periods could allow themselves to believe that they too would eventually achieve a high degree of political sovereignty, analogous to that of David in ancient times.

This identification with David was also congruent with the latent messianism in Zionism because, according to Jewish tradition based on prophetic texts, the Messiah will be of the House of David. This is undoubtedly the significance of the tremendous popularity of the folk song based on the traditional Jewish liturgical expression "*David melekh yisra'el ḥai veqayyam*" ("David King of Israel lives") in the pre-State and early State periods. It was most convenient for Israel's first prime minister, Ben-Gurion, that his first name was David, thereby suggesting in a subliminal way to his fellow Israelis that the Kingdom of David was in some sense reestablished with the founding of the State of Israel. This identification of political leaders with King David survived into the period of the ascendance of the right-wing Likud party to political power beginning in the late 1970s, when it became customary for supporters of Likud leaders such as Menachem Begin and Ariel Sharon to chant the declaration that their leader is the King of Israel: "*Begin melekh yisra'el*" and "*Arik melekh yisra'el.*"[8]

In the period between the end of the War of Independence and Israel's next major war with an Arab enemy, the Sinai Campaign of 1956, Israeli vulnerability was felt keenly during Arab terrorist attacks over the borders between Israel and the West Bank and Israel and Gaza. One reason Israel went to war against Egypt in the Sinai Campaign was to stop the terrorist incursions from Gaza. Just as Ben-Gurion discovered in Joshua and Judges biblical parallels for what he believed would be the victory of Israel over its Arab enemies, a few months before the outbreak of the Sinai Campaign the Israeli general Moshe Dayan spoke of the vulnerability of Israel in the face of Arab terrorism as analogous to the story of Samson in Judges. He delivered his remarks in April 1956, at the funeral of Roi Rothberg, a member of Kibbutz Nahal Oz near the border of Gaza, who was killed by Arabs from Gaza whom he tried to chase away when they attempted to harvest wheat in the fields of the kibbutz.[9] The Samson story works well as an analogy to this situation because the name Arabs call the Land of Israel, Palestine, derives from Samson's enemy the Philistines, who lived in ancient times in the area of Gaza. In his remarks Dayan displays a marked sensitivity to the suffering of the Arab refugees in Gaza that has led to such violent attacks on Israelis. "What right have we to dispute their strong hatred of us?" Dayan rhetorically asks. "For eight years they have been sitting in the refugee camps in Gaza, and before their eyes we have been taking possession of the land and the villages in which they and their ancestors dwelled."[10]

From Dayan's point of view, Israelis do not take seriously enough the danger to Israel's security that is the result of the understandable hostility of the Palestinian refugees. Israelis, Dayan argues, do not fully appreciate the crucial role that the young members of Kibbutz Nahal Oz have assumed in risking their lives so that Israel would survive, and they forget that only by means of military strength and constant vigilance will Israel overcome the attempts by Arabs to destroy it. By settling near the border of Gaza and serving as a protective wall between Gaza and Israel, Dayan suggests, Roi Rothberg and his fellow youthful kibbutzniks are "carrying on [their] shoulders the heavy gates of Gaza,"[11] thereby demonstrating the courage and strength that Samson did when he foiled the Philistines' plot to kill him by leaving the city of Gaza carrying its gates on his shoulders (Judges 16). Given Roi Rothberg's fate, however, Dayan feels impelled to connect him as well with the period of Samson's defeat, when he was captured, blinded, and imprisoned by the Philistines (Judges 16). "The longing for peace," Dayan declares, "deafened his ears, and he did not hear the murderous cry of the ambusher. The gates of Gaza were too heavy for him and they subdued him."[12]

More recently, representatives of both ends of the political spectrum have seen the issue of Israeli control of the territories it conquered in 1967 as analogous to the Samson story. Shimon Peres, who as foreign minister of Israel played a central role in the negotiations with the PLO that led to the beginning of Israeli withdrawal from the West Bank and Gaza in 1994, published a book at the time of these negotiations. In this book Peres writes that Israel's agreement to withdraw from Gaza in effect saved it from a suicidal destruction that would have been analogous to that of Samson in the Philistines' temple (Judges 16). If an accommodation had not been made with the Palestinians, then the Palestinian uprising against Israel known as the Intifada, which began in Gaza, would have eventually overwhelmed Israel. "Samson in his time," Peres declares, "took a drastic step, bringing down the columns of the shrine in Gaza. There was no point in our repeating it."[13] At the other end of the political spectrum, shortly after the Jewish West Bank settler Baruch Goldstein was killed when he massacred Arabs in the mosque in the Tomb of the Patriarchs in Hebron in 1994, the extremist *Kahana' Hai* organization issued a statement in support of Goldstein, associating his suicidal attack on gentiles in their house of worship with Samson's self-destruction in the Philistine temple. "Happy is the lot of Baruch Goldstein," the statement read, "may the memory of the righteous be for a blessing, who sanctified the Name [of God] in his life, but even more so sanctified the Name [of God] in his death, as Samson once did."[14]

A more pervasive biblical association with the Goldstein massacre was the struggle between the ancient Israelites and the people of Amalek. Even before the massacre, the Arab-Israeli conflict was often associated in the minds of Israelis with the struggle between ancient Israel and Amalek. At a Sabbath morning service that I attended in the early 1970s on the Sabbath preceding the Jewish holiday of Purim, known as *Shabbat Zakhor* (the Sabbath of Remembrance), the man who was presiding over the Torah reading called on all those in attendance to listen carefully to the special additional Torah reading for that Sabbath (Deut. 25:17–19), in which the ancient Israelites are commanded to obliterate their enemies the Amalekites. He exhorted those in attendance to listen carefully to every word that was about to be read from the Torah while concentrating their thoughts toward Heaven so that God would "help us to destroy our enemies."

It was clear to me that for this religious Israeli Jew the significance of the special Torah reading was its application to Israel's struggle for survival with its Arab neighbors. The Arabs, he believed, were the reincarnation of Amalek, who according to the biblical passage read on that Sabbath had committed the heinous offense of attacking the weak stragglers at the end of the ancient Israelites' procession in the wilderness.

Undoubtedly, for this man the association with Amalek included not only the reference to their attack on the Israelites in the wilderness. He must have had in mind as well the traditional Jewish notion that ever since the period of the Exodus, there has been an ongoing struggle between the people of Israel and the people of Amalek and their descendants. On the Sabbath preceding Purim, the special Torah reading that recounts the attack of the Amalekites in the wilderness is supplemented in the synagogue by the prophetic reading that tells of the divine command to King Saul to destroy the Amalekites of his day, including their king, Agag (I Samuel 15). On Purim, Jews read in the synagogue the book of Esther, which tells of the third major event in this ongoing struggle between these two peoples by imaginatively declaring Haman, the villain of the Purim story who sought to destroy all the Jews in the kingdom of Ahasuerus, to be a descendant of the Amalekite king Agag, and Mordecai, the Jewish hero of the story who together with his cousin Esther saved the Jews from annihilation, to be a descendant of King Saul.

In postbiblical Jewish tradition Amalek, particularly in its incarnation as Haman, has come to be seen as the archetypal representative of the enemy who wishes to destroy the Jews. This archetypal enemy has been of central concern to Jews because of the traditional Jewish assumption, captured so succinctly and directly in the words of the Passover Haggadah, "for not just one has attacked us to destroy us, but in every generation they have attacked us to destroy us, but the Holy One Blessed be He saves us from their hand." Thus, the need to fully destroy Amalek was transformed by Jews from an act of revenge in Saul's time to one of self-defense; in each generation the anti-Jewish manifestation of Amalek, from Haman to Rome to Hitler, had to be defeated by the Jews with the help of God if the Jewish people were to survive. By associating the Arab enemies of Israel with Amalek the man who presided over the Torah reading, in effect, gave Israel the license to do whatever it needed to do, including presumably engaging in the mass slaughter of Arabs, at any point that Israelis believed that the Arabs were close to achieving their desired goal of destroying Israel. Clearly once this association of the Arabs with Amalek had been established in the mind of the man presiding over the Torah reading, he would not be inclined to believe that the Arabs were capable of playing any role in his life other than that of the latest manifestation of the never-ending hatred of the Jews. Given this mode of thinking, there could not have been any room in his mind to consider the Arab position that they were fighting for the legitimate national territorial rights of a Palestinian people.

Arab officials contributed to the perception by Jews of Arabs as latter-day Amalekites, for until recently—in fact, since before the establishment of the State—so many have declared their opposition to the existence of Israel. The frequently repeated declaration by Arab leaders that they would liberate Palestine by "throwing the Jews into the sea" has left an indelible mark on the psyche of Jewish Israelis. This image may have had a particularly strong resonance among Jews, for it substituted the drowning of the modern Israeli Jews in the Mediterranean Sea by Egypt and other Arab states for the drowning of the Egyptians in the Sea of Reeds in biblical times after the Exodus of the Israelites from slavery in Egypt (Exodus 14). It was as if the Arabs were claiming to have the power to reverse the fortunes of the Jews by turning the Exodus-like national triumph of the establishment of the State of Israel into the catastrophe of destruction.[15]

Amos Oz writes of a week in April 1987 when Israeli diplomatic activity lent itself to an association between Amalek and the enemies of the Jews. During that week the president of Israel visited Germany, which for so many Israelis still bears the guilt of the Holocaust, and the foreign minister of Israel visited Spain, which had expelled the Jews in 1492, and Rome, the capital of the empire that destroyed Jerusalem in 70. In Rome he met with representatives from the Soviet Union, which had such a long history of anti-Semitism and at the time widely discriminated against its Jewish citizens. According to Oz, this diplomatic fraternization with the historical enemies of the Jews aroused opposition in Israeli public opinion. This opposition, Oz adds, was fueled by the fact that the purpose of the foreign minister's trip was to establish "an international peace conference under the auspices of 'the evil Gentile world,' in hope that such a conference would further the peace process with [the Arabs, whom some Israelis view as] 'the inheritors of the seven biblical enemy nations of Canaan.' "[16] Some of those who objected, Oz notes, saw the week as

"Amalek Week." Oz believes this persistent tendency to see all gentiles as Amalek creates a mythic view of reality that can bring Israel to a dangerous political paralysis based on a paranoid view of the world.

As Yehoshafat Harkabi notes, the specific identification of the Palestinian residents of the Land of Israel with Amalek has not been a universal feature of Jewish thought. In recent times, he notes, "some nationalistic religious extremists frequently identify the Arabs with Amalek."[17] In the secular education he received in the Land of Israel in the 1920s, however, he was "taught that this was a relic of a bygone and primitive era, a commandment that [according to rabbinic sources] had lapsed because Sennacherib the Assyrian king had mixed up all the nations so it was no longer possible to know who comes of the seed of Amalek."[18]

On Purim 1994, however, Baruch Goldstein, who had strong connections to the politically extreme political movement *Kakh,* did make the connection between Palestinians and Amalek when he embarked on his suicidal massacre in Hebron. His action represents an extreme application of the Bible to contemporary Israeli existence. Although in its extremity the massacre is atypical, it is worthwhile to explore in detail because it provides an instructive example of the negative effect of biblical analogies often questioned by writers of Israeli biblical allusion poetry. To understand how the Amalek association contributed to the massacre, it is important to review the events in Hebron that reinforced that association for Goldstein. During the week before Purim of that year, Muslim mosques near the West Bank Jewish settlement of Kiryat Arba outside of Hebron had broadcast nightly cries of "slaughter the Jews" (*idbah al-yahud*) an expression that had been used by Arabs who massacred Jews in Hebron in 1929.[19] On Purim night, Goldstein, an American-born religious Jewish resident of Kiryat Arba, attended the service and reading of the book of Esther in the Jewish prayer section of the Tomb of the Patriarchs in Hebron. One of his fellow settlers recounted Goldstein's reaction to the taunting of the Jews by the Arabs in the tomb during the Purim service: "The Arabs were screaming out during our prayers that the Jews should be slaughtered. . . . The fact that he could not even say his prayers greatly upset him."[20] The next morning, on Purim day, Goldstein entered the Muslim prayer section of the Tomb of the Patriarchs and fired over one hundred rounds of ammunition from an M-16 automatic rifle at the Muslim Arab wor-shipers participating there in the Friday services of the holy month of Ramadan, killing twenty-nine people and wounding tens of oth-ers.[21] Those in the Tomb who survived the attack beat Goldstein to death.

As a physician who had treated Jewish victims of Arab terrorist attacks, Goldstein had become greatly distressed at the Jewish suf-fering he had witnessed. He also had become extremely wary of the peace negotiations underway at that time between Israel and the Palestine Liberation Organization, which he feared could lead to a new Holocaust in the form of the destruction of Israel. According to the account in the *New York Times,* Goldstein's attack on the Muslim Arab worshipers "appears to have been the culmination of weeks, even months, of bitterness and anger at what Dr. Goldstein consid-ered a betrayal by the [Israeli] Government, and frustration at mounting attacks by Arab militants, an enemy many settlers freely equate with Nazis."[22] One of Goldstein's fellow settlers quoted him as saying that "Jews should never again be led like sheep to the slaugh-ter."[23]

Many of Goldstein's fellow settlers in Kiryat Arba saw Goldstein as a hero. As a fellow American-born settler put it, "This act, which sanctified God's name, shows the Arabs that we will not remain silent and watch them spill Jewish blood with impunity."[24] *Kakh* praised Goldstein as "a martyr and a righteous man" (*qadosh vetsad-diq*).[25] On the front page of the *New York Times* an ultra-Orthodox Jew was pictured in the funeral procession for Goldstein carrying a sign in Hebrew quoting the conclusion of Moses' poem in the book of Deuteronomy: "For [God will] avenge the blood of His servants, wreak vengeance on His foes, and cleanse the land of His people" (Deut. 32:43), a declaration in effect that Goldstein was not the per-petrator of a crime, but rather the martyred victim of the Arab ene-mies' violent opposition to Israel, whose death must some day be avenged.[26]

Soon after the Goldstein massacre, Israeli President Ezer Weizman paid a condolence call to the Hebron municipality and condemned the attack as "anti-Jewish and anti-Israeli."[27] In a speech to the Israeli Knesset responding to Goldstein's Purim attack Prime Minister Yitzhak Rabin issued what was in effect a secular excommunication of the extremist Jewish settlers, declaring, "You are not part of the

community of Israel. . . . You are not partners in the Zionist enter-
prise. You are a foreign implant. You are an errant weed. Sensible Ju-
daism spits you out. You placed yourself outside the wall of Jewish
law."[28]

The chief rabbis of Israel also condemned Goldstein's Purim mas-
sacre. Sephardic Chief Rabbi Eliyahu Bakshi-Doron suggested that if
it could be determined that Goldstein had not been insane, it would
be appropriate to apply to him the traditional Jewish practice of
burying evil people and those who commit suicide outside the ceme-
tery wall.[29] Ashkenazic Chief Rabbi Yisrael Meir Lau was particularly
outraged that the slaughter took place in a house of worship,
thereby denying the fundamental "right of every person to pray to
his God to the best of his faith."[30] The general secretary of the Jewish
settler Council of Judea, Samaria, and Gaza, Uri Uriel, declared that
Goldstein's act was beyond acceptable Jewish practice: "This is an
act that is not Jewish, not humane, and in the end, which is less im-
portant but still important, it leads to nothing and only causes the
situation to deteriorate."[31]

While most religious and secular Israeli leaders considered Gold-
stein's act to be beyond the pale of Jewish and Israeli values, it was
no accident that he chose Purim day to take his revenge against the
Palestinians whom he undoubtedly saw as the descendants of
Amalek, Haman, and Hitler. One can imagine the forceful effect on
Goldstein of the words of the book of Esther that had been read on
Purim night at the same service that he heard Arabs calling for the
slaughter of the Jews. The book of Esther recounts Haman's genoci-
dal plot, which was supported by King Ahasuerus: "to destroy, mas-
sacre, and exterminate all the Jews, young and old, children and
women, on a single day, on the thirteenth day of the twelfth month—
that is the month of Adar—and to plunder their possessions" (Esther
3:13). Toward the end of the story, due to the intercession of Esther,
the king grants official permission to the Jews to militarily oppose
Haman's plot by doing to their would-be attackers what Haman had
planned to do to them: "The king has permitted the Jews of every
city to assemble and fight for their lives; if any people or province at-
tacks them, they may destroy, massacre, and exterminate its armed
force together with women and children, and to plunder their pos-
sessions—on a single day in all the provinces of King Ahasuerus,
namely, on the thirteenth of the twelfth month, that is, the month of

Adar. . . . The Jews should be ready for that day to avenge themselves on their enemies" (Esther 8:11–13).

In a statement of support for the massacre the politically extremist *Kahana' Hai* movement declared that Goldstein "committed precisely the act of the Jews in Shushan [the capital city of the kingdom of Ahasuerus] about whom it is said, 'So the Jews struck at their enemies with the sword, slaying and destroying; they wreaked their will upon their enemies (Esther 9:5).' "[32] A fellow political extremist, Barukh Ben-Yosef, head of the Temple Mount Yeshiva saw the connection as clear: "[Purim] is the festival of vengeance," he declared.[33]

As the reaction of many political and religious leaders of Israel makes clear, a strong consensus of opinion emerged in Israel opposed to the horrifyingly literal way that Baruch Goldstein applied the traditional association between Amalek and Israel's enemies to the Arab-Israeli conflict. The non-normative nature of Goldstein's act was confirmed by the finding of the Shamgar Commission that investigated the massacre that Goldstein acted alone and therefore was not part of even a small conspiracy of fellow Israelis. Furthermore, no such occurrence of a lone gunman perpetrating a massacre inspired by the Bible had happened in the history of the State of Israel. Nevertheless, the Goldstein massacre provides one of the most striking recent examples of the powerful role that the Bible has played in the development of discourse in Israel on the Arab-Israeli conflict and the potentially destructive danger in allowing the Bible to influence contemporary perceptions of this conflict.

The examples of biblical allusions we have examined so far, primarily from the stories of Joshua, Samson, David and the struggle between Israel and the descendants of Amalek, have been used to convey approaches by Israelis to their relationship with the Arab enemies with whom they have been in violent conflict throughout the period of the State. Biblical allusions have also been used to deal with the conflict between the nation's desire to glorify the heroism of its soldiers in Israel's wars with the Arabs and the senseless nature of the deaths of these youths in war.

To bolster the morale of those who have fought to defend the State, Israeli culture has drawn on images of the meritorious sacrifice of life for the good of the country, which have been such a prevalent feature of modern nationalism. One of the most powerful examples of such an image is the statement allegedly made by the early Zionist military leader Yosef Trumpledor when he was about to die defending the Jewish settlement of Tel Hai in 1920, "*Tov lamut be'ad 'artsenu*" ("It is good to die for our country"). Hebrew literature from the pre-State Zionist period onward saw the sacrifice of human beings fighting to defend the Zionist cause and the State as analogous to the divine command of Abraham to sacrifice his son in the story of the binding of Isaac (Genesis 22).[34] The Palmach generation writer Moshe Shamir went so far as to declare that the story of the binding of Isaac was *the* story of his generation, reflecting their experience of the fathers sending their sons off to die in war.[35] In his remarks at the funeral of the kibbutznik Roi Rothberg killed by Arabs from Gaza in 1956, Dayan compared his death not only to that of Samson in the Philistine temple but also to Isaac's experience of almost being sacrificed. Roi, Dayan suggested, was like Isaac in the biblical story naively unable to perceive that he could be a victim, and so Roi was taken by surprise: "the light in his heart blinded his eyes and he did not see the flash of the slaughtering knife [*hama'akhelet*, the Hebrew term used in Genesis 22 for the knife that Abraham almost used to slay his son]."[36]

After the establishment of the State, however, the notion of unquestioning willingness to die for one's country was increasingly challenged. Yael Zerubavel recounts that already in the 1940s jokes were being told in paramilitary Palmach units and Zionist youth groups deflating the glorious image of Trumpeldor, often by making fun of the fact that one of his arms had been amputated.[37] Beginning in the early years of the State, especially after the Sinai Campaign of 1956, intellectuals and writers began to raise serious questions about Israel's military activities. The sense of vulnerability that followed the Yom Kippur War, the unpopularity of the Lebanon War, and the moral revulsion felt as Israel fought the civil Palestinian uprising of the Intifada have all been part of a growing disillusionment with the glorification of war that has created a bigger gap between the biblical view of war and that of Israeli intellectuals and writers. More than anything, this disillusionment was fueled by the loss of Israeli youths in the wars Israel has fought. This disillusionment is expressed most forcefully in Renen Schorr's antiwar film of 1987, *Bluz lahofesh hagadol (Late Summer Blues)*, in which Israeli high school seniors about to be drafted into the army at the time of the War of Attrition in 1970 prepare to present a scathingly satiric song and dance routine based on Trumpeldor's famous dying words.

The comparisons between the deaths of Israel's youths in war and the binding of Isaac presented in the early years of the State by Moshe Shamir and Moshe Dayan suggested that such a comparison could help convey meaning to this sacrifice of life. Over time, however, the binding of Isaac story has often been used to express disillusionment with the image of young heroic Israeli youths sacrificing themselves in war. In discussing the application of the binding of Isaac story to the Israeli war casualties, Yoseph Milman refers to the process by which "contemporary poetry has secularized the sacrifice and transformed it from an act of religious faith commanded by God to a sacrifice for the nation dictated by history and the Zionist destiny."[38] When Israeli writers have compared national sacrifice with the binding of Isaac, Milman notes, they have often omitted the redeeming feature of the image of the angel staying the hand of Abraham, and typically Isaac, not the ram, is sacrificed. This omission radically undermines the meaning of this ultimate sacrifice demanded of Israeli youths fighting in Israel's wars.

This use of the binding of Isaac story to protest the sending of the younger generation by the older generation to die in war has persisted throughout most of the history of the State. One of the earliest examples of the use of the binding of Isaac story to protest the deaths of Israeli youths in war appeared in S. Yizhar's novel of the Israeli War of Independence, *Yemei tsiqlag (Days of Ziklag)*, published in 1958. In a passage in the novel a soldier protests his role as a potential war victim by expressing his anger at what happened in the binding of Isaac story:

> I hate our father Abraham going to sacrifice Isaac. What right does he have over Isaac? Let him sacrifice himself. I hate the God that sent him to sacrifice and closed all other paths for him—only the way to the *'aqedah* he left open. I hate the fact that Isaac is nothing but material for an experiment between Abraham and his God. . . . Scoundrels, for what do the sons have to die?[39]

In 1970, during the War of Attrition, the controversial Israeli satirical revue *Malkat 'ambatyah (Bath Queen)*, by Hanoch Levin, featured a scene in which the binding of Isaac story was used to critique the older generation for sending young soldiers to their deaths during that period.[40] At the time of the Lebanon War, Yitzhak Laor published a poem *"Hametumtam hazeh Yitshaq"* ("This Idiot Isaac"),[41] in which the speaker expresses his opinion that Isaac, who here represents the Israeli soldier, is an idiot to go along with the plan of Abraham, who represents the older generation in Israel, to kill him. Isaac, the speaker believes, should not trust Abraham: a father who was capable of expelling his other son Ishmael from their household (Genesis 21) is capable of almost anything. Instead, the speaker declares, Isaac should lock his crazy father up before he does something terrible to him.

Sensitivity to the Suffering of the Enemy

Biblical allusion poems about the Arab-Israeli conflict have addressed the two primary concerns evoked by the Arab-Israeli conflict that I have discussed: the nature of the relationship of Israelis to their Arab enemies and the conflict between celebrating the heroism of Israel's soldiers and coming to terms with the meaninglessness of their deaths. In assessing the nature of the relationship of Israelis to their Arab enemies, several poets have focused on how to make sense of the pain and suffering that Israel has inflicted (whether morally justifiable or not) on its Arab enemies each time it has defeated them. The Bible portrays the conquest of Canaan as a divinely sanctioned enterprise and the spilling of the enemy's blood and the destruction of his cities as necessary acts. Israeli biblical allusion poems about the military struggle between the Israelites and residents of Canaan in the days of Joshua, Deborah, Samson, and David reflect a discomfort with the violence of war and a preoccupation with the suffering of the enemies of ancient Israel not found, for the most part, in the Bible. The authors of these poems have been educated in the Western humanistic tradition and have also been influenced by experiences of Jewish Diaspora and Israeli vulnerability, which have led them to this new perspective. It is important to them to recast the biblical stories of the conquest of the land of Canaan in order to bring the Bible closer to their own moral qualms about warfare and to challenge what they see as the biblical manner of insensitive self-confidence that plays such a central role in Israelis' views of the Arab-Israeli conflict.

This sensitivity to the suffering of the Arab enemy was expressed early in the history of the State. Two poems from the 1950s provide powerful examples of how poets used the Bible to express this sensitivity. In "*David hatsaʿir*" ("Young David")[42] Yehuda Amichai challenges the adequacy of the David and Goliath myth as a basis for understanding the experience of fighting as a soldier in the Arab-Israeli wars:[43]

דָּוִד הַצָּעִיר

אַחַר הַתְּשׁוּאוֹת הָרִאשׁוֹנוֹת
חָזַר דָּוִד אֶל כָּל הַנְּעָרִים,
וּכְבָר הָרוֹעֲשִׁים בַּשִּׁרְיוֹנוֹת
הָיוּ כָּל כָּךְ מְבֻגָּרִים.

בַּחֲבָטוֹת כָּתֵף, בִּצְחוֹק צָרוּד.
וּמִישֶׁהוּ קִלֵּל וַאֲחָדִים
יָרְקוּ. אֲבָל דָּוִד הָיָה גַּלְמוּד
וְחָשׁ לָרִאשׁוֹנָה שֶׁאֵין עוֹד דָּוִדִים.

וְלֹא יָדַע פִּתְאֹם הֵיכָן יָנַח
אֶת רֹאשׁ גָּלְיַת שֶׁמִּשּׁוּם מָה שָׁכַח
וְעוֹד הֶחֱזִיק אוֹתוֹ בְּתַלְתַּלָּיו.

כָּבֵד וּמְיֻתָּר הָיָה עַכְשָׁו
וְצִפֳּרֵי הַדָּם שֶׁנָּדְדוּ הַרְחֵק
שׁוּב לֹא שָׁמְעוּ, כָּמוֹהוּ, אֶת הָעָם צוֹעֵק.

YOUNG DAVID

After the first cheers
David returned to all the youths,
and already the armored revelers
were so grown up.

With slaps on the shoulder, with a hoarse laugh.
And someone cursed and others
spit. But David was lonely
and felt for the first time there were no more Davids.

And suddenly he did not know where to put
Goliath's head that somehow he forgot
and he still held it by its locks.

Heavy and superfluous it now was
and the birds of blood that wandered far
again heard not, like him, the people shouting.

One of the most important ways in which Amichai questions the significance of the original biblical story is by eliminating almost all of the story of David and Goliath recounted in I Samuel 17. The Philistine threat, Goliath's taunting of the Israelites, the Israelites' fear, the humble bravery of young David based on his unswerving faith in God are simply not mentioned in the poem. Instead, the poet focuses on the period immediately following David's victory. Such a shift of focus challenges the prevailing national tendency to celebrate each Israeli victory over its Arab foes as analogous to the divinely inspired victory of young David over Goliath.

This challenge to the mood of national celebration is expressed as David returns to his fellow youthful soldiers, whose noisy revelry is nothing more than the haughty attempts of insecure adolescents to play at being adult by imitating the actions and speech that to them are so adultlike: slapping the hero on the shoulder, laughing hoarsely, cursing, and spitting. The speaker's negative evaluation of these young soldiers vicariously celebrating with the only true warrior among them comes through clearly when the speaker sarcastically describes them as "already . . . / . . . so grown up" ("ukhevar . . . / . . . kol kakh mevugarim").

David cannot celebrate with his fellow soldiers. They relate to him as if he were a soccer hero who saved the game by scoring a goal. Unlike them, however, David has actually shed the blood of the enemy, and he therefore knows this is not a game. The biblical David triumphantly brought the head he had severed from Goliath's body to King Saul as concrete proof of the victory he had accomplished. The David of the poem, however, does not know what to do with Goliath's head, which he sees as "superfluous." Indeed, as the speaker notes, David realizes that in modern times there are no more David-like heroes because the celebration of victory in the unself-conscious manner of David in biblical times is no longer possible.

In the biblical story Goliath had taunted David by declaring that if David came near him, he would soon become flesh eaten by the birds of heaven and the beasts of the field. The birds ('of hashamayim) of Goliath's taunt return in this poem as "the birds of blood" (tsipporei hadam) who come to prey on the dead body of Goliath. As in the natural order of things, they eat their prey and then wander off, oblivious, like David, to "the near absurdity" of the cheering people's cry.[44] As Glenda Abramson notes, the position of the word kamohu ("like him") in the final line ("again heard not, like him, the people shouting") creates an effect of ambiguity: did the birds not hear the cries, but David did, or did neither? It is most likely that neither David nor the birds heard the shouting.[45] Only he who actually sheds the blood and the birds who feed off the dead victims of war are fully in touch with the reality of violence that war brings. This process of war as a spectator sport contrasted with the reality of war happens again and again (shuv), and those who are fully conscious of the violence inherent in war must therefore be oblivious to the shouts of those who celebrate it from afar.

Ziva Shamir makes the point that this poem must be read in the context of Amichai's membership in the Palmach generation who in their youth fought for Israel's independence. She notes that the superficially masculine behavior of David's fellow soldiers represents the typical behavior of "Palmach [fighters] around the campfire."[46] Amichai, Shamir suggests, questions in this poem the conviction of the Palmach generation that their actions were those of heroes devoted to a righteous cause. The poet feels alienated internally from the external celebration of that conviction he has witnessed in the struggle to establish and defend the State.

The poem "'Immo" ("His Mother"),[47] by Haim Gouri, is another relatively early example of a tendency in Israeli biblical allusion poems to challenge the biblical approach to war and argue for a more modern sensibility toward the suffering of Israel's enemies. "'Immo" presents the response of the speaker to his reading of the song sung by Deborah in celebration of the defeat of the Canaanite general Sisera (Judges 5).

In the book of Judges toward the end of her song, Deborah focuses on two women: Jael, the Kenite, whose murder of Sisera when he slept in her tent brought the victory over the Canaanite military leader to a final conclusion, and Sisera's mother, whom Deborah

imagines to be waiting in vain for the return of her son. Deborah cele-
brates the cleverness and courage of Jael, whom she declares to be
"most blessed of women" (Judges 5:24). In the song Deborah takes
particular delight in describing in gory detail the spilling out of Sis-
era's brains when Jael hammered a tent peg into his head. Deborah
then mocks Sisera's mother who, she imagines, is falsely reassured
by her attendants that Sisera's army has been victorious but delayed
while Sisera and his fellow warriors distribute the spoils of war
among themselves. She concludes her song with a plea to God to de-
feat in a similar fashion all of His enemies, which include, she as-
sumes, all who oppose Israel.

Neither the battle between the Israelites and the Canaanites nor
Jael's murder of Sisera in his sleep described in Judges 4 and cele-
brated by Deborah in her song in Judges 5 are preserved in Gouri's
poem. The focus of the poem is on the aftermath of war and the ef-
fect of war on those who fought, particularly the defeated. The
speaker begins by responding to the final comment of the narrator of
Judges that appears after Deborah's song: "And the land was tran-
quil forty years" (Judges 5:31). The original Hebrew verb of this sen-
tence, *vatishqot,* means "to be quiet" as well as "to be tranquil."
Gouri's speaker is less interested in the peace that followed the vic-
tory of the Israelites over the Canaanites than in the silence of death
that followed that victory. For him this silence is a more significant
part of the aftermath of war than either Deborah or the narrator of
Judges believed:

אִמּוֹ

לִפְנֵי שָׁנִים, בְּסוֹף שִׁירַת דְּבוֹרָה,
שָׁמַעְתִּי אֶת דּוּמִיַּת רֶכֶב סִיסְרָא אֲשֶׁר בּוֹשֵׁשׁ לָבוֹא,
מַבִּיט בְּאִמּוֹ שֶׁל סִיסְרָא הַנִּשְׁקֶפֶת בַּחַלּוֹן,
אִשָּׁה שֶׁפַּס כֶּסֶף בְּשַׂעֲרָהּ.

שְׁלַל צְבָעִים רִקְמָה,
צֶבַע רִקְמָתַיִם לְצַוְּארֵי שָׁלָל, רָאוּ הַנְּעָרוֹת.
אוֹתָהּ שָׁעָה שָׁכַב בָּאֹהֶל כִּנְרְדָּם.
יָדָיו רֵיקוֹת מְאֹד.
עַל סַנְטֵרוֹ עִקְּבוֹת חָלָב חֶמְאָה וָדָם.

הַדּוּמִיָּה לֹא נִשְׁבְּרָה אֶל הַסּוּסִים וְאֶל הַמֶּרְכָּבוֹת,
גַּם הַנְּעָרוֹת שָׁתְקוּ אַחַת אַחַר אַחַת.
שְׁתִיקָתִי נָגְעָה בִּשְׁתִיקָתָן.
אַחַר זְמַן-מָה שָׁקְעָה הַשֶּׁמֶשׁ.
אַחַר זְמַן-מָה כָּבוּ הַדִּמְדּוּמִים.

אַרְבָּעִים שָׁנָה שָׁקְטָה הָאָרֶץ. אַרְבָּעִים שָׁנָה
לֹא דָהֲרוּ סוּסִים וּפָרָשִׁים מֵתִים לֹא נָעֲצוּ עֵינֵי זְכוּכִית.
אֲבָל הִיא מֵתָה, זְמַן קָצָר אַחַר מוֹת בְּנָהּ.

His Mother

Long ago at the end of Deborah's song
I heard the silence of Sisera's chariots that were late.
I looked at Sisera's mother gazing through the window there,
A woman with a streak of silver in her hair.

Maidens saw "a spoil of varicolored embroidery,
Of varicolored embroidered cloth on the captive's neck."
He lay as if asleep in the tent then.
His hands were very empty.
Traces of milk, butter and blood on his chin.

The silence lay unbroken by horse or chariot.
The maidens kept silent one by one
My silence touched their own.
After a while the sun went down,
The setting rays went out.

For forty years the land was stilled, forty years
Horses did not race. Dead riders did not pierce with glassy
eyes.
But she died shortly after her son was killed.

The poem is filled with auditory images of silence and visual images of emptiness, endings, and death. The lack of sound that is the result of Sisera not returning home has a palpable existence that the speaker can actually hear. This haunting silence "is unbroken by horse or chariot," for all vestiges of war have disappeared. The maidens who had falsely misled Sisera's mother with their optimistic explanation for his delay have subsequently been silenced, as well.

As in Deborah's song Sisera's mother is portrayed as looking out the window in expectation of her son's return. Unlike Deborah, however, the speaker in Gouri's poem does not mock Sisera's mother. As William J. Ubrock notes, the very title of the poem "His Mother" without an explicit reference to the enemy general evokes sympathy by associating Sisera's mother with the positive associations of motherhood that are undermined when Deborah refers to her as "the mother of [the enemy] Sisera."[48] Furthermore, by referring to the "streak of silver in her hair" the speaker arouses the reader's sympathy for this aging woman who will never again see her son.[49] This sympathy is intensified at the end of the poem when the speaker introduces a detail not found in the book of Judges: Sisera's mother "died shortly after her son was killed," presumably because of the great sadness of her bereavement.

Unlike Deborah, who triumphantly celebrates Jael's murder of Sisera, the speaker makes no reference to this act. He refers only to the image he sees of Sisera lying "as if asleep in the tent then. / His hands were very empty. / Traces of milk, butter and blood on his chin." The final images of the setting sun, the extinction of the sun's rays, the "dead riders" whose horses are no longer heard, and the death of Sisera's mother, presumably in response to the death of her son, all emphasize that from the speaker's point of view the primary effect of war is the shedding of the blood of the warriors.

The images of silence are reinforced by the prevalence of the sound "sh" throughout the poem, which is the first sound of the two most commonly used roots for silence in Hebrew—*sh-q-t-* and *sh-t-q*— and is for Hebrew speakers, as for English speakers, a sound used to quiet people down. The harshness of the pain experienced by the participants in the war is expressed by means of the "k" or "q" sound that appears in the roots for silence as well as in other words in the poem. Gouri also plays effectively with the sounds "d" and "m." These sounds are expressed in the two consonants in the Hebrew word for blood, *dam,* and also appear in the words *dumiyyah* ("silence"), *nirdam* ("asleep"), and *dimdumim* ("setting rays"); thereby he emphasizes the direct connection between the shedding of the enemy's blood and the haunting deathlike silence that pervades the land after the war is over.

Gouri shares neither Deborah's conviction that she has defeated God's enemies nor the unqualified conviction of modern Israel's leaders that military victory is fully justified because it preserves the existence of Israel. He also rejects the tendency in ancient and modern Israel to mourn only one's own dead at the conclusion of a war. He is too troubled by the effect of death and bereavement to associate himself either with Deborah's song or with the songs of modern Israel that honor military victories. While Deborah concludes her song with the words, "So may all Your enemies perish, O Lord! But may His friends be as the sun rising in might!" (Judges 5:31), the speaker concludes his poem with the image of the setting sun.[50]

The stunning defeat of its Arab enemies in the Six-Day War of 1967 and the occupation of additional territories populated by Arabs brought not only celebrations of triumph but also poetic expressions of concern about the suffering of the Arabs so definitively defeated in that war. Biblical allusion poems about Jericho and Gaza continue the trend found in the earlier poems by Amichai and Gouri to write sympathetically about the enemies of ancient Israel and thereby to express dissent from the celebration of war in ancient and modern Israel. Jericho and Gaza could serve as powerful images after Israel's occupation of the West Bank and Gaza during the Six-Day War of 1967 brought Israelis back to direct contact with these parts of ancient Israel that they had not visited since the conclusion of the War of Independence.

In Anadad Eldan's poem "*Shimshon qorea' begadav*" ("Samson Tearing His Clothes"),[51] published in a collection that appeared a few years after the Six-Day War, the speaker meets Samson in Israeli-occupied Gaza, the once prominent city of the Philistines. The Samson whom he encounters resembles the biblical Samson after he was captured by the Philistines, yet his image conveys a different view of relations with the enemy than that conveyed in the book of Judges. There, Samson is portrayed as a superhuman hero who, after having been tricked by Delilah into revealing the secret of his power is captured and humiliated by the Philistines (Judges 13–16). His greatest humiliation occurs when he is brought to entertain the Philistines in their temple. While standing between the main pillars of the temple, he prays to God to restore his strength so that he can avenge his defeat. He regains his power and dies toppling the temple; as the biblical narrator notes, he kills more Philistines in his death than in his life.

Eldan transforms the biblical images of Samson's transition from power to defeat to the assertion of power in defeat into a set of images that portray the potential strength of those who suffer:

שִׁמְשׁוֹן קוֹרֵעַ בְּגָדָיו

כְּשֶׁהָלַכְתִּי
לְעַזָּה פָּגַשְׁתִּי אֶת
שִׁמְשׁוֹן יוֹצֵא קוֹרֵעַ בְּגָדָיו
בְּפָנָיו הַשְׂרוּטוֹת זָרְמוּ נְהָרוֹת
וְהַבָּתִּים נִכְפְּפוּ לְאַפְשֵׁר לוֹ
מַעֲבָר
כְּאֵבָיו עָקְרוּ אִילָנוֹת וְנֶאֱחַזוּ
בִּסְבַךְ
הַשָּׁרָשִׁים. וּבַשָּׁרָשִׁים קְוֻצּוֹת
שַׂעֲרוֹתָיו.
רֹאשׁוֹ הִבְהִיק כְּגֻלְגֹּלֶת סְלָעִים
וּפִרְפּוּר צְעָדָיו קָרַע אֶת בִּכְיִי
שִׁמְשׁוֹן הָלַךְ גּוֹרֵר שֶׁמֶשׁ עֲיֵפָה
שִׁבְרֵי שְׁמָשׁוֹת וְשַׁרְשְׁרוֹת שָׁקְעוּ
בַּיָּם שֶׁל עַזָּה. שָׁמַעְתִּי אֵיךְ
הָאֲדָמָה נֶאֶנְחָה תַּחַת צְעָדָיו,
אֵיךְ רָטַשׁ אֶת בִּטְנָהּ. שִׁמְשׁוֹן
הָלַךְ וְחָרְקוּ נְעָלָיו.

SAMSON TEARING HIS CLOTHES

When I went
to Gaza I met
Samson going out tearing his clothes
on his scratched face rivers flowed
and the houses bent to permit him

        passage
his pain uprooted trees and was caught

        in the thicket
of the roots. And among the roots the locks

        of his hair.

His head shone like a stony skull
and the quivering of his steps tore my cry
Samson walked towing a tired sun
pieces of suns and chains sank
in the sea of Gaza. I heard how
the earth sighed under his steps,
how he trampled its belly. Samson
walked, his shoes grating.

At first, Samson displays signs of his defeat at the hands of the
Philistines: he is "tearing his clothes," presumably in mourning for
his fate; rivers of blood flow from the scratches in his face. As he
walks in Gaza, however, Samson exerts his power over nature and
civilization: "the houses bent to permit him/passage;" his pain up-
roots trees, creating a kind of reverse Absalom image of hair caught
in the roots of upturned trees, rather than in the branches (II Samuel
18). His head is stonelike, and he walks with such a heavy tread that
he crushes the belly of the earth. We learn by means of a play on the
name Samson (*Shimshon*) and the Hebrew word for sun (*shemesh*)
that Samson has overcome the power of the sun itself as well as his
chains. Both the setting sun and Samson's chains sink defeated into
the sea along the Gaza Strip. Unlike Samson in his final act of re-
venge, however, Samson in Eldan's poem does not really accomplish
anything in his expression of power. In response to Samson's pa-
thetic appearance, the speaker, deeply moved, declares: "the quiver-
ing of his steps tore my cry." Our final view of Samson is of his con-
tinuing to walk in grating shoes, with no apparent goal in mind.

In this poem Samson, the ancient Israelite hero who struggled
with the Philistines in Gaza, is transformed into an image represent-
ing the modern Palestinians of Gaza, whose pain of poverty and mili-
tary occupation is great. Eldan insistently calls attention to their
plight at a time when most of his fellow Israelis would wish to ignore
it. This poem was published more than fifteen years before the out-
break of the civil uprising of the Palestinians, the Intifada, which
began in Gaza. Nevertheless, it seems that even then Eldan sensed
the potential strength of the Palestinians to assert themselves, al-
though at the time they appeared incapable of a sustained effort to
achieve political independence. His sense of the Palestinians' poten-

tial strength impels him to portray them as not only pathetic victims to be pitied but also a potential time bomb that might some day seriously threaten the State that occupies them.

As in his poem *"Immo"* in his later post–Six-Day War poem *"Yeriho"* ("Jericho")[52] Haim Gouri reflects on the aftermath of war. In this poem he focuses, however, not on the death and destruction that is the result of war but rather on the vulnerability of the defeated enemy. He once again reverses the biblical perspective on the defeat of an enemy of ancient Israel. In Joshua 6 the defeat of Jericho is accomplished by the miraculous upheaval of its walls effected by the blowing of rams' horns while circling the city for seven days. The inhabitants of Jericho are all killed, except for Rahab the harlot and her relatives, whom the Israelite spies had promised to save in gratitude for the help she had earlier accorded them. All property in Jericho is destroyed, except for valuable utensils that are taken for "the treasury of the House of the Lord" (Joshua 6:24), and the city is burned to the ground. Joshua insists that this complete defeat never be reversed and utters a curse on anyone who would try to rebuild the city. The biblical narrator triumphantly declares that this victory was a sign to all that "the Lord was with Joshua and his fame spread throughout the land" (Joshua 6:27) as a result of this great accomplishment.

The speaker in Gouri's poem is not at all interested in the event from the point of view of the victorious Israelites; he considers instead the point of view of the defeated residents of Jericho. We can sense in the speaker's concern for Jericho the poet's analogous concern for the fate of Palestinians living in Jericho and other parts of the West Bank and Gaza, who were taken by surprise in the Six-Day War of 1967. The speaker wonders in this poem how it was possible for Jericho to be defeated:

יְרִיחוֹ שֶׁאֵינֶנָּה יוֹדַעַת.
יָמִים מְרֻבִּים לְפָנֵי שֶׁרָאוּהָ בְּאוֹר הַחַמָּה הַשּׁוֹקַעַת
הַבְהָבָה, חֲלוּמָה, בִּשְׁנָתָם.
הָיְתָה חוֹמָתָהּ חוֹמָתָם.

בַּכְּתוּבִים וּבָאֶבֶן אֵין סִימָן לְרוֹאֵי הַשְּׁחֹרוֹת, שֶׁעָבְרוּ בֵּין דְּקָלִים
וּפִרְחֵי בּוּגוֹנְוִילְיָה, לֵילָךְ וְשָׁנִי, וְאָמְרוּ לָהּ דְּבַר-מָה.
זֶה נִשְׁמָע מְשֻׁנֶּה.
אֲסוֹנוֹת כָּאֵלֶּה אֵינָם מַתְחִילִים לְלֹא סִימָנִים רִאשׁוֹנִים.

נָפוֹצוּ שְׁמוּעוֹת עַל זָרִים וּשְׂעִירִים, חֲמוּצֵי בְּגָדִים מֵאֱדוֹם,
שֶׁהִגִּיעוּ אֵלֶיהָ, רוֹחֲצִים רַגְלֵיהֶם בַּפְּלָגִים הַקְּרִירִים.

עִיר גְּדוֹלָה לֵאלֹהִים אֵינָה מִתְרַשֶּׁמֶת מִכָּךְ.

רַק זוֹנוֹת צְעִירוֹת, שֶׁהָיוּ חֲפוּרוֹת, עַד שֶׁשָּׁחַר עָלָה בְּמוֹאָב,
בְּבַרְזֶל אַמָּתָם,
יָדְעוּ לְסַפֵּר, הַפּוּכוֹת וְלֵאוֹת, עַל רָעָב נוֹרָאִי.
הֵם הִשְׁאִירוּ שָׁם רֹשֶׁם חָזָק כְּמוֹ מִדְבָּר.

יְרִיחוֹ, יְרִיחוֹ הַיָּפָה.
יְרִיחוֹ שֶׁאֵינֶנָּה יוֹדַעַת. שׁוּם אִישׁ שֶׁצֵּרֵף בָּהּ פְּרָטִים לִפְרָטִים
לִתְמוּנַת מוֹדִיעִין,
שֶׁנִּחֵשׁ בָּהּ תְּרוּעַת שׁוֹפָרוֹת.
לֹא מַשְׁתִּין וְלֹא קִיר,
רַק עָפָר.

JERICHO

Jericho unknowing.
Long before they saw her in the dying light
She glittered, dreamily, in their sleep.
Her wall was their wall.

Inscriptions lack all trace of the doomsayers, moving among
the palm trees,
Amid the purple crimson bougainvillea, to tell her something.
It does sound odd.
Such disasters don't unfold without some warning.

Rumors were rife about strangers, hairy, red-garbed from
Edom,
Coming there, washing their feet in the cold streams.

A mighty city is heedless of such talk.

Only young whores, gouged by their virile iron
Till dawn rose in Moab,
Understood, confusedly, wearily, the fierce hunger.
They left an impression as forceful as the desert.

Jericho, gorgeous Jericho.
Jericho unknowning. No one put bits and pieces together
For a clear picture,
No one foresaw the blast of the rams' horns.
No one to piss, no wall,
Only dust.

The speaker concludes that the defeat of Jericho occurred because in the period leading to the Israelite attack on the city the residents of Jericho had been lulled into a false sense of security. The speaker cannot understand how it was possible for the city not to have been prepared for such a great disaster, and he is surprised that now that the war is over there is no evidence in the city that anyone could foretell the attack. "It does sound odd," he declares. "Such disasters don't unfold without some warning." He imagines that at the very least there were rumors in the city of the arrival of hairy strangers, but this sign of the attack was ignored by the residents of Jericho in their overly confident assessment of their security: "A mighty city is heedless of such talk."

Gouri transforms the interaction between the spies and Rahab the harlot portrayed in Joshua 2 into a scene of lustful interaction between the Israelites and the young harlots of Jericho who know all too well of the Israelites' "fierce hunger" for conquest. The harlots' understanding of the impending danger is, however, never communicated to the rest of the city. Jericho remains "unknowning. No one put bits and pieces together / For a clear picture, / No one foresaw the blast of the rams' horns."

The poem concludes with an allusion to the biblical expression *mashtin baqir* ("he who urinates on the wall"), used in a number of biblical verses to refer to males who will be defeated in war. Gouri plays with the words of this expression and the association between the two Hebrew words for wall *qir* (used in *mashtin baqir*) and *homah* (used in the Bible to refer to the wall of Jericho toppled by the Israelites) to express the utter ruin of Jericho: "No one to piss, no wall,

/ Only dust." The destructiveness that mirrors that of the original account of the conquering of Jericho calls attention to the tragic fate of innocent civilians who are victims of the lustful drive to conquer that is central to any victorious army.

In the poem "*Yeriho: shir politi*" ("Jericho: A Political Poem")[53] Moshe Dor expresses his discomfort with Israel's military conquest of the Palestinians in his day by portraying his ancient Israelite forebears as even more brutal and arbitrary in their relations with Jericho than they are in the Bible. Although the ancient Israelites totally destroyed the city of Jericho, they did save Rahab and her relatives. Rahab in Dor's poem, it would appear, will die along with the others:

יְרִיחוֹ: שִׁיר פּוֹלִיטִי

הַלַּיְלָה חוּט הַשָּׁנִי שֶׁל רָחָב שׁוּב
מָתוּחַ כִּפְתִיל שֶׁל דָּם קָרוּשׁ עַל
אֶדֶן חַלוֹנָהּ, בִּירִיחוֹ יְרֵחִית, קְפוּאָה
בִּשְׁתִיקָה עַתִּיקָה,
בְּטֶרֶם שׁוֹפָרוֹת.

וְרַק הַגַּחֲלִילִיּוֹת מְהַבְהֲבוֹת בֵּין
עַנְפֵי הַצֶּאֱלוֹן כְּמוֹ לַהֲבוֹת הַלַּפִּידִים
שֶׁתִּשְׁתַּקֵּפְנָה בְּעֵינֵיהֶם, מִשְׁתָּאוֹת בְּאֵימָה
לֹא-מְבִינָה, שֶׁל כְּבָשִׂים וּפָרוֹת וַחֲמוֹרִים
שְׁמוֹתָם יִהְיֶה פִּתְאֹמִי וּמֻחְלָט,
בִּידֵי אָדָם וּבִגְזֵרַת אֱלֹהִים.

JERICHO: A POLITICAL POEM

Tonight Rahab's scarlet thread marks
her windowsill again like a trail
of congealed blood, while a Jericho
frozen in moonlight and ancestral
silence, awaits the trumpets' blast.

And in the poinciana, fireflies flare
like torches in the eyes of stupefied
ass and ox and sheep, whose slaughter,

108

swift and absolute, shall be exacted
by human hands, at God's decree.

The scarlet thread, which in the biblical account was the sign put in
the window by Rahab to signal the conquering Israelites that she and
her family were to be saved, is compared by the speaker to "a trail of
congealed blood," which is presented as part of a never-ending cycle
of war from ancient to modern times: "Tonight Rahab's scarlet
thread marks / her windowsill again [*shuv*] like a trail / of congealed
blood." The quiet that modern Jericho experiences before the next
attack makes Jericho seem "frozen in moonlight and ancestral si-
lence," in a paralysis that renders it unable to defend itself. The He-
brew for "Jericho / frozen in moonlight" is a play on the consonants
common to the Hebrew name Jericho and to the Hebrew term for
moon: *yeriho yerehit.* The very name of the city therefore connotes
an inherent tendency of these victims to see themselves as in a
moonstruck, deathly state of powerlessness. Such a state is all too
often experienced by the victim in the cyclical return of violent con-
flict. The inevitability of the coming conquest is suggested by the
flickering light of the fireflies that anticipates the flames of the
"torches" that will soon destroy the city. Like animals the residents
of Jericho, in both ancient and modern times, have a strong sense of
fear as they are about to confront a people who claim divine sanction
for their act of conquest "by human hands, at God's decree."

When Dor calls his poem "A Political Poem,"[54] he signals to his
readers that he wants them to discern a political message in this por-
trayal of Jericho on the verge of defeat. The strong empathy for the
enemy of Israel that the speaker expresses is an effective counter-
balance to the nationalistic celebration of war that accompanied the
conquest of the West Bank in 1967. This indirect way of challenging
such insensitive militarism is, in a sense, more effective than a direct
political message opposing the occupation of the territories by Is-
rael. In particular, the final line, which states that the conquest of
Jericho was "by human hands, at God's decree" (*bydei 'adam uvi-
gezerat 'elohim*) comments ironically on the assumption of some Is-
raelis that what they accomplished in 1967 was the will of God.
Adding to the irony is the poet's choice of the word *gezerah* (decree)
rather than, for instance, *ratson* (will), because the former often
has a negative connotation of divine punishment or of an arbitrary

decree imposed by an insensitive royal power. In rabbinic literature the term frequently refers to a decree by a foreign ruler prohibiting the Jews from observing their religious traditions. Thus, what some in Israel see as the positive expression of God's will, from the point of view of the Arab enemy is an evil, oppressive fate.

In a poem published in the early 1980s Yehudit Kafri responds to the ongoing moral concerns of people like herself who more than a decade after Israel's occupation of the West Bank and Gaza cannot make peace with Israel's role as ruler over another people. In this poem, "*Yosef*" ("Joseph"),[55] images drawn from Joseph's brothers throwing him into a pit in the Valley of Dothan (Genesis 37) convey the suffering of the defeated Arab enemy. At the beginning of the poem the speaker responds to an inquiry addressed to her regarding the location of the biblical site of the Valley of Dothan:

יוֹסֵף

בֶּאֱמֶת אֲנִי מוֹדָה
שֶׁתְּפַסְתֶּם אוֹתִי לֹא מוּכָנָה,
שֶׁבְּקֹשִׁי יָדַעְתִּי
אֵיפֹה הוּא עֵמֶק דֹּתָן
וּמַה זְכֻיּוֹתֵינוּ עָלָיו
וּמֵאֵיזֶה צַד עוֹבֵר אוֹתוֹ
הַקַּו הַיָּרֹק.

JOSEPH

Really I admit
that you caught me unprepared,
that I barely knew
where the Valley of Dothan is
and what our rights to it are
and from what side of it crosses
the green line.

The speaker understands the issue raised by the questioner to be related to the larger question of the territorial rights of the Jews to the

Land of Israel. Her initial inability to answer the question and her lack of knowledge regarding on what side of "the green line," that is the pre-1967 border between Israel and the West Bank, it is located suggest how absurd and arbitrary are the constant battles over territory fought by Jews and Arabs. The speaker then recounts what happened when she remembered a scene from that valley:

רַק מִקֵּץ שָׁבוּעַ
זָכַרְתִּי פִּתְאֹם
שֶׁיֵּשׁ שָׁם בּוֹר עָמֹק
וְאִישׁ אֶחָד יוֹשֵׁב בּוֹ עַל עַקְרַבִּים
וְצוֹרֵחַ כְּמוֹ מְשֻׁגָּע.
וְכָל הָאֲנָשִׁים בּוֹרְחִים מִפָּנָיו,
צְעָקוֹת מְשֻׁגָּע זֶה דָּבָר מַבְהִיל.
רַק אִשָּׁה אַחַת אַמִּיצָה בִּמְיֻחָד
נִגֶּשֶׁת עַד שְׂפַת הַבּוֹר וְאוֹמֶרֶת :
אִלְמָלֵא הָיִיתָ נִרְגָּשׁ כָּל כָּךְ
אֶפְשָׁר הָיָה לְהָבִין אֶת דְּבָרֶיךָ.
וְהוּא צוֹרֵחַ מֵרֹב כְּאֵבִים,
רִבּוֹנוֹ שֶׁל עוֹלָם, רַחֵם עָלָיו!

Only after a week passed
I remembered suddenly
that there is there a deep pit
and a man sits in it on scorpions
and screams like a crazy man.
And all the people flee from him,
the shouting of a crazy man is an alarming thing.
Only one especially brave woman
approaches the edge of the pit and says:
If you weren't so emotional
it would be possible to understand your words.
And he screams from much pain,
Master of the universe, have mercy on him!

Her memory of this scene transforms the territorial conflict between the Jews and the Arabs from an abstract exercise into one fraught with the human suffering that has continued to accompany that conflict. The image of Joseph thrown into the pit represents the plight of the Palestinians who as a people have suffered the most in this conflict. Their suffering, however, is not taken seriously by the world. The Joseph figure is portrayed as crazy, and the woman who approaches him makes clear that he will have to take a more rational approach to his suffering if anyone is to understand and help him. Only from God can he expect any mercy. Nevertheless, Kafri appears to be saying, even if the Palestinians come across as crazed and unable to rationally articulate their case, it is still the obligation of Israelis to relate to their suffering with empathy.

The speaker then arrives at a new realization:

עַכְשָׁו אֲנִי כְּבָר יוֹדַעַת בְּוַדָּאוּת
שֶׁעֵמֶק דֹּתָן הוּא
בְּסֵפֶר בְּרֵאשִׁית.
וְהַזְּכוּת הַיְחִידָה שֶׁלָּנוּ עָלָיו,
שֶׁעָשִׂינוּ שָׁם מַעֲשִׂים נוֹרָאִים
לְאָחִינוּ הַקָּטֹן.   לְאָחִינוּ.

Now I already know for certain
that the Valley of Dothan is
in the book of Genesis.
And our only right to it is
that we did there awful deeds
to our little brother.   To our brother.

It is significant that when considering the Arab-Israeli conflict the speaker rejects the trend to seek biblical justification for holding onto the territories conquered by Israel in 1967. She insists on returning the Valley of Dothan to the book of Genesis and keeping it there, with the suggestion that its presence in the Bible does not in and of itself guarantee to the Jewish people the right to control it. Indeed, her ironic comment that the brothers' torture of Joseph gives their descendants the right to that valley suggests the opposite: the suffering caused the Palestinians ("our brother") negates that very right claimed by Israeli annexationists.

Soldiers as Victors and Victims

Biblical allusion poems published in the aftermath of the Six-Day War of 1967, the Yom Kippur War of 1973, and the Lebanon War that broke out in 1982 express the response of poets to the role that Israeli soldiers have played as both victors and sacrificial victims in defense of the State. Following the Six-Day War, when he was in his mid-forties Haim Gouri published a poem that expressed his response as a middle-aged Israeli to the young soldiers who had executed the triumphant victory over Israel's Arab enemies. The poem is a good source for understanding the role that young men play in Israeli society as defenders of the State and how that role contributes to the image of masculinity that stays with men even after they are no longer obligated to serve in combat. In the poem "*Shimshonay*" ("My Samsons")[56] the speaker is in awe of the physical strength and virile attractiveness of the returning victorious Samson-like soldiers of the Six-Day War. They return from Gath, one of the ancient Philistine cities in the area of Gaza, which had just been conquered by the Israeli army. Their strength is portrayed in terms of several images from the Samson story (Judges 13–16): the gates of Gaza, Delilah, the lion Samson tore apart, the valley of Sorek, Samson's wedding feast Samson's riddle, and the foxes with burning tails that Samson sent into the fields of the Philistines.

שִׁמְשׁוֹנַי

הִנֵּה שָׁבִים שִׁמְשׁוֹנַי וְשַׁעֲרֵי עַזָּה עַל כִּתְפֵיהֶם:
עוֹבְרִים, חִיּוּךְ, לְיַד זְקִיפִים עִוְרִים.
זַעְתַּר. רוּחַ. צְרָצְרִים.

הִנֵּה שָׁבִים שִׁמְשׁוֹנַי, דְּלִילוֹתֵיהֶם לְרַגְלֵיהֶם;
נָעִים לְאֹרֶךְ שְׂדֵרָתִי.
אֲנִי עֵר.

הִנֵּה שָׁבִים שִׁמְשׁוֹנַי וְזֵכֶר אֲרָיוֹת בִּידֵיהֶם;
פּוֹסְעִים, יַחֲפוּת קַלָּה,
בִּרְחוֹב אֵין קוֹל וְאֵין בּוֹעֵר.

הִנֵּה שָׁבִים שִׁמְשׁוֹנַי וּצְפַרְדְּעֵי נַחַל-שׂרֵק בְּאָזְנֵיהֶם;
הוֹלְכִים לָהֶם, תָּמִיד הוֹלְכִים לָהֶם,
מָתַי נָשָׂאתִי שְׁעָרִים בָּאַחֲרוֹנָה?

הִנֵּה שָׁבִים שִׁמְשׁוֹנַי וְזֶבַח הַמִּשְׁתֶּה לְשִׁנֵּיהֶם;
וְהַלְּחִים קְרוּעִים וְהַחִידוֹת פְּתוּרוֹת,
שֵׁיבַת רֹאשִׁי הָרִאשׁוֹנָה.

הִנֵּה שָׁבִים שִׁמְשׁוֹנַי, לֹא מַסְמְרִים בְּעֵינֵיהֶם;
חוֹזְרִים אֵלַי מִגַּת,
כְּתֹם הָאֵשׁ.

הִנֵּה שָׁבִים שִׁמְשׁוֹנַי אֶל מַעֲבֶה לֵילוֹתֵיהֶם
הַמּוּאָרִים בְּשׁוּעֲלֵי הָאֵשׁ.

My Samsons

Look, my Samsons are coming back, the gates of Gaza on their
   shoulders;
smiling, they pass unseeing sentries.
Mint. Wind. Crickets.

Look, my Samsons are coming back, their Delilahs at their
   feet;
they move along my spine.
I'm awake.

Look, my Samsons are coming back, the memory of lions in
   their hands;
they march by in bare feet,
soundlessly in the unlit street.

Look, my Samsons are coming back, the frogs of the Vale of
   Sorek in their ears;
they make their way, they always make their way,
when was it I last lifted the gates?

Look, my Samsons are coming back, the slaughter of the feast
   in their teeth;

the wet ropes are torn, the riddles are solved,
my first grey hairs.

Look, my Samsons are coming back, no nails in their eyes;
they come back to me from Gath,
after the fire.

Look, my Samsons are coming back to the gloom of their
    nights
luminous with fox fire.

As he views these newly returned soldiers moving along the avenue where he lives (a preferable translation for the original Hebrew *sederati*), the middle-aged speaker, whose hair is just beginning to turn gray, feels somewhat inferior: "When was the last time I carried gates on my shoulders?" he asks himself. Because he is no longer fighting Israel's enemies on the front line, as he had once done when he was at his physical prime, he cannot live up to the ideal of heroic masculinity that these young soldiers embody. It is possible that the jealous admiration the speaker feels toward his younger compatriots may be tempered by irony. Warren Bargad connects this poem with the "common theme in the literature produced after the 1967 war, when the soldiers of 1948 [including Gouri and Amir Gilboa] were well into their forties and fifties and did not believe that war was the only course of action."[57] According to this reading the speaker may be seen as distancing himself from the follies of the youthful victors: after all, the victories of his youth were of limited effect because they were followed by a new cycle of war in 1967; who could say that the victory in 1967 would be of lasting significance?

In another poem that he wrote in the aftermath of the Six-Day War, *"Avshalomay"* ("My Absaloms")[58] Gouri presents a more clearly sober assessment of the young Israeli soldier. In this poem he makes use of the story of Absalom's rebellion against his father King David (II Samuel 15–19) to convey the older generation's response to the deaths of soldiers in Israel's wars. As in *"Shimshonay"* of the same period, the fate of the Israeli soldiers is presented as a multiple reenactment of the fate of a biblical hero. The long hair of many Absaloms is caught in the branches of oak trees while their horses continue to run. The aesthetic beauty of the scene is accompanied by a sense of futility:

אַבְשָׁלוֹמַי

הִנֵּה נִפְרָדִים אַבְשָׁלוֹמַי מִסּוּסֵיהֶם
וְנֶאֱחָזִים בִּשְׂעָרָם —
מַה נָּאוֹת הָאֵלוֹת הָאֵלֶּה!

הִנֵּה בָּאוֹת צִפֳּרִים גְּדוֹלוֹת לְהַבִּיט בְּעֵינֵיהֶם
וְאֵין קוֹל פַּחִים
לְאוֹר הָעֶרֶב,

הִנֵּה נִפְרָדִים אַבְשָׁלוֹמַי מִסּוּסֵיהֶם
לְרוּחַ הָעֶרֶב.

MY ABSALOMS

Look, my Absaloms are separated from their horses
and held by their hair—
How beautiful are these oaks!

Look, large birds are coming to look into their eyes
and there's no sound of traps
in the evening light,

look, my Absaloms are separated from their horses
in the evening wind.

Ironically, the speaker sees the dead bodies of the soldiers hanging
from the trees as if they were life-sustaining fruit. Sadly the horses,
perhaps representing the more impersonal forces that keep war
going, survive the deaths of these soldiers. The sequence happens
all too often: their deaths provide some measure of peace for the
country, but that peace lasts only for a limited time until the next
war, which official political rhetoric will justify, even though it will kill
more young soldiers:

וּבָאָה הַשֶּׁמֶשׁ לְרַגְלֵיהֶם
וְהֵם נִרְאִים מֵרָחוֹק, פֵּרוֹת מָאֳרָכִים,
עַל אִילָנוֹת הַדּוּמִיָּה הָאֵלֶּה;

שָׁם נִפְרָדִים אַבְשָׁלוֹמַי מִסּוּסֵיהֶם
הַמּוֹסִיפִים לִדְהֹר לִדְהֹר
אַחַר הַכֶּתֶר,

בְּשֵׁם הַגַּעְגּוּעִים וּבְשֵׁם פָּרָשֵׁיהֶם
צְמוּדֵי הָרַגְלַיִם
וּבְשֵׁם הַמִּלְחָמָה הַצּוֹדֶקֶת.

תָּמִיד, כַּנִּרְאֶה, נִפְרָדִים אַבְשָׁלוֹמַי מִסּוּסֵיהֶם
וְלִזְמַן־מָה קְצָת שֶׁקֶט.

And the sun sets at their feet
and they are seen from afar, elongated fruits,
on these trees of silence;

there my Absaloms are separated from their horses
that continue galloping galloping
after the crown,

in the name of longings and in the name of their riders
legs joined together
and in the name of the just war.

Always, it seems, my Absaloms are separated from their
horses
and for a while there's a little quiet.

It should be noted that in the titles of both poems, "*Shimshonay*" and "*Avshalomay*" Gouri has made the names Samson and Absalom into plural forms and attached to each one a first-person singular possessive ending. These poems are not about one particular soldier, but about all Israeli soldiers, who as defenders of the State belong, in a sense, to the older speaker of the poem. These soldiers are linked to Samson and Absalom in Gouri's imagination because both biblical characters were mighty warriors with long hair, a physical characteristic that sometimes characterizes youthful rebellion against adults in contemporary society. As strong as they were, both biblical characters were ultimately defeated by events related to their long hair; thus, they serve aptly as figures representing both the great strength and the vulnerability of the young Israeli soliders.

Nathan Yonathan also makes use of the David and Absalom story to write about the relationship of the older generation to the soldiers who died in battle. In "*Od shir ʿal ʾAvshalom*" ("Another Poem on Absalom"),[59] published in a collection that appeared a few years after the Six-Day War, Yonathan uses the untimely death of David's son Absalom (II Samuel 18) to convey the anguish of a bereaved father of a dead Israeli soldier. Although, as Zvi Luz notes, we can read this poem as an expression of the emotional suffering of any father whose son dies before him, the pervasive Israeli experience of young soldiers dying before their parents in battle must be seen as a significant aspect of the meaning of the poem.[60] The title of the poem, "Another Poem on Absalom," may be understood in two ways. On the one hand, it signals the poet's recognition that Absalom has been a figure that has fascinated many modern poets because of his great beauty, his long hair, his rebellion against his father, and his tragic death, and this poem will add to the tradition of writing poetry about Absalom. On the other hand, it conveys the sense that the poet is weary of all the deaths in war of youthful soldiers and that he is greatly displeased at having to witness yet another death.

In the biblical story on which Yonathan's poem is based, David's defeat of the rebellion in which his son Absalom took part is marred for him by Absalom's death. The king's anguish is captured powerfully by his repeatedly calling out to his dead son: "My son Absalom! O my son, my son Absalom! If only I had died instead of you! O Absalom, my son, my son!" (II Samuel 19:1). In the poem David's lament for Absalom is presented in a more articulate and reflective manner:

עוֹד שִׁיר עַל אַבְשָׁלוֹם

עָרוֹם כָּאִשָּׁה יָפֶה כַּנָּחָשׁ בִּישָׁן כָּאֱלִיל
תָּמִיד עִם חֶבֶר מֵרֵעָיו, בַּסּוּסִים, בַּזָּהָב,
וְעַכְשָׁו, אִמְרוּ, אֵיפֹה עָרְמַת נָשָׁיו
יְפִי נְחָשָׁיו, אֱלִילוֹ הַבִּישָׁן,
חֲלוֹמוֹת מַלְכוּתוֹ אַיָם?
עֵץ בַּיַּעַר, זֶה מַה שֶּׁנִּשְׁאַר מִכָּל אַבְשָׁלוֹם
וּבְכִיוֹ שֶׁל הָאָב, הַמְאַהֵב הַזָּקֵן, אִישׁ הַמִּלְחָמוֹת

אֲפִלּוּ רַכָּבוֹ פּוֹנֶה הַצִּדָּה לִבְכּוֹת;
כָּכָה לִשְׁבֹּר גַּב שֶׁל אָב,
לַעֲשׂוֹת צְחוֹק מֵהַמָּוֶת, מֵהַכֹּל!

ANOTHER POEM ON ABSALOM

Cunning as a woman beautiful as a snake shy as an idol,
Always with his crew of cronies, on horses in gold,
And now, tell me, where is the cunning of his women,
The beauty of his snakes, his shy idol?
The dreams of his kingdom—where are they?
A tree in the forest—that's all that's left of Absalom,
And the tears of the father, the old lover, the man of wars;
Even his charioteer turns aside to weep;
Thus to break a father's back,
To make a joke of death, of everything!

David expresses his anger at Absalom for wanting so much to have the power his father had. David's anger is not because he had been reluctant to turn over his power to his son, but rather because he knew so much better than Absalom how dangerous it was to enter battle and try to be the heroic warrior he had been:

אַבְשָׁלוֹם, בְּנִי בְּנִי אַבְשָׁלוֹם
לֹא יָכֹלְתָּ לְחַכּוֹת,
יֶלֶד מְפֻנָּק — עַד שֶׁנַּזְקִין,
שֶׁהַכֶּתֶר יוֹרִידֵנוּ בְּיָגוֹן.
וְתַלְתַּלֶּיךָ מָה, תַּלְתַּלֶּיךָ —
לֹא יָדַעְתָּ אֵיזוֹ סַכָּנָה טְמוּנָה בְּכָאֵלֶּה תַּלְתַּלִּים?

Absalom my son my son Absalom
You couldn't wait,
You spoiled child, until we aged,
Until the crown brought us down in agony.
And your curls, what of your curls—
Didn't you know the danger that hid in such curls?

David regrets that he never conveyed to Absalom how little he val-
ued heroic fighting by the end of his life. Having failed to convey this
message, he apparently feels guilty that he was unable thereby to
save his son and enjoy his presence in the coming years. His guilt re-
sembles the survivor guilt of David in the Bible, who in his lament ex-
pressed the wish that he, not his son Absalom, had died in the vio-
lent conflict between them:

וְלָמָּה דֶּרֶךְ הַיַּעַר דַּוְקָא
שָׁכַחְתָּ מַה קָּרָה לִיוֹנָתָן?
אֵינְךָ מַכִּיר אֶת הָאֵלוֹת?
אָבִיךָ אָהַב בְּךָ כֹּל מַה שֶׁהוּא לֹא,
תִּרְאוּ אֵיךְ הַגֶּבֶר רוֹעֵד כֻּלּוֹ, לָמָּה
אַתָּה חוֹשֵׁב, לֹא נָתַתִּי לְךָ מְלוּכָה —
מֵרֹב דְּאָגָה לָעָם? בִּגְלַל גִּילְךָ?
לוּ יָכֹלְנוּ לְדַבֵּר עַל כָּךְ בְּשֶׁקֶט
הָיִיתָ מֵבִין שֶׁאֲנִי כְּבָר לֹא אוֹתוֹ דָּוִד
תּוּגַת אִמְּךָ, רַק מֶלֶךְ בָּא בַּיָּמִים
שָׁאֵל מוֹתוֹ הוֹלֵךְ בְּלִי שִׂמְחָה
וְעוֹד כָּמַס בְּלִבּוֹ מְזִמָּה אַחֲרוֹנָה
לְהַצִּיל לְפָחוֹת יֶלֶד אֶחָד שֶׁלּוֹ
מֵהַכֶּתֶר, מֵהַמִּלְחָמוֹת.
רָצִיתִי, טִפְּשׁוֹן שֶׁלִּי, רַק אוֹתְךָ, אַבְשָׁלוֹם

And why through the forest, of all ways—
Did you forget what happened to Jonathan?
Don't you know the terebinths?
Your father loved in you all that he was not,
See now this man trembles all over, why
Did you think I would not make you king,
Because of my concern for the people? Because
You were too young? If we'd only been able to speak of it
        calmly
You'd have understood that I'm no longer the same David,
Your mother's sorrow, but just an aging king
Going joylessly to his death,
With one last intrigue concealed in his heart:

To save at least one of his sons
From the crown and the wars.
I wanted, my little fool, only you, Absalom.

Authors of Israeli biblical allusion poetry have made their contributions to the trend in Israel of comparing the older generation sending the younger generation to war to the binding of Isaac story (Genesis 22). This use of the binding of Isaac story can be found in biblical allusion poems responding to the last three major Arab-Israeli wars: the Six-Day War, the Yom Kippur War, and the Lebanon War.[61] In a poem published in a collection that appeared a few years after the Six-Day War, "*Ha'aqedah*" ("The Akedah," or "The Binding")[62] Alizah Shenhar expresses the anguish of the parents, and in particular of the mothers, when they contemplate the deaths of their sons in war. She makes use of the story of the binding of Isaac as the basis for a fundamental challenge to the ways that Israeli culture typically attempts to find meaning in the deaths of its young soldiers:

הָעֲקֵדָה

הָרָמְקוֹל צָרַח
"קְחִי נָא אֶת יְחִידֵךְ,
אֶת זֶה אֲשֶׁר אָהַבְתִּי".
וְהַמִּזְבֵּחַ הָרוּס. עֲצֵי
הַמַּעֲרָכָה פְּזוּרִים. הַנְּעָרִים
מְגֻלְגָּלִים כַּדּוּרֵי
אַהֲבָה עַל-פְּנֵי דֶשֶׁא
צְעִירוּתָם. לְשׁוֹנָם
חַמָּה. הַמַּאֲכֶלֶת נוֹצֶצֶת
בַּוָּאדִי לְאוֹר יָרֵחַ
שֶׁל אֶמְצַע הַגְּבוּל.
הַמַּלְאָךְ הַלָּבָן, זֶה
שֶׁתָּמִיד צוֹעֵק
"אַל נָא תִּשְׁלְחִי יָדֵךְ"
בְּחֻפְשָׁה רְגִילָה.

THE AKEDAH

The loudspeaker screamed
"Take your only one
the one you love."
And the altar is destroyed.
Wood of the burnt offering is scattered.
The youths roll balls of love
on the grass of their youth.
Their tongues are hot.
The knife is shining in the wadi
in the light of the moon
of mid-border.
The white angel, the one
who always cries
"Please don't lay a hand"
is on leave.

There is a great degree of similarity between the language of the biblical account of the binding of Isaac and that of the contemporary poem. The voice of God and the voice of the loudspeaker are perceived as representing authorities to be obeyed. The special status of the beloved son is expressed in both texts. Shenhar, however, has radically challenged the meaning that the biblical narrative attributed to the event. In the original Hebrew of the poem the gender of the addressee is feminine, and so the hero of Shenhar's poem is not the male Abraham, but an unnamed female figure, perhaps Sarah. The commanding voice of God, who had protected and nourished Abraham for so many years, becomes in Shenhar's poem an anonymous human voice screaming over an impersonal loudspeaker. God in the biblical story clearly explains for what purpose Abraham is to "take" his son, to offer him as a sacrifice. The voice over the loudspeaker comes across as arbitrary and mysterious when it provides no more than an unexplained command to the woman to take her son.

The "taking" of the son in the poem is not for the purpose of offering him to God. In fact, the altar on which he might have been sacrificed is destroyed. The images that are left from the binding of Isaac story suggest that the context of a divine offering has been transformed into the context of war. The wood that Abraham arranged on the altar (*vaya'arokh 'et ha'etsim*) (Genesis 22:9) has become the scattered wood of a battle (*'atsei hama'arkhah pezurim*). Furthermore, Isaac is not to be the victim; a whole group of youths supplants him. In the biblical version, the source of pathos is that God commands Abraham to sacrifice his son and thereby apparently to undo God's promise to multiply Abraham's descendants. In the poem the pathos is in the deaths of these youths, who should be allowed to keep "rolling balls (*kadurim*) of love" but instead are playing with bullets (*kadurim*) of death. The hot tongue of sexual passion has become the tongue burned in battle. These youthful soldiers are not bound to an altar; rather, they are under the threat of the violent knife of war, which "shines in the wadi in the light of the moon" in the border between Israel and its Arab enemies. However, unlike the biblical story, which ends with the angel staying Abraham's hand, in war no angel arrives to stop the slaying of the soldiers. The angel is just part of the institution of the military, and like any soldier he is on his "regular leave" (*behufshah regilah*).

The poem is about the sacrifice that Israeli mothers make when they send their sons off to wars conducted by the governmental authorities. It is also about the biblical story of the binding of Isaac and later Jewish tradition that viewed that story as a paradigm of Jewish martyrdom. The Bible and later Jewish tradition discerned in God's command a meaningful obligation of self-sacrifice. In contrast, Israeli mothers are unable to find meaning in the deaths of their sons in war. Shenhar's version makes God, who represents the State's power to sacrifice youths in war, look even more arbitrary than He does in the Bible. It also questions the view, whether ancient or modern, that death for the sake of a higher purpose (divine will or national survival) is really worthwhile.

An example from the post–Yom Kippur War period of the use of the binding of Isaac to protest the deaths of Israel's youths in war is a poem by Matti Megged. Megged's poem appears in an appendix to his novel *Mem: (shem sha'ul) (M: [A Borrowed Name])*.[63] It is presented by the narrator as a poem by M., the central character of the novel, a poet of the Palmach generation who became increasingly disillusioned with the Zionist ideals of his youth in the course of the first decades of the State of Israel. The poem appears as an endnote to an incident in which M. discusses with a friend the death of the friend's son when he was held as a prisoner by the Syrians in the aftermath of the Yom Kippur War of 1973. As is typical of the indeterminate style of the narrator in the novel, he speculates about a reference that M. might have made to the binding of Isaac story:

> Or perhaps he spoke in the ears of that bereaved father about the binding of Isaac, about the generation of the fathers, the senders, as it were, of their sons in the face of the difficult battle. About the unintentional sin of the fathers, who were not wise enough to prevent their sons from experiencing what had fallen to their lot, when they were their age.[64]

By means of the narrator's comments Megged makes clear the subversive nature of this use of the binding of Isaac story to critique the sacrifice of young soldiers in war. The narrator states that he strongly suspects that even if M. did draw an analogy between the binding of Isaac and the deaths of the young soldiers he did not fully believe in it and "was embarrassed by [his words]."[65] In the appendix the narrator also distances himself from this analogy by introducing M.'s poem with a disclaimer: "If I had permission I would erase the allusion to the binding of Isaac, which is all falsehood and lack of respect."[66] Then, after quoting the poem, the narrator declares, "As far as I know, M. never showed this poem to anyone. And justifiably so."[67]

In this poem the soldier who goes off to war is a contemporary version of Isaac led to the slaughter:

וְכַאֲשֶׁר הָלַכְתִּי שׁוּב אֶל הָעֲקֵדָה
(לֹא בְּרֶגֶל. לֹא רָכוּב עַל חֲמוֹר. כָּלוּא
בְּבִטְנָהּ שֶׁל מִפְלֶצֶת-פְּלָדָה)
יַד אָבִי הַחַמָּה
לֹא אָחֲזָה בְּיָדִי.
לֹא שָׁאַלְתִּי אַיֵּה הַשֶּׂה לְעוֹלָה,
וְלֹא הָיָה מִי שֶׁיָּשִׁיב עַל הַשְּׁאֵלָה.

גַּם מַלְאָךְ לֹא בָּא
לַעֲצֹר בַּמַּאֲכֶלֶת.

רַק אֲנִי לְבַדִּי —
הָאָב.
וְהַבֵּן.
וְהָרוּחַ אֵין
לְקַדֵּשׁ אֶת דָּמִי
שֶׁנִּגַּר עַל אַבְנֵי הַבַּזֶּלֶת.

אֲנִי זוֹכֵר
רַק שָׁמַיִם זָרִים, עֲשֵׁנִים,
אֲדִישִׁים לְחַיַּי, אֲדִישִׁים לְמוֹתִי.

רַק לִרְגָעִים אֶשְׁמַע עוֹד
מִבַּעַד לָעֲנָנִים
קוֹל אַשְׁמַאי זָקֵן
שׂוֹחֵק לְמִשְׁבַּתִּי.

And when I went again to the binding
(not on foot, not riding on a donkey. Imprisoned
in the belly of a steel monster)
my father's warm hand
didn't hold my hand.
I didn't ask where is the lamb for the offering,
and there was no one to answer the question.

Nor did an angel come
to stop the knife.

Only I alone—
the father
and the son.
And no spirit was there
to sanctify my blood
that flowed on the basalt stones.

I remember
only strange, smoky skies,
apathetic to my life, apathetic to my death.

Only every so often I still hear
from beyond the clouds

the voice of an old sinner
laughing at my destruction.

This latter-day Isaac will be slaughtered without the comforting hand of his father, without the sense that anyone can explain his death to him, and without the divine intervention that saved Isaac's life at the last moment. He is brought to his death in a steel tank, deep in its belly from which he will not be born, but rather will die.[68] There is nothing holy about the victim's spilled blood. His experience only proves the apathy of the cosmos toward him and the disturbing sense that the universe is ruled by an amoral force that maliciously laughs at his death.

Israel's least popular war, the Lebanon War of the early 1980s, evoked much public political opposition, including the publication of many protest poems.[69] One such poem was the biblical allusion poem mentioned above, "*Hametumtam hazeh Yitshaq*," by Yitzhak Laor. In his poem of this period, "*Hagibbor ha'amitti shel ha'aqedah*" ("The Real Hero of the Sacrifice of Isaac")[70] Yehuda Amichai puts a different twist on the comparison of Israel's wars to the binding of Isaac by having the ram represent the contemporary victim, thereby making him the real hero of the story:

הַגִּבּוֹר הָאֲמִתִּי שֶׁל הָעֲקֵדָה

הַגִּבּוֹר הָאֲמִתִּי שֶׁל הָעֲקֵדָה הָיָה הָאַיִל
שֶׁלֹּא יָדַע עַל הַקְּנוּנְיָה בֵּין הָאֲחֵרִים.
הוּא כְּמוֹ הִתְנַדֵּב לָמוּת בִּמְקוֹם יִצְחָק.
אֲנִי רוֹצֶה לָשִׁיר עָלָיו שִׁיר זִכָּרוֹן,
עַל הַצֶּמֶר הַמִּתְלַתֵּל וְעַל עֵינָיו הָאֱנוֹשִׁיּוֹת
עַל הַקַּרְנַיִם שֶׁהָיוּ שְׁקֵטוֹת כָּל כָּךְ בְּרֹאשׁוֹ הֶחָי
וְאַחַר שֶׁנִּשְׁחַט עָשׂוּ מֵהֶן שׁוֹפָרוֹת
לְקוֹל תְּרוּעַת מִלְחַמְתָּם
אוֹ לְקוֹל תְּרוּעַת שִׂמְחָתָם הַגַּסָּה.

אֲנִי רוֹצֶה לִזְכֹּר אֶת הַתְּמוּנָה הָאַחֲרוֹנָה
כְּמוֹ תַּצְלוּם יָפֶה בְּעִתּוֹן אָפְנָה מְעֻדָּן:
הַצָּעִיר הַשָּׁזוּף וְהַמְפֻנָּק בִּבְגָדָיו הַמְגֻנְדָּרִים

וְלִידוֹ הַמַּלְאָךְ הַלָּבוּשׁ שִׂמְלַת מֶשִׁי אֲרֻכָּה
לְקַבָּלַת פָּנִים חֲגִיגִית.
וּשְׁנֵיהֶם בְּעֵינַיִם רֵיקוֹת
מַבִּיטִים אֶל שְׁנֵי מְקוֹמוֹת רֵיקִים

וּמֵאַחוֹרֵיהֶם, כִּרְקַע צִבְעוֹנִי, הָאַיִל
נֶאֱחָז בַּסְּבַךְ בְּטֶרֶם שְׁחִיטָה.
וְהַסְּבַךְ יְדִידוֹ הָאַחֲרוֹן.

הַמַּלְאָךְ הָלַךְ הַבַּיְתָה
יִצְחָק הָלַךְ הַבַּיְתָה
וְאַבְרָהָם וֵאלֹהִים הָלְכוּ מִזְּמַן.

אֲבָל הַגִּבּוֹר הָאֲמִתִּי שֶׁל הָעֲקֵדָה
הוּא הָאַיִל.

The Real Hero of the Sacrifice of Isaac

The real hero of the sacrifice was the ram
Who had no idea about the conspiracy of the others.
He apparently volunteered to die in place of Isaac.
I want to sing a memorial song about the ram,
His curly wool and human eyes,
The horns, so calm in his living head.
When he was slaughtered they made *shofars* of them,
To sound the blast of their war
Or the blast of their coarse joy.

I want to remember the last picture
Like a beautiful photo in an exquisite fashion magazine:
The tanned, spoiled youngster all spiffed up,
And beside him the angel, clad in a long silk gown
For a formal reception.
Both with hollow eyes
Observe two hollow places,

And behind them, as a colored background, the ram
Grasping the thicket before the slaughter.

The angel went home
Isaac went home
And Abraham and God left much earlier.

But the real hero of the sacrifice
Is the ram.

We can discern in this poem the sense of some Israelis at the time of the Lebanon War that there was a secret conspiracy of the government to send youths off to war without giving the nation the true story of why they were fighting. As Yair Mazor suggests, in the line stating that the ram "apparently (in Hebrew: *kemo*, "as if") volunteered to die in place of Isaac," it is clear that the ram really had no choice, and correspondingly neither did the Israeli soldiers who died in Lebanon. Thus, here Amichai is ironically undermining the Israeli army value of volunteerism in a war such as the Lebanon War, which does not seem to be justified.[71]

Like the ram in this version of the binding of Isaac story the deaths of the youths are not taken as seriously as they should be. They are treated like animals, whose deaths are generally not mourned by human beings as much as human deaths are mourned. They provide an opportunity to further pursue war and vulgar celebration. As Mazor notes, the image of the celebration accompanied by the blowing of rams' horns may allude to the blowing of the shofar that accompanied the conquering of the old city of Jerusalem in the Six-Day War.[72] From the perspective of the seemingly pointless Lebanon War the postwar celebrations of 1967 do indeed look vulgar. The casualties of war are soon abandoned and leave the society's consciousness more quickly than they deserve. There is something obscene about the image of Isaac and the angel posing for a picture in a fashion magazine as if the death of the ram could not possibly disrupt society. The shift of tense from the beginning to the end of the poem is significant. At the beginning of the poem, the real hero *was* the ram; at the end of the poem the real hero *is* the ram. This archetypal victimization that began in biblical times persists to this day, and it is the poet's role to remind his society to be more sensitive to the cruelty of using youths as cannon fodder to achieve the nation's military ends.[73]

Recently, Yitzhak Laor returned to the binding of Isaac story in the poem "*Hametumtam hazeh Yitshaq (girsah me'uheret)*" ("This Idiot

Isaac [Late Version]"), which presents a less angry and more compassionate view of the older generation than does his earlier poem:[74]

הַמְטֻמְטָם הַזֶּה יִצְחָק (גִּרְסָה מְאֻחֶרֶת)

שָׁנִים שֶׁעָקַבְתִּי אַחֲרֵי כָּל מַעֲשָׂיו שֶׁל אָבִי (הֻמְלַץ לָנוּ לִגְלוֹת עֵרָנוּת
הַשָּׂפוֹת שֶׁדִּבְּרוּ לֹא הָיוּ בְּרוּרוֹת) הוּא עָבַד כְּמוֹ חֲמוֹר וַאֲנִי יָשַׁבְתִּי
עַל עֲרֵמַת הָעֵצִים (רַק עִנְיָן אֶחָד הֶעֱלַמְתִּי תָּמִיד : אָבִי הָיָה חֲסַר כָּל
הִתְמַצְּאוּת בַּחֲיֵי הַצָּבָאִי) וְלִפְעָמִים כָּתַבְתִּי שִׁירִים נֶגֶד הָעֲקֵדָה
(וְנֶגֶד הָאָבוֹת) אֲנִי זוֹכֵר אֶת לֵילוֹת הַשָּׁעוּל. הוּא מָרַח לִי
שֶׁמֶן חַם עַל הֶחָזֶה וְעַל הַגַּב וְרִפֵּד בְּצֶמֶר גֶּפֶן וְעָטַף בְּבַד וּבִשְׁמִיכָה
וְיָצָא אִתִּי הַחוּצָה לֶחָצֵר. אֲנִי זוֹכֵר עַד הַיּוֹם אֶת בִּרְכָּיו, אֶת יָדָיו
הָרַכּוֹת, אֶת צַמֶּרֶת הַתּוּת בַּחֹשֶׁךְ וְאֶת שִׁיר הָעֶרֶשׂ שֶׁשָּׁר לִי בְּקוֹלוֹ הָרַךְ
בְּלִי מִלִּים (בִּגְלַל הַשָּׂפוֹת שֶׁדִּבְּרוּ וכו'). אֲנִי, מִצְּדִי, פָּחַדְתִּי לָמוּת
(וְשֶׁלֹּא יִקְחוּ אוֹתִי לַצָּבָא)
וְהוּא אָמַר לִי בְּקוֹל מָלֵא אַהֲבָה :
אַל תִּפְחַד, הִנְנִי, בְּנִי יִצְחָק

(וְהַיֶּלֶד הִשְׁתָּעֵל וְקָדַח וְאָמַר : מִי אַתָּה?
וְהָאִישׁ עָנָה בְּמִבְטָא קְצָת זָר :
לֹא אֶתֵּן לָהֶם, בְּנִי, לָקַחַת אוֹתְךָ
אֲנִי הָאַיִל
אֲנִי הַמַּלְאָךְ
אֲנִי אַבָּא שֶׁלְּךָ)

THIS IDIOT ISAAC (LATE VERSION)

For years I followed all my father's actions (we were told to
    stay alert
the tongues they spoke weren't clear) he worked like an ass
    and I
sat on the woodpile (only one thing I always concealed: my
    father was completely
ignorant of my military experience) and sometimes I wrote
    poems against
the Sacrifice (and against the Fathers) I remember nights of
coughing. He'd rub warm oil on my chest and back which he'd
    soothe with cotton

and wrapped in a sheet and blanket he'd take me out into the
yard.
To this very day I remember his knees, his soft hands, the
crown
of the mulberry in the dark and the lullaby he'd sing in his soft
voice
without words (because of the tongues they spoke, etcetera).
I, for my part, was scared to die
(and that they wouldn't draft me into the army)
and he'd tell me in a voice brimming with love:
don't be scared, here I am, my son Isaac

(and the boy coughed and burned and said: who are you?
and the man answered with a slight foreign accent:
I won't let them, son, take you
I am the ram
I am the angel
I am your father)

In this poem the speaker indicates that his anti-binding of Isaac
poems, which attacked his father's generation, are in the past; he now
can affectionately remember his father as a hard-working and caring
man. Nevertheless, there are differences between the speaker and his
father: his father's native language is not Hebrew, he apparently never
served in the army, and the speaker has always hidden from him his
experiences in the army. The most significant difference between
them, however, is apparent when the father reassures the son by say-
ing "don't be scared, here I am, my son Isaac," and the son asks him
"who are you?" The father then claims that he can take the place of
the ram and the angel that saved the biblical Isaac from death, while
the speaker knows this really is not true. Here Abraham does not rep-
resent the State out to kill youthful Israeli soldiers, but rather the Is-
raeli parent powerless to change the fate of his son, who, while he
succumbs to the underlying cultural assumption that to serve in the
army is a central experience of Israeli youth (he is scared that he will
not be drafted), is also scared that he will die in war, for he knows nei-
ther God nor human beings can make sure he will survive.

The poem is introduced by a quotation from the ballad, "*Erl-
könig,*" by Goethe in German and in Hebrew translation:

"Mein Sohn, was birgst du so bang dein Gesicht?"—
"Siehst, Vater, du den Erlkönig nicht?"

"בְּנִי, לָמָּה פָּנֶיךָ בְּפַחַד תַּחְבִּיא?!"
— "לֹא תִרְאֶה אֶת שַׂר-הַיַּעַר, אָבִי?!"

In the first stanza of the ballad from which these lines are taken a father holds his child tightly as they ride in the night. At the beginning of the second stanza, in the lines quoted by Laor at the beginning of the poem, the father notices that the boy is covering his face. When the father asks him why, the son replies, "Don't you see the elf king [or "prince of the forest," as Laor translates it], my father?" As the poem progresses the son keeps seeing and hearing the ever-threatening elf king, while the father keeps insisting that the son is only seeing and hearing natural phenomena. The father recognizes the danger that the elf king represents only at the end of the ballad, when it is too late, and the child dies in his arms as the father rides home in horror.

The passage by Goethe throws light on the meaning of Laor's poem. As in the Goethe ballad, the son is distant from his father because the father cannot understand the son's fears. Like the father in the ballad, who is deluded into thinking there is no danger, so the father in Laor's poem does not fully appreciate the mortal danger his son faces in war, and he therefore can never fully understand his son's terror as he faces the prospect of battle. When the father in Laor's poem tries to comfort the son with the words, "I won't let them, son, take you," he refuses to realize how little power he has to protect his son. By associating war with the supernatural power of a German legendary elf king, Laor removes war from its Israeli context and presents the dangers of death in battle as an ominous, uncontrollable force that has nothing to do with the sense of purpose that Israeli society has attributed to army service. The parents are portrayed as less malicious than they are in the earlier version of "*Hametumtam hazeh Yitshaq.*" They are not crazy murderers trying to kill their children by sending them into battle; instead, the parents are portrayed as helpless victims unable to face the truth that the momentum of war that takes their children's lives is dangerously out of control.

Poems by Yehudit Kafri and Dalia Ravikovitch draw on other biblical material to respond to the events of the Lebanon War. As in her poem *"Yosef,"* in *"Vehu' nofel"* ("And He Falls," dated December 1982)[75] Yehudit Kafri makes use of the Joseph story, this time as a means to express her response to the Lebanon War. The speaker tells of observing Joseph on his way to see his brothers in the Valley of Dothan:

וְהוּא נוֹפֵל

אִישׁ הוֹלֵךְ בְּעֵמֶק דֹּתָן
לָבוּשׁ כְּתֹנֶת פַּסִּים.
הַשֶּׁמֶשׁ וְהַיָּרֵחַ וְהַכּוֹכָבִים
מִשְׁתַּחֲוִים לְפָנָיו.
מַה פֶּלֶא שֶׁהוּא לֹא שָׂם לֵב
לַבּוֹרוֹת שֶׁבַּדֶּרֶךְ,
אוֹ לְמַה שֶּׁבֶּאֱמֶת חוֹשְׁבִים עָלָיו אֶחָיו.
הַשֶּׁמֶשׁ וְהַיָּרֵחַ וְהַכּוֹכָבִים
מִסְתַּחְרְרִים סָבִיב עֵינָיו.
זוֹ סְחַרְחֹרֶת אַחֲרוֹנָה שֶׁל אוֹר
לִפְנֵי הַנְּפִילָה
אֲבָל הוּא עוֹד לֹא יוֹדֵעַ.

AND HE FALLS

A man walks in the Valley of Dothan
dressed in a coat of many colors.
The sun and the moon and the stars
bow down to him.
What's the wonder that he doesn't pay attention
to the pits on the way,
or to what his brothers really think of him.
The sun and the moon and the stars
swirl around his eyes.
This is the final swirling of light
before the fall
but he still doesn't know it.

The man, like the biblical Joseph, walks naively believing in his dreams of greatness and oblivious to the jealousy and hatred that his brothers feel toward him. He represents the naive Israeli soldier going into battle in Lebanon without knowing the real reason why he is fighting and without full awareness of how mortally dangerous war can be. The soldier's persistent lack of awareness finally leads him to his "fall," which may be seen as referring to his death in battle because "fall" (*nafal*) is the Hebrew euphemism for such deaths. At the last moment the speaker seeks to warn him, but it is too late:

יוֹם וְלַיְלָה וְיוֹם
הוּא הוֹלֵךְ בָּאוֹר הָרַב
רֹאשׁוֹ בַּשָּׁמַיִם
רַגְלָיו מְרַחֲפוֹת;
בָּרֶגַע הָאַחֲרוֹן לִפְנֵי שֶׁהוּא מַגִּיעַ לִשְׂפַת הַבּוֹר
אֲנִי מַתְחִילָה לִצְעֹק.
אֲנִי צוֹעֶקֶת
וְהוּא נוֹפֵל.

Day and night and day
he walks in the abundant light
his head in the sky
his feet hovering;
at the last moment before he arrives at the edge of the pit
I start to shout.
I shout
and he falls.

"*Eglah 'arufah*" ("Blood Heifer," or "Broken-Necked Heifer"),[76] a poem published by Dalia Ravikovitch a few years after the outbreak of the Lebanon War, addresses the questions of the meaning of the Arab-Israeli conflict and the moral obligation toward Israel's enemies and its dead soldiers. It does so by placing the Arab-Israeli conflict in a different biblical context from the other poems we have seen. The poem, ignoring the more common biblical associations with the period of the conquest of the Land or the binding of Isaac, instead views the Arab-Israeli conflict as related to laws of moral responsibility promulgated by Moses in the wilderness. The poem begins with the description of a figure stumbling to his death. The initial description of his weakness, with his glasses and skullcap falling to the ground, give the figure Diaspora associations, as if the description is of a Jew at the time of a pogrom. As the stanza progresses, however, the speaker makes clear that the context is Israel. Furthermore, the speaker suggests, the victim may be a Jew or an Arab. The identity of the victim, however, is irrelevant; all that matters is that a human being has been shot:

עֶגְלָה עֲרוּפָה

הָלַךְ עוֹד צַעַד
הָלַךְ עוֹד כַּמָּה צְעָדִים,
נָפְלוּ לוֹ הַמִּשְׁקָפַיִם
נָפְלָה לוֹ הַכִּפָּה.
הָלַךְ עוֹד צַעַד
שָׁטוּף בְּדָם,
מוֹשֵׁךְ רַגְלַיִם
אַחֲרֵי עֲשָׂרָה צְעָדִים
כְּבָר לֹא יְהוּדִי
לֹא עֲרָבִי,
עַרְטִילָאִי.

BLOOD HEIFER

He took one step,
then a few steps more.
His glasses fell to the ground,
his skullcap.
Managed another step,
bloody, dragging his feet.
Ten steps
and he's not a Jew anymore,
not an Arab—
in limbo.

Because the identity of the victim is unknown, both Jews and Arabs react as if one of their people has been attacked. They can discern no

justification for this death at the hands of the enemy, so each side
feels justified in avenging the spilled blood of its brother:

מְהוּמַת אֱלֹהִים; אֲנָשִׁים צוֹעֲקִים; לָמָּה אַתֶּם רוֹצְחִים אוֹתָנוּ?
וַאֲחֵרִים מִתְרוֹצְצִים
מְמַהֲרִים לַעֲשׂוֹת נְקָמָה.

Havoc in the marketplace; people shouting, Why
are you murdering us?
Others rushing
to take revenge.

The death of this victim defies all the religious expressions that
might be put forth to neutralize the pain and anguish associated with
such a death. The speaker insists on moving beyond such clichés
and the anonymity of the victim that they reinforce. This real human
being has a very specific identity, and neither side can rightfully
deny its responsibility for his death:

וְהוּא מְחַרְחֵר עַל הָאָרֶץ
גּוּף קָרוּעַ,
וְהַדָּם שׁוֹתֵת מִתּוֹךְ הַבָּשָׂר.
הַדָּם שׁוֹתֵת מִתּוֹךְ הַבָּשָׂר.

הוּא מֵת פֹּה אוֹ שָׁם
אִי בְּהִירוּת יֶשְׁנָהּ פֹּה.
מָה אֲנַחְנוּ יוֹדְעִים?
נִמְצָא חָלָל בַּשָׂדֶה.

אוֹמְרִים, יִסּוּרִים מְמָרְקִים עָוֹן.
אָדָם כְּאָבָק פּוֹרֵחַ,
אַךְ מִי הָאִישׁ
שֶׁכָּךְ בִּבְדִידוּת
שָׁכַב מְעֻלָּע אֶת דָּמָיו?
מָה הוּא רָאָה
מָה הוּא שָׁמַע

בְּתוֹךְ הַמְּהוּמָה
מֵעָלָיו?
וְיֵשׁ הָאוֹמְרִים,
חֲמוֹר שֹׂנַאֲךָ
עָזֹב תַּעֲזֹב עִמּוֹ.

כִּי יִמָּצֵא חָלָל בַּשָּׂדֶה,
כִּי יִמָּצֵא חָלָל בָּאֲדָמָה
וְיָצְאוּ זְקֵנֶיךָ וְשָׁחֲטוּ עֶגְלָה
וְאֶת אֶפְרָהּ בַּנַּחַל יְפַזְּרוּ.

And he lies on the ground: a death rattle,
a body torn open,
blood streaming out of the flesh,
streaming
out of the flesh.

He died here, or there—
no one knows for sure.
What do we know?
A dead body lying in the field.
Suffering cleanseth from sin, it is said,
man is like dust in the wind,
but who was that man
lying there lonely in his blood?
What did he see,
what did he hear
with all that commotion around him?
If thou seest even thine enemy's ass
lying under its burden,
it is said, thou shalt surely help.

If a dead body is found lying in the field
if a body is found in the open,
let your elders go out and slaughter a heifer
and scatter its ashes in the river.

The references to the Mosaic laws of the obligation to help your
enemy's ass (Exodus 23:5) and of the ritual of the heifer practiced in

response to the discovery of a dead body between two cities (Deuteronomy 21:1–9) make clear that it really does not matter whether an Arab killed a Jew or a Jew killed an Arab. Both sides have fallen far short of the moral standards put forth in the Torah. If ancient Israelites were expected to help their enemies' fallen asses, then how much more of a responsibility do Jews and Arabs have to the fallen soldiers of their enemies? Indeed, they need to take seriously the prayer prescribed by the Torah for the elders of the two cities between which the dead body lies that the sin of murder be expiated. The connection between this ritual and the theme of the poem is reinforced by the fact that the passage describing the ritual of the heifer in Deuteronomy 21 is preceded and followed in the biblical text by laws of war. This association with laws of war reinforces the poet's concern that the Arab-Israeli conflict has degenerated into violent confrontations that defy any attempt to modify them by the application of moral principles.

Ravikovitch introduces a significant change in her allusion to the ritual of the heifer. In Deuteronomy the elders do not scatter the ashes in the river. This image may have been suggested to the poet by the passage describing the ritual of purification in which the ashes of a red cow are mixed with water (Numbers 19). For Ravikovitch, in a moral, if not a ritual, sense the Land of Israel has been polluted by acts of violence. Only when both Arabs and Jews can transcend the rhetoric that seeks to justify the continuation of their conflict, she believes, will the land recover from this plague of war.

Each biblical allusion poem we have examined challenges the ways that Israeli public discourse has resorted to the Bible to enlist public support for Israeli war efforts and to grant meaning to the sacrifices Israelis have made in their violent struggle with their Arab neighbors. For the authors of these poems there is a significant flaw in comparing the contemporary Arab-Israeli conflict with battles against the residents of ancient Canaan led by Joshua, Deborah, Samson or David; as far as these poets are concerned, the attitude of the Bible to the military conflicts of its day is unacceptable.

These poets are extremely sympathetic to the plight of Israel's Arab enemies who have suffered in war, and thus they cannot celebrate Israel's victories the way ancient Israelite warriors did without being acutely aware of what has happened to the defeated enemy. Furthermore, they are driven to seriously question any attempt to place the sacrifice of Israel's youthful soldiers in battle in the meaningful context of divine providence. God, as far as they can tell, has not cared much for His people during the decades of warfare in Israel that have produced so many bereaved parents. Stories of divine intervention such as the binding of Isaac and the Joseph story, therefore, must be retold without their heroes being saved. These poets are troubled by comparisons of the Arab-Israeli conflict to the Bible because they reinforce such disturbing trends in Israeli culture as insensitivity to the Arab enemy, the reliance by men on war heroism to bolster their status in society, and a tendency not to want to come to terms with the soldiers' deaths. Dalia Ravikovitch's poem "'Eglah 'a-rufah" has a somewhat different relationship to the Bible than do the other poems because it asserts that the Bible itself contains a kernel of sensitivity to the deaths of Israelis and Arabs in war that is absent in the biblical stories about the conquest of Canaan. Israelis have much to learn, she suggests in the poem, from the Mosaic law that is so concerned with the responsibility of humanity for the shedding of blood.

CHAPTER THREE

IT IS I
WHO AM
SLAUGHTERED
MY SON | **THOSE WHO**
EXPERIENCED
THE HOLOCAUST
AND THOSE
WHO DID NOT

Although the destruction of European Jewry in World War II took place outside the Land of Israel, Israeli culture has been greatly preoccupied by this historical event. For Jews engaged in the Zionist enterprise in the Land of Israel during and immediately after World War II, Hitler's genocidal attack on the Jews of Europe grimly confirmed their conviction that Diaspora Jewry was doomed and that the only viable alternative for Jews was the development of the Land of Israel into a sovereign Jewish state. As Dina Porat observes, "Tragically, it was a far stronger confirmation than the Zionist movement had wanted or needed."[1]

At the same time, as Tom Segev has noted, even if the Zionists were powerless to stop the Nazis' program of genocide, the destruction of European Jewry put Zionism in a position of defeat, for "the Zionists were unable to convince the majority of the world's Jews to come to Palestine before the war, while that was still an option."[2] This failure of Zionism was experienced on a particularly painful level by the many Jews who had emigrated from Europe to the Land of Israel before the war and had to come to terms with the fact that their grandparents, parents, siblings, cousins, aunts, uncles, and friends were among the victims of the Holocaust. For those mourning such personal losses the issue was how to live with a sense of guilt for having saved themselves in time by emigrating to the Land of Israel and having failed to influence or help their loved ones to do the same.

The Jews living in the Land of Israel in the years since the end of the war have related to the Holocaust not only as an historical event of the past. Living representatives of that period, the survivors, flooded the Land of Israel in the years immediately before and after the establishment of the State. From 1946 until 1951, so many Holocaust survivors emigrated from Europe to the Land of Israel that almost one-quarter of the population of Israel in 1951 were Holocaust survivors.[3] Eventually, Israel became the country with the highest percentage of Holocaust survivors relative to the Jewish population.[4] The living legacy of the Holocaust survivors has continued with the birth of a second and a third generation of descendants of the survivors, who on some level have been personally affected by their forebears' sufferings.

Those who were in the Land of Israel during World War II, as well as Israelis born after the war, initially had an uneasy relationship with the survivors. As Segev notes, the Jews of the pre-State Zionist settlement period had developed an image of the fighting, native-born sabra as the ideal to replace the Jew of the Diaspora who was seen as weak and defenseless, and the survivors of the Holocaust were viewed as seriously falling short of that ideal. Not only were the survivors viewed as flawed, but their very presence was seen as a threat to the Zionist program to liberate the Jews from what Zionism saw as the negative qualities of Diaspora Jewish life. As Segev puts it, "The survivors forced the Israelis to realize that the [Zionist] vision of the 'new man' was not to be."[5]

Segev refers to an account of Yoel Palgi: when he returned to the Land of Israel in 1945 from a paratrooper mission in Hungary he saw that Jews who had spent the war years in the Land of Israel were ashamed of the Holocaust victims and kept asking him, "why did [the Holocaust victims] go like lambs to the slaughter?" Because his fellow Jews who had not experienced the Holocaust saw the survivors as worthless, Palgi realized, "unconsciously, [they had] accepted the Nazi view that the Jews were subhuman."[6]

On arriving in his early teens in the Land of Israel in 1946, the Israeli Holocaust survivor novelist Aharon Appelfeld recounts that he became painfully aware of the fact that the survivors had been fit there into a national myth that questioned their political sagacity as well as their moral character. This mythic interpretation of the Holocaust, Appelfeld relates, "swooped down on us [the survivors] . . . and without mercy established parallels: exile—redemption, Zionism versus assimilation, the guilty as opposed to the blameless, the wise as opposed to the naive. There was a terrible transparency to these analogies."[7] As Porat observes, the survivors were suspected of having morally compromised themselves during the war "because they had been unwilling to sacrifice themselves in the struggle against the Nazis." Furthermore, Porat notes, "comparisons were often made between the Zionist image of a productive person, imbued with universalistic humanistic values, who worked for the common good, and the survivors, who seemed, at first sight, to be the polar opposites of that ideal type."[8] One kibbutz Haggadah went so far as to blame the deaths of the victims on their passivity, declaring, "If they had known that the Jew has power, they would not have all been butchered . . . the lack of faith, the ghettoish-exilic self-denigration . . . contributed its share to this great butchery."[9]

Even though, as Porat observes, the heroism of the survivors in their role of courageous illegal immigrants and soldiers in the Israeli army often belied their image as the opposites of the ideal Zionist type, Israelis who had not experienced the Holocaust continued to have a problematic relationship with that period in the years immediately following the establishment of the State. This difficulty of connecting the experience of national rebirth in Israel with the experience of defeat in the Holocaust apparently was one reason why in the early years of the State Israelis rarely brought the Holocaust to conscious awareness. The Holocaust, in fact, played a miminal, if any, role in the curriculum of Israeli schools, in the university research agenda, drama, poetry, and fiction.[10] Appelfeld describes this period of public avoidance of the Holocaust in Israel as one in which both the survivors and those who had not been in Europe during World War II tacitly agreed to refrain from talking about an historical event that seemed too horrible to contemplate. "A kind of secret covenant was created," Appelfeld relates, "between the survivor witness and the one to whom, as it were, this testimony was directed, a

141

covenant of silence, by means of which much misunderstanding accumulated."[11]

Over time, however, the Holocaust has been gradually transformed in Israeli culture from a human experience that Israelis felt to be radically different from their own experience to one with which Israelis have increasingly identified. In the early years of the State public discourse linked Israelis with the Holocaust victims and survivors by focusing on aspects of the Holocaust with which Israelis could most readily identify. Dina Porat, Charles S. Liebman, and Eliezer Don-Yehiya point out that the Israeli Knesset decided to call the day that was officially established in 1951 to commemorate the Holocaust *Yom hasho'ah umered hageta'ot* (Holocaust and Ghetto Uprising Day) in an attempt to bridge the gap between the images of the fighting Israeli and the Holocaust victims and survivors.[12] The choice of this name and the name that eventually replaced it, *Yom hasho'ah vehagevurah* (Holocaust and Heroism Day), was part of a larger tendency to envision the Holocaust as being closely connected to the period of national rebirth of the establishment of the State. As Porat notes, by emphasizing Jewish armed resistance during World War II in the name of the day, the Knesset attempted to depict European Jews as fitting the image of "the fighting, independent Israeli."[13]

This process of bridging the gap between the Holocaust victims and Israelis found concrete expression in the law passed by the Knesset in 1953 establishing Yad Vashem, the Martyrs' and Heroes' Remembrance Authority, which called upon the Authority "to confer upon the members of the Jewish people who perished in the days of the Holocaust and the resistance the commemorative citizenship of the state of Israel, as a token of their having been gathered to their people."[14] In granting this symbolic citizenship, James E. Young explains, it was as if there really were no historical distinction between the Holocaust and Israel, and World War II was as important a factor in establishing the State of Israel as was Israel's War of Independence in 1948. "If the state came about by virtue of the blood spilt in both places," Young observes, "it is little wonder that the murdered Jews of the Holocaust would be conferred posthumous Israeli citizenship, for in this scenario they, too, have given their lives for Israel."[15]

The main problem with this association established between those who experienced the Holocaust and those who fought for Israel's independence was that it suggested the denigration of those who did not engage in armed struggle against the Nazis. The addition of the reference to "the ghetto uprisings"—later changed to the more general term "heroism," in the name of the day that commemorated the Holocaust—reinforced the narrow view that those victims and survivors who did not fight were of little worth. "The emphasis on bravery during the Holocaust," Porat observes, "prevented a realistic understanding of the desperate situation of the Jews in Europe and of their quiet daily and hourly struggle that demanded no less a degree of spiritual stamina than did the actual fighting."[16]

As many observers have noted, the trial of the Nazi war criminal Adolf Eichmann in Jerusalem in 1961–1962 made an important contribution to Israeli identification with all Holocaust survivors and victims, whether or not they participated in armed struggle. The opportunity the survivors had to tell their stories to the nation when they testified in the trial broke what Appelfeld has characterized as "the covenant of silence" between the survivors and Israelis who did not experience the Holocaust.[17] The impact of the Eichmann trial is reflected in statements by the native-born Israeli writers Moshe Shamir (1921–), Dalia Ravikovitch (1936–), and Haim Gouri (1922–), none of whom had any direct personal experience of the Holocaust.

In an article that appeared in the Israeli newspaper *Ma'ariv* at the time of the Eichmann trial, an interviewer reported that Shamir was deeply affected by the extreme contrast between the life he experienced in Israel and the lives of the Holocaust victims described in the trial. "The force of testimonies of death at the trial, against the background of our *dolce vita,*" Shamir stated, "have caused me, more than anything else, to feel the catastrophe for the first time as a personal problem of my own."[18] In the same article the interviewer conveys Ravikovitch's assertion that although she had not experienced the Holocaust she felt very connected to it as she heard the survivors' testimonies: "Even I . . . who am the third generation in this country, felt during the trial as if I were experiencing these things for the second time."[19] In the conclusion to a collection of his journalistic reports from the Eichmann trial Gouri expressed his conviction that consciousness of the Holocaust is essential for Israelis because it serves as an important reminder of the potential vulnerability of human existence. "This feeling, wrote Gouri, "accompanies the one

143

who walks in the footsteps of the destruction, who sees how the se-
cure, the certain, the solid are nothing but an illusion."[20]

Even before the Eichmann trial, Israeli experience had been linked
to that of the Holocaust when Israelis began to identify with the vul-
nerability of the victims and survivors of the Holocaust. Over time
there developed within Israel a trend to associate the Arab threat to
militarily destroy Israel with the Holocaust and thereby to suggest
an identification between Israel's potential destruction and the ac-
tual fate of the Jewish victims of the Nazis in World War II. In the pe-
riod leading to the Sinai Campaign of 1956, Segev relates, "The Israeli
press, like that of Britain and France, often compared [Egyptian Presi-
dent] Nasser to Hitler in both articles and cartoons."[21] In the tense
weeks that preceded the Six-Day War in 1967, comparisons between
Egypt's President Nasser and Hitler were frequent.[22] The surprise
military attack by Egypt and Syria that launched the Yom Kippur War
in 1973 evoked a feeling of vulnerability among Israelis that was, ac-
cording to Holocaust scholar Leni Yahil, "similar to the sense of help-
lessness that gripped the Jewish people during the Second World
War."[23] Segev also notes that terrorist attacks before and after the
Yom Kippur War, such as the terrorist attack on the Israeli Olympic
team in Munich in 1972 and the hijacking of an Air France jet flying
from Tel Aviv to Paris, which was rescued by Israel in Entebbe,
Uganda, in 1976, were often associated in the minds of Israelis with
the Holocaust. By undermining the sense of invincible superiority
that Israelis had once felt over the Jews of the Diaspora, these ter-
rorist attacks forced Israelis to view the Holocaust and its Jewish vic-
tims and survivors with more understanding. As Liebman and Don-
Yehiya note, "for some Israelis, especially since the Yom Kippur War,
it is Jewish suffering and the indifference of the world to that suffer-
ing which evokes an identification with the Holocaust, rather than
the physical resistance or any other acts of courage by Jews."[24]

With the rise of Menahem Begin to political power, the Holocaust
became increasingly central to political rhetoric. "In June, 1981,"
Segev notes, "Begin justified the demolition of an Iraqi nuclear fa-
cility with the words, "We must protect our nation, a million and a
half of whose children were murdered by the Nazis in the gas cham-
bers."[25] In particular, Segev points out, Begin saw the violent opposi-
tion of Yasser Arafat's Palestine Liberation Organization to Israel as
historically parallel to Hitler's war against the Jews. Begin used this

historical analogy to justify Israel's invasion of Lebanon in June 1982 by declaring at the time to the Israeli government cabinet, "Believe me, the alternative is Treblinka, and we have decided that there will be no more Treblinkas."[26]

The Israeli experience in the Persian Gulf War of 1991 further solidified the Israeli identification with the Holocaust. In part, as Segev writes, Israeli reaction at that time was a continuation of the association between the Arabs and the Nazis that had been prevalent in previous wars (an association, it should be noted, that played an important role in the rhetoric of President George Bush at the same time as he sought political support for American military intervention in the Persian Gulf). The connection between the Gulf War and World War II was strengthened by the commonly held assumption that "Sadam Hussein . . . had chemical weapons manufactured with the help of German firms."[27] A Holocaust survivor wrote a newspaper article explaining why he had refused to accept a gas mask offered to him by the authorities during the Gulf War: "I did not survive the Auschwitz death camp and the gas chambers of Birkenau [declared the survivor] in order, more than forty-five years later, to walk around an independent Jewish state with antigas equipment, against gas developed and manufactured by Germans."[28] This association between Sadam Hussein and the Nazis was put forth in a documentary produced by the Israeli Broadcast Authority immediately after the war. In the documentary, "*Naḥash tsefaʿ,*" by Yarin Kimor, the narrator notes the curious coincidence that the Israeli authorities distributed the gas masks on the day that Germany was reunited, and he makes an explicit comparison between Sadam Hussein's aggression against Israel and the Nazis' attempt at a "final solution to the Jewish problem."[29]

In January 1995, a Palestinian suicide bomber killed eighteen and wounded sixty-two people in an attack that nearly coincided with a commemoration of the fiftieth anniversary of the liberation of Auschwitz held at Yad Vashem. At the commemoration, education minister Amnon Rubinstein, representing Prime Minister Yitzhak Rabin (who went to the scene of the attack instead of attending the ceremony) made a connection between those two events: "Today too the human monsters are trying to hit at our lives here and the chance of peace."[30] In an editorial, the Israeli newspaper *Ma'ariv* even more explicitly declared that the suicide bombing "reminds us that as long as Jews are killed because they are Jews . . . the evil spirit of Auschwitz has not left us. The Islamic fanatics are the Nazis of our day: they are killing Jews and threatening world peace."[31]

This developing perception of Israel's armed conflict with its Arab enemies as reenactments of World War II may partly account for the fact that, as Segev notes, over time the Holocaust was transformed in Israel from a subject to avoid to one central in the minds of Israelis. In 1979, for the first time the Israeli Ministry of Education made the Holocaust a mandatory part of the national school curriculum.[32] Segev observes that beginning in the 1980s the Holocaust became a central concern in Israeli news, literature, cinema, theater, and television; institutes to study the Holocaust were formed; and it became very popular for Israeli high-school students to go on organized trips to see the remnants of the European concentration camps.[33] Segev also notes that the increasing connection Israelis have felt to the Holocaust has over time made the destruction of European Jewry in World War II an essential aspect of Israeli identity, for Jews of Middle Eastern and North African origin, as well as those of European origin. A convincing indication of this fact is that "a 1992 study of Israeli identity among teachers' college students found that close to 80 percent of those asked identified with the statement, 'We are all Holocaust survivors.' "[34]

Attempts to connect the Holocaust with the Bible have also contributed to closing the gap that Israelis initially felt between their lives and the Holocaust. To the extent that the Holocaust was seen as reenacting biblical events, it made that European event more relevant to Israelis who had not experienced it. This assimilation of the Holocaust to the Bible was effected, in part, by the use of biblical Hebrew terms in discourse about the Holocaust. By considering such terms we can learn about not only how the Holocaust has been linked to the Bible in Israel but also the role of these words in conveying to Israelis the meaning of that historical event.

It is significant that Israeli speakers of Hebrew did not choose the Hebrew word *ḥurban* (destruction), which was used by Yiddish speakers to refer to the period (as *ḥurbn* in Yiddish pronunciation). The Yiddish choice of *ḥurban* suggested that the Holocaust was parallel to the destruction of the First and Second Temples in ancient Jerusalem, known in Hebrew as *ḥurban habayit.* Indeed, as David Roskies notes, Yiddish speakers and writers have often referred to the Holocaust as *der driter hurbn* (the third destruction).[35] Because Zionist thought rejected the legitimacy of Jewish culture in the Diaspora, it would have been unthinkable for Jews of the Land of Israel to associate the destruction of Diaspora communities with that of the Temples in Jerusalem. Furthermore, associated with *hurban* is the notion of an eventual *ge'ulah* (redemption) of divine origin. After the destruction of the First Temple, the Jews returned to Zion to build the Second Temple, and Jewish tradition teaches that the building of a Third Temple in Zion in the messianic era will conclude the long exile of the period after the destruction of the Second Temple. If Zionists were not particularly interested in rebuilding the Temple in Jerusalem, they certainly had no interest in rebuilding the Yiddish-speaking European Jewish culture that Hitler destroyed.

Not long after World War II, the biblical Hebrew term *sho'ah* emerged as the Israeli equivalent of the English term Holocaust and the Yiddish term *hurbn*. Its presence in Israel's Declaration of Independence in 1948 attests to the fact that it had become widely accepted by then among the Jews of the Land of Israel. A careful analysis of forms of the term *sho'ah* in the Bible can provide a key to understanding possible associations Hebrew speakers had with it and what those associations tell us about how the culture has understood the meaning of the Holocaust.[36] For the most part, in the Bible the term *sho'ah* connotes a sudden, often stormlike, act of destruction that comes without warning. In some verses this destruction comes about as a divine punishment directed at either Israel or her enemies (Isaiah 6:11, 10:3, 47:11). The term is sometimes used in prophetic visions of an apocalyptic end of time (Ezekiel 38:9; Zephaniah 1:15).

Passages in Proverbs and Psalms apply the term not so much to a nation or to the end of time, but rather more to groups of people deserving divine punishment (Proverbs 1:27, 3:25). The term may also refer to the struggle between the speaker of a poetic passage and his enemies. In two verses in Psalms and one in Job it connotes the destructive intentions of the speaker's enemies (Psalms 35:17, 63:10; Job 30:14). In another verse in Psalms it refers to the well-deserved end of the psalmist's enemies (Psalms 35:8). Some passages make use of the term to describe the effect of such destruction on a particular area (Job 30:3, 38:27; Isaiah 6:11).

147

It is likely that for most Israeli speakers of Hebrew, the term has been less associated with the biblical connotation of divine punishment and more with that of a sudden arrival of a dark, stormlike destructive force from the outside that brings unexpected desolation to people who do not understand why they are being attacked. This suggests that the Holocaust was an event in which mysterious forces were unleashed to wipe out Jewish existence in Europe, analogous to a natural disaster. In this way the term echoes the Hebrew name that the late nineteenth-century European Hebrew and Yiddish writer S. Abramovich gave to the pogroms in Russia and the Ukraine in 1881–1882, *sufot banegev* (storms in the south), taken from Isaiah 21:1.[37]

Shulamith Hareven suggests that in its meaning as a natural disaster the term *sho'ah* conveys that human beings were not responsible for what happened.[38] Her suggestion makes sense because such an interpretation would have relieved the Jews of the Land of Israel of their feeling of guilt for not having done enough to save European Jewry in World War II. After all, human beings are not generally held accountable for natural disasters. A. B. Yehoshua suggests that the connotation of the term *sho'ah* as an unexplained catastrophe is appropriate because he believes that no meaning can be attributed to the Holocaust. "The Jewish people's terrible sacrifice in the Holocaust," Yehoshua maintains, "was for no purpose.... Those whom the concentration camp flames consumed did not die for any idea, for any world view; they did not meet their deaths for the continued existence of the Jewish people or for its imminent redemption."[39]

Another biblical term that came to be associated in Israel with the Holocaust was *tevah* (slaughter). The writers of the Israeli Declaration of Independence refer to the Holocaust as "the *sho'ah* that was brought upon the people of Israel in recent times, in which millions of Jews in Europe were forced to the slaughter (*hukhre'u latevah*)." A review of biblical uses of the term *tevah* suggests that its primary meaning was the slaughter of an animal for food but that it came to be used figuratively to refer to the murder of human beings as defenseless as sheep before the slaughterer. The term *hukhre'u latevah* alludes most directly to a verse in Isaiah, in which the prophet warns those who do not heed the divine word that they will receive the punishment of abject slaughter by divine power (Isaiah 65:12). Other verses make more explicit references to the image of leading a domesticated animal to the slaughter as a metaphor for the deaths of defenseless people: for example, "like an ox going to the slaughter" (*keshor 'el tevah*, Proverbs 7:22); "like a sheep being led to slaughter" (*kaseh latevah yuval*, Isaiah 53:7); "we are regarded as sheep to be slaughtered" (*nehshavnu ketson tivhah*, Psalms 44:23). The point suggested by the writers of the Israeli Declaration of Independence that the Holocaust should be seen primarily as the imposition of Nazi destructiveness on a helpless Jewish people was reinforced subsequently by the pervasive use in Israeli discourse of the expression "like sheep to the slaughter" (*katson latevah*) to refer to the victims of the Holocaust.

The Declaration of Independence refers to the survivors of the Holocaust as "the remnant that was saved (*she'arit hapeletah shenitslu*) from the terrible Nazi slaughter in Europe." This expression makes use of the biblical lexicon in a way that has continued in the everyday language of Israel. In Israel, the survivors came to be known as *pelitim* ("refugees") or more commonly *nitsolim* ("those who were saved"). Whereas the English word "survivor" can suggest actions having been made on the part of the survivor to stay alive, the Hebrew terms suggest that the essentially passive survivors merely fled the destruction in Europe to find refuge in Israel and were thereby saved.

The choice to name the central Israeli museum that commemorates the Holocaust after a biblical term, *yad vashem*, reflects this Israeli trend to assimilate the Holocaust to the Bible. The term is taken from a passage in Isaiah:

> For thus said the Lord: "As regards the eunuchs who keep My sabbaths, who have chosen what I desire and hold fast to My covenant—I will give them, in My House and within My walls, a monument and a name (*yad vashem*) better than sons or daughters. I will give them an everlasting name which shall not perish." (Isaiah 56:4–5)

Perhaps the term was chosen with the poignant realization that so many Holocaust victims died together with their children or died before they had the opportunity to have children. This museum, its name suggests, will be a substitute for the continuation into eternity

149

that future generations would have provided if the Holocaust had not occurred.

Because biblical terminology has played such an important role in bridging the gap between Israelis and the Holocaust, it is not surprising that some poets, preoccupied with that gap, have turned to the genre of biblical allusion poetry in an attempt to come to terms with it. Significant poems of this type were composed by two poets personally affected by the Holocaust: Dan Pagis, a Holocaust survivor, and Amir Gilboa, who left Europe before the outbreak of World War II but lost his entire family in the Holocaust.

Dan Pagis: Holocaust Victims Address Israelis

As a survivor Dan Pagis felt the obligation to break through the difficulties in communication between those who experienced the Holocaust and those who did not. Even greater than the gap between survivors and those who were not in the war is the gap between the victims, who belong to the world of the dead, and those not in the war, who belong to the land of the living. Pagis explores this gap between the dead and the living in two biblical allusion poems based on the Cain and Abel story (Genesis 4). In both poems Pagis provides the victims of the Holocaust with a voice that attempts to transcend the dividing line between death and life.[40]

In the poem "*Katuv be'ipparon baqaron hehatum*" ("Written in Pencil in the Sealed Railway-Car")[41] a Holocaust victim, represented here by Eve, communicates with those who were not in the war by means of a note she has left behind in the train that took her to her death in a concentration camp.

כָּתוּב בְּעִפָּרוֹן בַּקָּרוֹן הֶחָתוּם

כָּאן בַּמִּשְׁלוֹחַ הַזֶּה
אֲנִי חַוָּה
עִם הֶבֶל בְּנִי
אִם תִּרְאוּ אֶת בְּנִי הַגָּדוֹל
קַיִן בֶּן אָדָם
תַּגִּידוּ לוֹ שֶׁאֲנִי

WRITTEN IN PENCIL IN THE SEALED RAILWAY-CAR

here in this carload
i am eve
with abel my son
if you see my other son
cain son of man
tell him that i

In this poem elements of what the Bible records as the first murder in human history represent the very concrete Holocaust image of Jews being shipped by train to a concentration camp. Unlike the biblical story, both Eve and Abel are victims. This emphasizes the limitations of the application of the Bible to the Holocaust. The Holocaust is more than just another set of murders. It constitutes an even more basic attack on the value of life itself, represented by Eve (*Havvah*), to whom Adam gives that name because she is "the mother of all the living" (*'em kol hai*) (Genesis 3:20). The main purpose of the note appears to be an attempt by Eve to restore the human moral consciousness of her victimizers. There cannot, however, be communication between the Jewish victims and the Nazi victimizers because the latter, represented by Cain, Eve's other son (or as the original Hebrew text says, *beni hagadol,* "my big son") has forgotten that he is a *ben 'adam,* the expression "son of Adam," which in Hebrew connotes a human being in the highest sense of the word.

Although perhaps not intended as such, the note functions as a posthumous means of communication between the dead victim and the living readers of the note who did not experience the Holocaust. In trying to restore the humanity of the Nazi victimizers, the victim reminds those who live in the postwar world that the very essence of human experience was at stake in the war and that the moral issues raised by the Holocaust must still be taken seriously. The effect of this communication, however, is uncertain. The original story of Cain's murder of Abel, which makes its readers aware of the moral issues at stake in every murder, is written in the Torah scroll with permanent ink on parchment; it has been passed down for centuries from one generation to the other. In contrast Eve's message, written in pencil, is vulnerable to fading or even erasure. Furthermore, the readers of her message cannot fully know what she is trying to communicate because she never completed writing it.

In the poem *"Otobyografyah"* (*"Autobiography"*)[42] communication between the Holocaust victim and those who were not in the Holocaust is represented by Abel's attempt to address the readers of the poem. Abel, the first victim of murder, speaks here for all such victims, including the six million Jews who were killed by the Nazis in World War II. It is clear, however, that he feels he can never fully communicate his experiences to those who have not been victims of murder. Even the title "Autobiography" distances this victim from those whom he addresses. If they chose to compose them, *their* autobiographies would be about their lives; in contrast, the autobiography Abel must tell is not the story of his life but rather the story of the effect of his death on those who have survived him.

Abel begins his autobiography with the impact of his death on his immediate family, whose claim to fame, like that of Abel, is connected with his death:

אוֹטוֹבִּיוֹגְרַפְיָה

מַתִּי בַּמַּכָּה הָרִאשׁוֹנָה וְנִקְבַּרְתִּי
בִּשְׂדֵה הַטְּרָשִׁים.
הָעוֹרֵב הוֹרָה לְהוֹרַי
מַה לַעֲשׂוֹת בִּי.

מִשְׁפַּחְתִּי מְכֻבֶּדֶת, לֹא מְעַט בִּזְכוּתִי.
אָחִי הִמְצִיא אֶת הַהֶרֶג,
הוֹרַי אֶת הַבְּכִי,
אֲנִי אֶת הַשְּׁתִיקָה.

AUTOBIOGRAPHY

I died with the first blow and was buried
in the rocky field.
The raven taught my parents
what to do with me.

My family's respected, largely due to me.
My brother invented murder,
my parents, tears,
I, silence.

Abel boastfully brags that he and his family pioneered the human experience of murder and grief. Adam and Eve were so unprepared for this event that they did not even know what to do with Abel's body, and so a raven had to show them how to bury their dead son.[43] All too easily, however, humanity became used to acts of murder. As history developed, Abel relates, human beings improved on Cain's primitive way of taking Abel's life and committed innumerable murders. Abel distinguishes himself from the readers of the poem in that he, unlike them, is fully conscious of the homicidal history of humanity. He knows, however, that there is no point in his recounting that history because his audience, which does not share his experience of being a victim, is most likely numbed by overexposure to the large numbers of murders in human history, including those perpetrated by the Nazis on six million Jews, and they are most likely tired of hearing about them:

אַחַר כָּךְ נָפְלוּ הַדְּבָרִים הַזְּכוּרִים הֵיטֵב.
הַהַמְצָאוֹת שֶׁלָּנוּ שֶׁכְלְלוּ. דָּבָר גָּרַר דָּבָר,
הוּצְאוּ צַוִּים. הָיוּ גַּם שֶׁהָרְגוּ לְפִי דַּרְכָּם,
בָּכוּ לְפִי דַּרְכָּם.

לֹא אַזְכִּיר שֵׁמוֹת
מִתּוֹךְ הִתְחַשְּׁבוּת בַּקּוֹרֵא,
כִּי בִּתְחִלָּה עֲלוּלִים הַפְּרָטִים לְהַבְעִית,
אֲבָל בְּסוֹפוֹ שֶׁל דָּבָר הֵם מְיַגְּעִים:

Later the really famous things happened.
Our inventions were refined. One thing led to another,
orders were issued. Some even killed their own way,
cried their own way.

I'll name no names
out of concern for the reader,
for at first the details might be frightful,
but in the end they're tiresome:

It would appear that this attempt by a victim to communicate with those who did not experience the Holocaust has not brought the two sides closer. Abel's tone of superiority, in particular, distances him from those whom he addresses. As Alan Mintz notes, when Abel contrasts his ability to die ten thousand times with the reader's ability to die no more than once, "[t]here is, now, no condition which the speaker and the reader can share."[44] For Abel, furthermore, the world is divided between victims and victimizers, and he proudly asserts the strength, rather than the weakness of the victims of this history of human violence. Over time the victims, he claims, have greatly outnumbered the victimizers. This triumph, however, is of little value to the victims: it is "a sour revenge" (or as the original Hebrew says, *hatsi neqamah,* a half revenge, a play on the Hebrew expression *hatsi nehamah,* a half comfort) because it can never compensate them for what was done to them:

אַתָּה יָכוֹל לָמוּת פַּעַם, פַּעֲמַיִם, אֲפִלּוּ שֶׁבַע פְּעָמִים,
אֲבָל אֵינְךָ יָכוֹל לָמוּת רְבָבוֹת.
אֲנִי יָכוֹל.
תָּאֵי הַמַּחְתֶּרֶת שֶׁלִּי מַגִּיעִים לְכָל מָקוֹם.

כַּאֲשֶׁר הֵחֵל קַיִן לִפְרֹץ עַל פְּנֵי הָאֲדָמָה
הַחִלּוֹתִי אֲנִי לִפְרֹץ בְּבֶטֶן הָאֲדָמָה,
וּמִזְּמַן עוֹלֶה כֹּחִי עַל כֹּחוֹ.
גְּדוּדָיו נוֹטְשִׁים אוֹתוֹ וּמִצְטָרְפִים אֵלַי,
וַאֲפִלּוּ זֶה רַק חֲצִי נְקָמָה.

You can die once, twice, even seven times,
but not ten thousand times.
I can.
My underground cells reach everywhere.

When Cain began spreading over the earth
I began spreading in the womb of the earth,
and my strength has long surpassed his.
His legions are leaving him and joining me,
though it's only a sour revenge.

Amir Gilboa: Contact With His Slaughtered Family

Amir Gilboa emigrated from Eastern Europe to the Land of Israel at the age of twenty in 1937, two years before the outbreak of

154

World War II. His parents, two brothers, and four sisters, who remained in Europe, were all killed by the Nazis in 1942.[45] His situation as an immigrant to the Land of Israel who lost family members in the Holocaust was, as we have seen, not unique. In many European Jewish families members of the younger generation in their late teens and twenties were adventuresome enough to move to the Land of Israel, often leaving behind their parents and siblings in Europe. By the time they became fully aware of the Nazi threat to their families, those who had emigrated to the Land of Israel were powerless to help them.

A person in Gilboa's position would undoubtedly experience a tremendous sense of frustration at being unable to save his family from destruction at the hands of the Nazis. In biblical allusion poems in which the speakers imagine seeing biblical characters who represent the victims, Gilboa attempts to come to terms with the fact that he was far away from the members of his immediate family when they were slaughtered in the Holocaust. Gilboa begins the poem "*Yitshaq*" ("Isaac")[46] with what appears to be a retelling of the binding of Isaac story:

יִצְחָק

לִפְנוֹת בֹּקֶר טִיְּלָה שֶׁמֶשׁ בְּתוֹךְ הַיַּעַר
יַחַד עִמִּי וְעִם אַבָּא
וִימִינִי בִּשְׂמֹאלוֹ.

כְּבָרָק לָהֲבָה מַאֲכֶלֶת בֵּין הָעֵצִים.
וַאֲנִי יָרֵא כָּל-כָּךְ אֶת פַּחַד עֵינַי מוּל דָּם עַל הֶעָלִים.

אַבָּא אַבָּא מַהֵר וְהַצִּילָה אֶת יִצְחָק
וְלֹא יֶחְסַר אִישׁ בִּסְעֻדַּת הַצָּהֳרָיִם.

ISAAC

Toward morning the sun strolled in the forest
Together with me and with father,
My right hand was in his left.

Like lightning flash, a knife between the trees
And I fear the terror of my eyes opposite the blood on the
leaves.

Father, Father, come quickly and save Isaac
That no one may be missing at the noon meal.

From the beginning the reader discerns significant departures from
the original biblical text. In the poem the story is told not from the
point of view of an omniscient third-person narrator but rather from
Isaac's point of view. In addition, the reference to the forest suggests
the European landscape of the poet's childhood. It is also peculiar
that when Isaac refers to the slaughtering knife he makes no refer-
ence to Abraham. The knife appears suddenly to Isaac "like a light-
ning flash," evoking in him stark terror. Sensing his father's absence
Isaac calls out to be saved. He does so in such a way that indicates
he is not fully aware of the impending danger: the worst that he can
imagine is "that no one may be missing at the noon meal."

Isaac is soon disabused of his naive perspective. His father Abra-
ham announces to him that the story has been reversed: the father,
not the son, is being slaughtered:

זֶה אֲנִי הַנִּשְׁחָט, בְּנִי,
וּכְבָר דָּמִי עַל הֶעָלִים.
וְאַבָּא נִסְתַּם קוֹלוֹ.
וּפָנָיו חִוְרִים.

It is I who am slaughtered, my son.
And my blood is already on the leaves.
Father's voice choked.
His face grew pale.

Isaac does not want to believe the sound of his father's choked voice
and the sight of his pale face—signs that he is indeed being killed. He
then awakes from what he now knows was a nightmare. Because he
slept on his right arm, Isaac's right hand that his father once reas-
suringly held is now drained of blood, like Abraham's face. Isaac
therefore is powerless to save his father:

וְרָצִיתִי לִצְעֹק, מְפַרְפֵּר לֹא לְהַאֲמִין
וְקוֹרֵעַ הָעֵינַיִם.
וְנִתְעוֹרַרְתִּי.

וְאָזְלַת-דָּם הָיְתָה יַד יָמִין.

And I wanted to scream, writhing not to believe
And I opened my eyes wide.
And I awoke.

Bloodless was my right hand.

In this poem Gilboa captures the sense of helplessness he experienced as a son living too far from his father to save him from the murderous actions of the Nazis. The father is geographically as far from the son as ancient Israel is distant in time from modern Israel. The scene of the father's death is as removed from the current reality of the son as the subconscious world of dreams is from the conscious world of waking existence. The choice to express this experience by means of the story of the binding of Isaac places the Holocaust in the context of the Land of Israel. It also conveys clearly the struggle of the poet to come to terms with the role reversal that the Holocaust brought to him. In Genesis 22 Abraham, the patriarch fully in charge, has the ultimate power of life and death over his son Isaac. In the poem Abraham the father is transformed into a powerless victim, and Isaac the son must face his responsibility as a grown adult to protect his weaker father. By casting the story of his inability to save his father in terms of the binding of Isaac story, the poet also holds on to some extent to his reluctance to accept responsibility for his father's death. When Isaac describes himself as lying in bed "writhing," we sense his continued identification with Isaac the helpless victim tied to the altar. This poem then is as much about the son's suffering for being unable to save his father as it is about the father's suffering in the Holocaust. Furthermore, this retelling of the binding of Isaac story without the presence of God makes clear the poet's inability to discern any meaning in the death of his father at the hands of the Nazis.

In another poem by Gilboa, *"Bamatsor"* ("Under Siege"),[47] the speaker goes further than Isaac in *"Yitshaq"* to bridge the geographical gap between the Land of Israel and the European Holocaust. The bridging of this gap is represented by the speaker traveling back in time to the period of the siege of Jerusalem by the Babylonians, which preceded the destruction of the First Temple. The use of a biblical scene to represent the Holocaust is in keeping with the trend in Israel to assimilate the Holocaust experience to the Bible as a way to connect more directly with that experience, even as it runs counter to the reluctance of Israelis to associate the Holocaust with the destruction of the Temples.

In the beginning of the poem the suffering of the people is captured by selected concrete images of hand-to-hand combat, walls crumbling, and a little girl scurrying about, while holding back any cry of fear. When the speaker sees the horrifying image of a man who has been blinded screaming, he calls out like a viewer of a suspenseful movie to one of the central characters of the period, the prophet Jeremiah, to do something to prevent the disaster. The speaker's great wish is that Jeremiah assassinate Nebuchadnezzar, the King of Babylonia, before that enemy of Judea can be victorious:

בְּמָצוֹר

יָד אִישׁ בְּרֵעֵהוּ
וְקִיר אַחַר קִיר מִתְמוֹטֵט.
דָּלְיָה הַקְּטַנָּה מִתְרוֹצֶצֶת
אֵין עִמָּהּ אִישׁ
וְהִיא אֵינָהּ בּוֹכָה.
מִיהוּזֶה אֶל מוּל הַשֶּׁמֶשׁ
שַׁצַוֵּוחַ.
אֲהוֹי, כְּבָר לֹא עֵינַיִם
בְּחוֹרָיו קוֹדְחוֹת.
יִרְמְיָהוּ, יִרְמְיָהוּ
קַח אֶת שְׁשָׁמוּר עַמִּי
אֶת הָאֶקְדָּח
וְכַדּוּר קָטֹן
בְּלִבּוֹ שֶׁל נְבוּכַדְרֶאצַּר
בֵּאלֹהֵינוּ יִשְׁתַּבַּח.

UNDER SIEGE

The hand of each man is against his neighbor
and wall after wall crumbles.
Little Daliah scurries about,
no one is with her
and she doesn't cry.
Whosthis facing the sun
screaming.
Aie, already not eyes in
his burning sockets.
Jeremiah, Jeremiah
take what I have been saving
the pistol
and for God's sake
a small bullet
in Nebuchadnezzar's heart
will be praised.

The speaker's decision to call out to Jeremiah is significant. In the period preceding the destruction of the First Temple, Judea, under the leadership of King Zedekiah, rebelled against the rule of the Babylonians. Jeremiah opposed the rebellion because he believed that the Babylonians had been sent by God to punish the people of Judea. He advised the king to submit to Babylonian rule, for rebellion against Babylonia was counter to the will of God and therefore would not succeed (Jeremiah 27). Jeremiah's position that the people could not succeed in militarily overthrowing their rulers represents in the poem the relative weakness of the Jews in their confrontation with the genocidal Nazis. The prophet's approach is problematic for an Israeli when applied to the Holocaust because it both suggests divine sanction for the power of the Nazis and eliminates the possibility of military victory over one's enemy.

The image of the blinded man alludes to the biblical account of the fate of King Zedekiah following the failure of the rebellion.[48] Nebuchadnezzar executed Zedekiah's sons in front of him, blinded him, and then sent him off to captivity in Babylonia (Jeremiah 39). This image of children being killed while their parents watch can be seen as a reflection of the Holocaust experience. This scene arouses the speaker to urge Jeremiah to reject his passive response to evil and to undertake the only violent response that could stop the disaster; the speaker tries to hand Jeremiah a pistol so that the prophet can assassinate Nebuchadnezzar. This image of the armed speaker trying to hand a weapon to the unarmed prophet may draw on Gilboa's wartime experience. On the very day in 1942 when his entire family was killed by the Nazis Gilboa was an armed soldier stationed in Egypt in the British Army. At that time he had the capacity to fight the Nazis militarily but was unable to transfer that capacity to his family.[49]

Because the readers know that neither Nebuchadnezzar nor Hitler were assassinated, they conclude that the speaker's cry to Jeremiah to take the pistol is futile. It must be seen, instead, as the cry of frustration of the poet who had as little influence on the events of the Holocaust in Europe as he could possibly have on the events of the Bible. The final lines of the poem may be understood as a protest against God's lack of intervention in the Holocaust. By translating the end of poem, "and a small bullet in the heart of Nebuchadnezzar in our God be praised" we get the impression that as much as the speaker would like to kill the Nazi murderer, he would also like to kill God for permitting the moral chaos of World War II.

The poems "*Yitshaq*" and "*Bamatsor*" reflect Gilboa's recurring sense of frustration at his inability to save his family from the Nazis. In his poem "*Penei Yehoshua*'" ("Joshua's Face")[50] the speaker tells of being regularly haunted by the spirit of his dead brother Joshua. Consideration of Gilboa's relationship with his brother whose name was Joshua may shed light on the significance of this poem.[51] In her monograph on Gilboa, Eda Zoritte notes that the poet had been very close to his brother Joshua. The image in the poem of the dead brother Joshua following the speaker to Israel has added poignancy when we consider that the brothers shared a strong commitment to Zionism in their youth. Together with another friend the two brothers established the local branch of a Zionist youth group in their town. Joshua acceded to their father's pressure to abandon his Zionist activities and learn the family trade of tailoring; Gilboa defied their father and insisted on emigrating to the Land of Israel to fulfill his dream of being a Hebrew writer in Zion.[52]

Folklore in many cultures is replete with stories of the living being haunted by the restless ghost of a person murdered before his or her time.[53] Having been dealt an untimely and unjust death by the Nazis, the speaker's brother Joshua appears to him in the form of the face people often discern in a full moon. In this case the face that the speaker sees is that of his brother Joshua. Gilboa has apparently drawn on an expression that appears in a talmudic interpretation of a passage describing the beginning of the transition of power from Moses to his successor Joshua. In that passage God commands Moses, "Invest him [Joshua] with some of your authority (*mehod-kha*)" (Numbers 27:20). According to the talmudic interpretation the biblical passage reads "some of your authority," not "all of your authority," because Joshua was less honored than his predecessor Moses, to such an extent that the elders of the generation in which the transition took place would state, "The face of Moses was like the face of the sun; the face of Joshua was like the face of the moon" (Baba Batra 75a).[54] In an analogous way, as he appears in Israel the speaker's brother's honor would be considered by some Israelis to be tarnished, for he did not fight during World War II in the Zionist spirit of armed self-defense:

פְּנֵי יְהוֹשֻׁעַ

וִיהוֹשֻׁעַ מֵעַל אֶל פָּנַי מַבִּיט. וּפָנָיו זָהָב
שָׁחוּט. חֲלוֹם קַר. חֲלוֹם חָנוּט.
וּלְרַגְלַי הַיָּם מַכֶּה נְצָחִים אֶל הַחוֹף.
אֲנִי חוֹלֶה נִהְיָתוֹ. דּוֹמֶה, אֲנִי עוֹמֵד לָמוּת.
אַךְ מֶכְרַחֲנִי, מֶכְרַחֲנִי לְחַכּוֹת חַי
אֶל-תָּמִיד.
אָחִי מֵעַל פָּנָיו עוֹלִים בָּעֲב
לְהַגִּיד עִקְּבוֹתַי בַּחוֹל הַנִּשְׁטָף.

הַיָּם מַכֶּה וְנָסוֹג. מַכֶּה וְנָסוֹג.
מִלְחָמוֹת אֵיתָנִים מֵתְנוֹת בַּחֹק.
אֲנִי. בָּרוּחַ. אַחֵר. בּוֹרֵחַ. רָחוֹק.
גַּם יְהוֹשֻׁעַ עַכְשָׁו נָח מִמִּלְחָמוֹת.
שֶׁהִנְחִיל נַחֲלָה לְעַמּוֹ,
אֲבָל קֶבֶר לֹא חָצַב לוֹ
בְּהָרֵי אֶפְרַיִם.

עַל כֵּן לַיְלָה לַיְלָה הוּא יוֹצֵא
לָשׂוּחַ בַּשָּׁמַיִם.
וַאֲנִי חוֹלֶה, דּוֹמֶה עוֹמֵד לָמוּת
מְיַחֵף בְּחוֹל יָרֵחַ קַר
בְּשׁוּלֵי הַמַּיִם
וְהוֹמֶה בִּי, הוֹמֶה בִּי סוֹף
הַמַּכֶּה לְרַגְלַי אֶת מוֹתִי
גַּל אַחַר גַּל —

עַל פְּנֵי חַיִּים רַבִּים
יִתְרוֹמָם וְיִתְגַּדֵּל.

JOSHUA'S FACE

And Joshua looks down on my face. And his face
is hammered gold. A dream embalmed. And cold.
And at my feet the sea strikes endless time.
I'm sick of its wailing. Perhaps, about to die.
But I am forced to stay alive
forever.
My brother's face rises in a cloud
to read my footsteps in the sea-washed sand.

The sea strikes and withdraws. Strikes and withdraws.
The wars of nature conditioned by laws.
Myself in the wind. Different. Running far.
Now Joshua also rests from war
and leaves his people a home
though he carved no tomb of his own
in the mountains of Ephraim.
Night after night
he walks the sky.
And I am sick, perhaps about to die
barefoot in cold moon sand
on the shore
while the end roars in me, a roar
that strikes my own death at my feet
wave after wave—

high over many lives
may he be raised and glorified.

The victim of the Holocaust in Europe has been brought, in the imagi-
nation of the speaker, to an Israeli setting. The association of the
moon with Joshua's face is significant in particular, as Hillel Barzel
notes, in terms of the image of the moon's symbolic death and re-
newal in the monthly cycle of waxing and waning.[55] The moon's
monthly cycle parallels the rhythmic coming and going of the waves
of the sea; the moon physically controls the movement of the sea's
tides as well. Like the moon, the dead brother Joshua is regularly res-
urrected and continually returns to haunt the speaker. As Warren
Bargad notes, the speaker must be seen as beset by survivor's guilt.
The line "Myself in the wind. Different. Running far," which in the He-
brew is expressed by five words isolated from each other by periods
(*'ani. baruaḥ. 'aḥer. boreaḥ. raḥoq*), may be read as the speaker's
barely articulate attempt to come to terms with his feeling of guilt for
having fled from the tragedy of the Holocaust in Europe and sparing
himself the fate of his family.[56]

As the speaker stands on the shore of the Mediterranean Sea, he
compares his brother Joshua to Joshua in the Bible. The life and
death of his brother, the Holocaust victim, stands in marked contrast
to the life and death of the biblical Joshua. Joshua led the ancient Is-
raelites in many battles with the residents of Canaan, and their vic-
tories gave Joshua the power to divide the land of Canaan, granting
an inheritance (*naḥalah*) to each tribe. When he died, the Bible re-
counts, Joshua was buried in the mountains of Ephraim (Joshua
24:30). The speaker's brother Joshua also experienced war, not as a
victorious fighter, but rather as a defeated victim. The rest granted
him after his battles as a young victim of the Nazis was very different
from that of Joshua, who was buried at the age of one hundred ten
after a long and successful life. The speaker's brother did not have
the benefit of being buried in the Land of Israel. Because he has not
fulfilled his youthful Zionist dream, "night after night / he walks the
sky" (*hu' yotse'/lasuaḥ bashamayim*), a description reminiscent of
Isaac, who "went out walking in the field" (*vayetse' ... lasuaḥ
basadeh,* Genesis 24:63) toward evening in the period between his
near sacrifice by his father Abraham and his marriage to Rebecca.
The speaker's brother Joshua is an actual victim, without the sense

of divine purpose that accompanied Abraham and Isaac in the story of the binding of Isaac, nor is he about to be granted the blessings of marriage that Isaac received with Rebecca. From his life remains only the memory of the struggle for Jewish survival in Europe in World War II, and what has followed his life is the continuing struggle for the survival of Israel in which the speaker participates.

There is a particular irony to expressions used by the speaker that play on references to the Song of Songs. As Arieh Sachs notes, the original Hebrew for the line translated as "I'm sick of its wailing" (*'ani ḥoleh nehiyyato*) may also be translated, "I'm sick from longing for him," alluding to the expression "sick with love" (*ḥolat ahavah*) in Song of Songs 2:5, 5:8. The original Hebrew for "many lives" (*ḥayyim rabbim*) and the sea water imagery in the poem constitute an allusion to the expression "vast floods (*mayim rabbim*) cannot quench love" in Song of Songs 8:7.[57] The pain of the speaker is reinforced by the ironic contrast between the unbridgeable gap separating him from his dead beloved brother and the celebration of union in love that is so central to the Song of Songs.

The speaker's longing for his unjustly murdered brother evokes in him a nearly overwhelming preoccupation with his own mortality. The poem is largely about the tension between his sense of the arbitrary cruelty of humanity's mortal condition and his acceptance of this reality. Indeed, the victimization of his brother and the mortal limitations of humanity stand in marked contrast to the sense of control of their fate that Israelis have felt they share with the victorious Joshua. As the speaker suggests, natural and historical forces set limits to the possibility of human accomplishments. The lines "The sea strikes and withdraws. Strikes and withdraws. / The wars of nature conditioned by laws" connect the reality of the Holocaust and the forces of nature and contrast them with the heady self-confidence of Israelis identifying with Joshua's conquest of Canaan. The Hebrew terms used to refer to striking and withdrawing (*makeh venasog*) have military associations. The waves of the sea reflect a static, eternal rhythm of aggression and acquiescence in which the Holocaust victims were caught. As an Israeli the speaker believes in his country's ability to assert power against its enemies, and he feels uncomfortable facing the possibility that Israel might have to acquiesce to those with greater power. Nevertheless, he must come to terms with this alternative experience of withdrawal in defeat as he contemplates the fate of the Holocaust victims at the hands of forces beyond their control.

The speaker can only accept human vulnerability and mortality when he is able to see the death of his brother and his own ultimate death as events that cannot be changed. By associating this healing acceptance of reality with the Joshua story, Gilboa points to the larger national question of how to make peace with the past limitations on Jewish power in Europe and the present limitations on Jewish power in Israel. At the end of the poem the speaker internalizes the wavelike reality of his mortality. In the last line of the poem he declares his acceptance of the ultimate victory of death with the words *yitromam veyitgadal* ("may he be raised and glorified") from the traditional Jewish memorial prayer, the Kaddish. This traditional prayer is actually not about death, but rather an affirmation by the believing Jew that God is worthy of praise and will one day establish His kingdom on earth. In the traditional Kaddish, the words *yitromam* and *yitgadal* are used to refer to human extolling of God (and in that context they could be translated "extolled" and "magnified"). Gilboa uses these words ironically: the speaker's death, not God, is the subject of these verbs. They therefore do not refer to a benevolent God who is worthy of praise, but rather to death, whose ultimate victory the speaker accepts. Like the traditional mourner, comforted by the words of the Kaddish that praise God, the speaker gains a measure of comfort in deciding not to fight the reality of his brother's death and his own mortality.

Over time Israeli public discourse has reflected a significant penetration of the original barrier between Israelis and the world of the Holocaust. Israel initially assimilated the Holocaust to its own image of the new fighting Jew by focusing its attention on the Jewish victims' armed resistance of the Nazis. It made use of biblical terminology to "biblicize" the Holocaust and thereby connect it to the history of ancient Israel with which Israelis so closely identified. Gradually Israelis connected more and more with the humanity of the Holocaust victims and survivors when Israel's vulnerability to her Arab enemies came to be identified with the vulnerability of the Jews in the Holocaust.

Pagis and Gilboa, however, explore more deeply than Israeli public discourse has allowed itself to do the unbridgeable gaps between the Holocaust and Israeli experience. They exploit the established tendency to "biblicize" the Holocaust by using biblical stories as the medium for writing about the Holocaust. Nevertheless, both Pagis and Gilboa establish in their poetry an analogous relationship between the distance from the present to the biblical past and the distance between current Israeli existence and the world of the dead inhabited by the Holocaust victims. Holocaust victims in Pagis's poetry address the contemporary audience from the ancient world of the Bible. Gilboa's speakers are either visited by a Holocaust victim from biblical times or required to travel back in time to the Bible to break through the barrier that separated Jews living in the Land of Israel during the war and the Holocaust victims they did not save. Having biblical characters address a contemporary audience or having contemporary figures travel back to biblical times in this poetry creates an atmosphere of fantasy in which the poet's imagination gives eloquent expression to the longings of those who suffered in the Holocaust and to the preoccupations with the Holocaust of those who did not suffer.

CHAPTER FOUR

EVE KNEW WHAT WAS HIDDEN IN THE APPLE

MEN AND WOMEN IN ANCIENT AND MODERN ISRAEL

Contemporary feminists have long held the Bible responsible for the inferior status of women in Western culture. As Ilana Pardes observes, such critiques of the Bible date back to the earliest stages of post–World War II feminism. "In the first major works of feminist criticism—Simone de Beauvoir's *The Second Sex* (1949) and Kate Millet's *Sexual Politics* (1969)—," Pardes notes, "the Bible is condemned as one of the founding texts of partriarchy."[1] When Western feminist consciousness began to penetrate Israeli culture in the early 1970s,[2] it is not surprising, given the central role of the Bible in Israeli culture, that feminists there pursued this notion of the Bible's responsibility for sexist attitudes in contemporary culture to which they were opposed. The biblical portrayal of women, the role of women in biblical law and in its later rabbinic developments, and even aspects of biblical Hebrew that survived in contemporary Hebrew have been seen by feminists as sources on which Israeli culture has continued to draw, thereby perpetuating the second-class position of women.

In her book *Israeli Women: The Reality Behind the Myths,* Israeli journalist Lesley Hazleton questions the image held by Israelis and others that Israel is, in the area of gender, an essentially egalitarian society. Among several historical and cultural factors that have led to gender inequality in Israel, Hazleton cites the Bible and the biblical origins of contemporary Hebrew. Like many feminists in the West, she considers the image of Eve in Genesis as an important factor in preserving the unequal status of women in her time. For Hazleton it is important that Israelis consider the strong impact on Israeli culture of the biblical figure of Eve and the figure of Lilith, who was, according to nonbiblical legendary sources, a feminine being created before Eve to be Adam's mate. Hazleton and other Jewish feminists in Israel and the Diaspora regard Lilith as an alternative liberated female model, largely because according to legend she resisted Adam's demand that she submit to him by lying under him when they engaged in sexual intercourse.[3] The stories of Eve and Lilith are important for Israelis, Hazleton maintains, because they "are unacknowledged foundation myths of woman's sexuality, and are particularly strong in Israel, where women are still living directly within the Jewish tradition."[4]

Hazleton believes that the story of Lilith's resistance to Adam's authority was largely suppressed throughout Jewish history, with the result of "establishing woman's submissive role in Hebrew and consequently Jewish society."[5] Because it is the biblical Eve about whom Israelis actually read, Hazleton argues, Israelis are subjected to a view of sexuality that degrades women. In the story of the Garden of Eden in Genesis 2, Hazletone argues, "Eve's very existence is merely a vehicle for introducing shame, guilt and the toil of labor into society, with no blame attached to man. The woman took the Fall, for she was set up for it from the start. And with that Fall, eroticism is conquered by guilt, and woman's sexuality is reduced to a male appendage."[6]

On the level of language, Hazleton and Israeli scholar Shalva Weil call attention to usages from biblical Hebrew in contemporary Hebrew that they believe reinforce a subordinate position for women in Israeli culture. Hazleton cites the Hebrew word *gever*, which is used in biblical and contemporary Hebrew to mean "man," in contrast to "woman." The use of the root of this word, *g-b-r,* in the Hebrew words for "hero" (*gibbor*) and "overcome" (*hitgabber*), associates strength primarily with masculinity.

Weil notes that remnants of biblical Hebrew in contemporary Israeli Hebrew reinforce a notion of men as the norm of humanity. She cites as a particularly illuminating example the definition of *'ishah,* the Hebrew word for woman, in the authoritative Israeli dictionary of modern Hebrew by Avraham Even–Shoshan: "she is 'the feminine (species) of the children of Adam' (*not* of Eve), 'the spouse of a man, married to a man, a wife,' while a 'man' (*'ish*) is 'Man, humanity, male, the masculine (species) of the children of Adam.' "[7] In this definition, the identity of a woman is more dependent on that of a man than vice versa. In addition, even the term used in the Even–Shoshan dictionary, as well as in general in contemporary Hebrew to refer to a human being is *ben 'adam,* literally "son of Adam"; this term confirms the privileged status conferred by biblical culture on the male descendants of Adam, who were the priests and for the most part the prophets and the political leaders in ancient Israel. Weil also points out that attitudes toward relations between men and women go beyond the use of particular terms and are actually reflected in the ways that in biblical and modern Hebrew "gender . . . pervades the entire structure of the language."[8] The masculine functions as the norm of humanity because "nouns whose gender is unknown (e.g., 'things:' *devarim;* 'people:' *'anashim*) are usually expressed in the masculine."[9] Another example of this nature not mentioned by Weil is the fact that pronouns, adjectives, and verbs that refer to groups containing both men and women are always in the masculine form in Hebrew.

In recent decades a number of feminist writers have moved beyond the wholesale condemnation of the Bible as a source of contemporary sexism. They have presented instead new ways of reading the Bible that might bring it in greater conformity to feminist values.[10] At times these new readings reveal that the Bible's view of relations between men and women is more complex than is sometimes allowed by feminist critics. At other times these new readings take the liberty of transforming biblical stories to reflect women's concerns not found in the original text and to present more detailed portraits of female characters that reflect the experiences of contemporary women.

Both male and female writers of Israeli biblical allusion poems share with writers of these feminist readings the tendency to take seriously the connection between biblical images and contemporary perceptions of relations between the sexes. In their poetry, biblical images are sometimes a powerful means to express their coming to terms with key aspects of relations between men and women and sometimes a means to raise questions about the biblical view of such relations that has survived into the present. Like Israeli feminists Hazleton and Weil, the Israeli writers of the biblical allusion poems I consider in this chapter are concerned in particular with the power relations between men and women. These poems explore the wide spectrum of relations—from tense hostility to satisfying intimacy—that has characterized relations between the sexes throughout human history.

Men Abandoning Women

A striking number of Israeli biblical allusion poems are about the failure of men and women to sustain a satisfying relationship. In some of these poems, men exploit their more privileged position in society to withhold sexual satisfaction from women. Not all the biblical stories on which these poems are based refer explicitly to men engaged in such withholding. By either introducing this element or putting it in a new context, the poets explore this self-centered tendency of men to abuse their power by withdrawing sexually from women. In each poem the speaker is clearly sympathetic to the plight of the woman who has been abandoned by a man in so cruel a fashion and doomed to a life of sexual frustration and loneliness.

In *"Eshet Potifar"* ("Potiphar's Wife")[11] Yehudit Kafri portrays the biblical account of the attempted seduction of Joseph by his master's wife in a manner very different from that of the original biblical story (Genesis 39). In the original story, Joseph's response to Potiphar's wife's seduction attempt represents a turning point in his development as a character; his refusal to agree to her bold sexual invitation signals his transformation from an insensitive dreamer of power who took advantage of his position as the favorite son of Jacob into a pragmatic, morally mature man. We see from his response to this temptation that he realizes the moral limits of power and the wisdom of not jeopardizing his status as the person in charge of Potiphar's household. In Kafri's poem, however, the speaker expresses her skeptical view of the biblical version of the story:

אֵשֶׁת פּוֹטִיפַר

נִשְׁאֶלֶת הַשְּׁאֵלָה
מַה בֶּאֱמֶת קָרָה
בֵּין יוֹסֵף וְאֵשֶׁת פּוֹטִיפַר.
מַה זָרַם בֵּינֵיהֶם בַּחֲשַׁאי, בְּאֵין רוֹאֶה,
אוּלַי הוּא חָפַר לָהּ
אַמַּת מַיִם כְּחֵלָה בַּמִּדְבָּר?
אוּלַי הוּא אָמַר לָהּ דְּבָרִים שֶׁלּוֹחֲשִׁים בִּיחִידוּת, בַּחֹשֶׁךְ,
אוֹ עֵינָיו אָמְרוּ?
אִשָּׁה לֹא מְבַקֶּשֶׁת סְתָם כָּךְ מֵאִישׁ
לָבוֹא לִשְׁכַּב עִמָּהּ.
מַשֶּׁהוּ קָרָה בֵּינֵיהֶם
אֲבָל הַתַּנַ"ךְ לֹא מְסַפֵּר.
יוֹסֵף אָמְנָם הֻשְׁלַךְ לַבּוֹר
אֲבָל הוּא הִסְתַּדֵּר.
תָּמִיד הָיָה מַגִּיעַ
לָעֶמְדָּה הַגְּבוֹהָה בְּיוֹתֵר,
לְפָחוֹת מִשְׁנֶה לְשַׂר.
חוֹלֵם הַחֲלוֹמוֹת הַזֶּה
הָיָה פְּרַקְטִי יוֹתֵר מִכָּל הַפּוֹלִיטִיקָאִים
מָכַר אֶת כָּל הָעָם עֲבָדִים לְפַרְעֹה בְּמִצְרַיִם,
אֶת הַשָּׂדוֹת, אֶת הַמִּקְנֶה.
צָבַר כָּבוֹד וּרְכוּשׁ
וְאֶת אָסְנַת בַּת פּוֹטִיפֶרַע.
הָיָה אִישׁ צַדִּיק וְאִישׁ יָשָׁר,
זֶה מַה שֶּׁהוּא הָיָה, כַּנִּרְאֶה.
אֲבָל מַה קָרָה בֵּינְתַיִם
לְאֵשֶׁת פּוֹטִיפַר (שֶׁאֲפִלּוּ שְׁמָהּ לֹא נִזְכָּר),
כְּשֶׁנִּשְׁאֲרָה לְבַדָּהּ עִם בִּגְדוֹ בְּיָדֶיהָ?
בִּגְדוֹתוֹ בְּיָדֶיהָ...
אֲנִי לֹא יְכוֹלָה אֲפִלּוּ לְהַתְחִיל לְסַפֵּר
מַה קָרָה לָהּ.
אַף כִּי אֲנִי יוֹדַעַת.

POTIPHAR'S WIFE

The question is
what really happened
between Joseph and Potiphar's wife.
What flowed between them secretly, unseen,
perhaps he dug her
a blue water canal in the desert?
Perhaps he said to her things that are whispered privately, in
    the dark,
or his eyes said it?
A woman doesn't just ask a man
to come and lie with her.
Something happened between them
but the Bible doesn't tell.
Joseph did get thrown in the pit
but he managed.
He always would achieve
the highest status,
at least viceroy.
This dreamer of dreams
was more practical than all the politicians
and sold the whole nation as slaves to Pharaoh in Egypt,
the fields, the cattle.
He amassed honor and property
and Osnat daughter of Potiphera.
He was a righteous and an honest man,
that's what he was, apparently.
But what happened meanwhile
to Potiphar's wife (whose name isn't even mentioned),
when she was left alone with his garment in her hands?
His treachery in her hands . . .
I can't even begin to tell
what happened to her.
Even though I know.

The speaker of the poem is disturbed by the biblical portrayal of
Potiphar's wife. In a mixture of literary and colloquial styles (the col-
loquial represented most prominently by the use of *lo'* as a negative

with a present participle), she makes clear her distance as a contemporary woman from the biblical point of view. She refuses to believe that any woman, Potiphar's wife included, would have so little self-respect that without any prior interaction with him she would have called out to a man, "Lie with me!" (Genesis 39:7). Potiphar's wife, she insists, must have had some encouragement from Joseph, although for its own reasons the Bible has covered up this part of the story. She speculates that Potiphar's wife and Joseph may have had sexual intercourse before the time of the story: "What flowed between them secretly, unseen, / perhaps he dug her a blue water canal in the desert?" In these lines the speaker uses sexually suggestive imagery: flowing water and a canal. The Hebrew word for canal in the poem, 'ammah, could be a euphemistic reference to the woman's vagina, but it also is a euphemism in rabbinic Hebrew for penis. The speaker rejects the negative portrait in the biblical text of Potiphar's wife as a powerful, vengeful woman with no compunctions about falsely accusing Joseph of trying to rape her. Instead, she declares that actually Joseph, who according to this version started the whole affair, made out very well in the long run, with his rise to wealth and power. In sarcastically referring to Joseph's status as "a righteous and an honest man, / that's what he was, apparently," the speaker expresses her empathy for Potiphar's wife, who is the real victim of the story, for she was abandoned by Joseph and did not even merit the mention of her name in the Bible. What Potiphar's wife went through in this affair is too painful for the speaker to recount, but as a woman the speaker is all too aware of what it is like to be seduced by a man, who as he rises to greater power and influence abandons her.

In his poem *"ʿAl ḥayyei hamin shel haʾish Mosheh"* ("On the Sex Life of the Man Moses")[12] Aryeh Sivan's portrayal of Moses' marital life resembles passages in the rabbinic tradition. In the Talmud it is related that Moses thought to himself that if God commanded the Israelite men to refrain from sexual relations with their wives for three days before the revelation at Sinai (Exodus 19:15), even more so should he refrain from sexual relations with his wife, "since every hour the presence of God speaks to me and does not set a particular time to do so" (Sabbath 87a). According to this talmudic passage, God approves of Moses' sexual abstinence. In another rabbinic text (*ʾAvot deRabbi Nathan* 9) this sexual abstinence is associated with

Moses' second wife, the Cushite woman. According to this text, Miriam and Aaron criticized Moses for withdrawing sexually from his Cushite wife (Numbers 12:1).

Like the passage in *'Avot deRabbi Nathan,* the poem is about Moses' sexual withdrawal from his Cushite wife. The speaker expresses his concern for the suffering Moses has caused his wife by repeatedly referring to her in the first two stanzas of the poem as he dwells on her sexual frustration:

עַל חַיֵּי־הַמִּין שֶׁל הָאִישׁ מֹשֶׁה

אִשָּׁה כּוּשִׁית שׁוֹכֶבֶת, מְחַשֶּׁבֶת עוֹנָתָהּ,
אִשָּׁה כּוּשִׁית בְּעוֹנָתָהּ פּוֹשֶׁטֶת אֶת כְּסוּתָהּ,
אִשָּׁה כּוּשִׁית רוֹאָה פִּתְאֹם, לְחֶרְדָתָהּ,
כִּי שְׁאֵרָהּ עוֹמֵד לִבְקֹעַ מְעוֹרָהּ.

וְאָז אִשָּׁה כּוּשִׁית בַּפֶּה תּוֹבַעַת,
אַחֶרֶת אֵין אִשָּׁה כּוּשִׁית יוֹדַעַת,
אַחֶרֶת אֵין אִשָּׁה כּוּשִׁית מַגַּעַת
גַּם לָגַעַת בְּגוּפוֹ שֶׁל בַּעֲלָהּ מֹשֶׁה.

ON THE SEX LIFE OF THE MAN MOSES

A Cushite woman lies, her mind on her conjugal rights.
A Cushite woman in season strips her raiment off.
A Cushite woman suddenly is horrified to see
that she is about to burst at her seams.

And then a Cushite woman loudly claims her rights.
There's no other way for a Cushite woman,
no other way for her to touch
the body of her husband Moses.

Although Moses' abstinence forces her to demand that he fulfill his conjugal responsibility, he feels neither desire nor need to respond to her:

וְהָאִישׁ מֹשֶׁה יָגֵעַ. זֶה הָאִישׁ מֹשֶׁה,
אֲשֶׁר יָדָיו כְּבֵדִים, נוֹגֵעַ וְאֵינוֹ נוֹגֵעַ,
וְרַק כְּשֶׁאֱלֹהִים דּוֹבֵר וְהוּא שׁוֹמֵעַ
נִדְרַךְ הָאִישׁ מֹשֶׁה וְקוֹמָתוֹ נִזְקֶפֶת

וְאֶת הָאֱלֹהִים מֹשֶׁה יוֹדֵעַ: אֵשׁ
בּוֹעֶרֶת בְּכַפּוֹת רַגְלָיו, וְאַחֲרֶיהָ
קוֹל דְּמָמָה דַקָּה בְּאֵבָרָיו
וּשְׂעַר-גּוּפוֹ רוֹחֵץ בְּאוֹר רוֹגֵעַ.

אִשָּׁה כּוּשִׁית אֶת שְׁאֵרָהּ בְּתוֹךְ דִּישׁוֹ חוֹסֶמֶת,
לוֹבֶשֶׁת אֶת כְּסוּתָהּ, כְּרוּתַת-יָדַיִם, מִתְנַשֶּׁמֶת.
שֶׁלֹּא בְּעוֹנָתָהּ נִרְדֶּמֶת וְחוֹלֶמֶת:
תְּבִיעָתָהּ הַמְקֻפַּחַת עַל צוּקֵי-סִינַי מוּנַחַת.

The man Moses is weary. This is Moses the man
whose arms are heavy, who touches and does not touch,
and only when God speaks and he hears
is he alert and holds himself erect

And Moses knows God: fire
burns under his feet, followed
by a still silent voice in his organs
and his body's hair is bathed in restful light.

A Cushite woman muzzles herself while her flesh threshes,
panting, her arms like stumps, she puts on her raiment.
Out of her season now she falls asleep and dreams:
on the cliffs of Sinai lies her unheeded claim.

In the first and last stanzas of this poetic portrait of what might be
more correctly called the "non-sex life" of Moses, the speaker uses
three terms that appear in Exodus 21:10: *she'erah* (translated in the
poem as "her flesh"), *kesutah* (translated in the poem as "her rai-
ment"), and *'onatah* (translated in the poem as "her season"). In the
original context of Exodus the terms are used by Moses to refer to
the obligations of a master to his maidservant. Later Jewish tradition
understands these as the marital obligations of every Jewish man to

his wife: food, clothing, and conjugal rights. The contrast between what tradition understands to be the obligation of sexual relations prescribed by Moses and the withholding of sex by Moses in the poem is clear. In so doing Moses violates the very law that he had given the Israelites in God's name. Ironically, Moses' engagement in the revelation at Sinai is the source of that law that leads him to violate it by devoting himself exclusively to God and thereby mistreat his wife by sexually abandoning her. By alluding to the legal category of ʿonah (conjugal rights), Sivan may be suggesting that the biblical attempts to legally control sexuality are an important factor in preventing Moses and his wife (and later Jewish men and women) from enjoying each other sensually in a spontaneous manner. This point comes across in the final image of the poem of Moses' wife's "unheeded claim" placed on the very Mount Sinai from which God gave the Israelites the Torah.

The poem suggests that part of the reason why Moses does not respond to the explicit demand for sexual intimacy that his wife makes is that he works too hard as the leader of God's people to have energy to make love to her. The expression "whose arms are heavy" (yadav kevedim) alludes to the battle with Amalek, during which Moses' hands became heavy because God told him to keep his hands up so that the Israelites would win the battle (Exodus 17:8–13). The speaker even repeats the grammatical anomaly of modifying the word for "his arms" (yadav), which is normally of feminine gender, with the masculine form of the adjective "heavy" (kevedim), just as the biblical narrator does in his account of the battle with Amalek.

Moses does not suffer from their celibate marriage, for he is able to sublimate his erotic desire in his vocation as a prophet of God. Only when Moses senses the divine presence does he experience physical arousal. As he holds himself erect and feels fire burning under his feet, he finds a more than adequate substitute for the erection of his penis and the fire of eros that he could experience in sexual relations with his wife.

The effect on a woman of her husband's withdrawal from sexual relations is explored as well in two poems by Edna Aphek; they portray, respectively, the marriages of David and Michal and of Abraham and Sarah. Aphek's poem "ʿOd huʾ" ("While He Still")[13] is based on the confrontation between David and his wife Michal at the time that he dances wildly in the procession to bring the ark to Jerusalem (II

Samuel 6:12–23). When, in the biblical account, Michal criticizes David for dishonoring himself by dancing in such a wild manner "in the sight of the slavegirls of his subjects," David angrily rebukes her for criticizing him, and the story concludes with the statement, "So to her dying day Michal daughter of Saul had no children" (II Samuel 6:23). It is not completely clear from the text whether Michal's childlessness was due to divine punishment for insulting the king or to David's refusal to have sexual relations with her.[14] In Aphek's poem the latter is understood to be the case. The poem does not focus on the poignant fate of Michal as a childless woman; rather, it emphasizes her frustrating experience of never receiving any response from David when she attempts to seduce him. The speaker links the dance of David condemned by Michal with Michal's later attempts to seduce him into sexual relations by describing both with the words *mefazez* and *mekharker*, which the Bible uses to describe David's dance before the ark. This connection suggests that the explicitly erotic expression of David's dance so offended Michal, and Michal's attack on his erotic self-expression so wounded him that he felt impelled to pay her back by maintaining his contempt for her sexual desire:

עוֹד הוּא
מְפַזֵּז לִפְנֵי הָאָרוֹן
מְכַרְכֵּר בִּתְרוּעַת נִצָּחוֹן
קָשְׁתָה אִשְׁתּוֹ
בּוּזָה בְגוּפוֹ.
וַתִּבֶז לוֹ בְלִבָּהּ,
עַל כֵּן לֹא יָדְעָהּ.

וּמֵאָז הָיָה
גּוּפָהּ
מְפַזֵּז לִפְנֵי גּוּפוֹ
מְכַרְכֵּר לִפְנֵי אוֹנוֹ
וְהוּא
אֶל גֵּוָהּ לֹא יָבוֹא.

וּלְמִיכַל בַּת שָׁאוּל
לֹא הָיָה בֵּן.
עַד יוֹם מוֹתָהּ.

While he still
danced before the ark
leaped with a victory shout
his wife shot
her contempt at his body,
and she despised him in her heart,
he therefore did not know her.

And since then
her body
would dance before his body
leap before his potency
but he
to her body would not come.

And Michal daughter of Saul
never had a son.
Until her dying day.

By delaying references to the names of any of the biblical characters
in the story until the end of the poem Aphek succeeds in universal-
izing the central issues of the story. In her version the issue is not
only the disrespect of Saul's daughter for his successor, her husband
David, but also the tensions in any marital relationship when mutual
respect and understanding are lacking in the attitudes that husband
and wife hold regarding each other's sexuality.

In *"Sarah haytah"* ("Sarah Was")[15] Aphek transforms the story of
the rivalry of Sarah and Hagar (Genesis 16;21) into an account of
Sarah's jealousy of Abraham's relationship with Hagar:

שָׂרָה הָיְתָה
אִשָּׁה
רַכָּה וְצִיְּתָנִית
תְּלוּמָה כְּמַעֲנִית
וְהוּא —
אֵצֶל הָגָר
תָּמִיד.

שָׂרָה הָיְתָה
רַכָּה וְצִיְּתָנִית

בְּלוּמָה וְשַׁתְקָנִית
אִשָּׁה
וְרַחֲמָנִית
וְהוּא —
אֵצֶל הָגָר
תָּמִיד.

שָׂרָה הָיְתָה
רַכָּה וְרַחֲמָנִית
אֲבָל
אִשָּׁה
כְּנוּעָה וְאַכְזָרִית
וְהוּא —
אֵצֶל הָגָר
תָּמִיד.

שָׂרָה הָיְתָה
פְּגוּעָה וְאַכְזָרִית
אִשָּׁה
. . . .
אַךְ כְּשֶׁעֶדֶן רָחֲמָה
בִּבְנָהּ
קָרָא לָהּ
צַחְקָנִית.

Sarah was
a woman
soft and obedient
well furrowed
and he—
with Hagar
always.

Sarah was
soft and obedient
closed and taciturn
a woman
and tender hearted

and he—
with Hagar
always.

Sarah was
soft and tender hearted
but
a woman
submissive and cruel
and he—
with Hagar
always.

Sarah was
marred and cruel
a woman
. . . .
but when her womb delighted
in her son
they called her
the laughing one.

In the biblical account Sarah actually encourages Abraham to have
sexual relations with the maidservant Hagar because it appears after
many years of childlessness that this is the only way they can have a
son. In the poem Abraham's relations with Hagar are not character-
ized as an attempt to use her as a surrogate mother, but rather as an
ongoing affair that distances Abraham from Sarah. In the Bible Sarah
drives Hagar out of their household for a brief period of time, and
later with God's support Sarah convinces Abraham to permanently
expel Hagar and her son Ishmael. In the poem Sarah, perhaps be-
cause of her personality, perhaps also because of her inferior status,
never openly challenges Abraham. She plays the role of obedient
wife, although inwardly she suffers in angry silence and wishes she
could respond to the situation in a cruel manner. It is significant that
the tension experienced by Sarah is not resolved by Abraham's re-
turn to sexual relations with her. Only when she is blessed with the
long-awaited experience of childbirth can she transcend her jeal-
ousy. Now she is no longer dependent on the insensitive male figure
of Abraham for her fulfillment as a woman. Motherhood has granted

her a more satisfying type of fulfillment that allows her to experience the joyous laughter which is the meaning of her son Isaac's name.

In the poem, *"Tamar"* ("Tamar"),[16] by Aryeh Sivan, a sexually deprived female biblical character does eventually find erotic fulfillment. In the original biblical story on which the poem is based (Genesis 38), Tamar tricks her father-in-law Judah into impregnating her. She does so because her first two husbands, Judah's sons Er and Onan, have died leaving her childless, and Judah has not honored his promise to her that when his third son Shelah grows up he will give him to her in marriage to provide her with the opportunity to procreate. Just as Aphek transfers the original biblical focus of Sarah's story from procreation to sexual jealousy, which is eventually resolved by an act of procreation, in this poem Sivan transfers the original biblical focus of Tamar's story from procreation to the rediscovery of sexual experience. In the poem the significance of her relations with Judah is not that she has succeeded in becoming pregnant but rather that she has experienced the sexual fulfillment that was denied her in widowhood:

תָּמָר

מֵעֲדֻלָּם וְעַד עֲרָד
הָיְתָה הָרוּחַ מְטַלְטֶלֶת אֶת פִּתְחָהּ בְּיַד קָשָׁה
וְהִיא, אַחֲרֵי כָּל הַמִּיתוֹת כֻּלָּן, אִשָּׁה
שֶׁאֲבָרֶיהָ בִּמְקוֹמָם, לֹא
לֹא פָּחוֹת מִן
הַכָּבוֹד.

עֵר מֵת עָלֶיהָ כִּפְשׁוּטוֹ. אוֹנָן
הָיָה מַבְלִיחַ וְכָבֶה, מַבְלִיחַ וְכָבֶה
כְּמוֹ נֵר לַח בְּחֶלְבּוֹ ;
אַךְ כְּשֶׁיָּרְדָה לְהִטָּבֵל, גִּלְּתָה, כִּמְעַט בִּבְעָתָה
כִּי אֲבָרֶיהָ עֲנֵפִים, שֵׁיָּם-
הַמָּוֶת סָר מֵעֲלֵיהֶם :
הָיְתָה בָּהֶם חִיּוּת קָשָׁה וּמְצֵרָה
לְאִשָּׁה אֲשֶׁר נוֹתְרָה בְּלִי גֶּבֶר לְבַשְׂרָהּ.

עַד אֲשֶׁר בָּא יְהוּדָה
עַל אֵם הַמִּשְׁעוֹלִים, עַד אֲשֶׁר בָּא יְהוּדָה

181

עִם הַמַּטֶּה וְהַפְּתִילִים, וְעִם שְׂעַר הַגְּדִי הָרַךְ, אֲשֶׁר נִמְשַׁךְ
מֵעֵבֶר לָעוֹנָה, כְּמוֹ בַּשָּׁנָה
שֶׁבָּהּ פָּקַד
הַגֶּשֶׁם אֶת מִדְבַּר עֲרָד.

TAMAR

From Adulam unto Arad
the wind would shake her opening with a hard hand
and she, after all the deaths, a woman
her organs in place, no
not less than
her honor.

Er simply died. Onan
would flicker and die out, flicker and die out
like a wet candle in its fat;
but when she went down to bathe, she saw, almost in fright
that her organs were branches, from which the sea
of death had departed:
they had a vitality hard and distressing
for a woman left without a man for her flesh.

Until Judah came
on the crossroads, until Judah came
with the staff and cords, with the soft lamb's hair, that ex-
tended
beyond the season, as in the year
in which the rain
revisited the desert of Arad.

After the deaths of Er and the impotent Onan, Tamar eventually tran-
scends her lifeless existence bathing in "the sea of death" (*yam
hamavet*) and realizes how difficult it is to live without physical con-
tact with a man. When Judah arrives and engages her in sexual inter-
course, this central difficulty of her life is resolved. This erotic expe-
rience, she discovers, is as crucial to her existence as rain is to the
parched desert. It is significant that in the poem Tamar is portrayed
as more passive than she is in the Bible. She does not engage in the

elaborate plan of deception to get Judah to have sexual relations with her that Tamar arranges in the Bible. The fulfillment of her erotic needs comes about only when Judah arrives on his own. It is poignant that Tamar has a need that she feels can only be fulfilled by a man, but she is not in a position to do anything about that need until a man is available to fulfill it. The language of the last two lines of the poem reinforces the image of Judah as a godlike superhuman savior of Tamar. By using the term *paqad* ("revisited") the speaker associates Judah with God, for *paqad* is a term often used in the Bible to describe God's remembrance or singling out of a person. Furthermore, when the speaker compares the arrival of Judah to a rainfall he suggests that Judah has the power of forces of nature beyond human control.

Women Unfulfilled in Marriage

Several biblical allusion poems portray female biblical characters assessing their lives after many years of marriage. In each case the female character has experienced a great lack of satisfaction in her marriage, and she attempts to come to terms with all that has been problematic during that period. In these poems, at the time of their reflection on the past these female characters are portrayed as not being in the presence of their husbands, as if this distance from their marital partners is necessary for their introspection.

In Asher Reich's poem *"'Eshet Lot: hamabat le'ahor"* ("Lot's Wife: The Look Backward")[17] Lot's wife describes for her apparently absent husband the experience of fleeing the destruction of Sodom, presumably just before she is turned into a pillar of salt (Genesis 19):

אֵשֶׁת לוֹט: הַמַּבָּט לְאָחוֹר

הִנְנִי אוּד, נָע וָנָד כְּגַרְגֵּר הָאָרֶץ.

מֵאֲחוֹרַי הִשְׁאַרְתִּי שׁוֹתֶתֶת שַׁחַר עִיר לְגוֹרָלָהּ.

מַה שֶּׁהִתְרַחֵשׁ שָׁם יָכֹלְתִּי לְנַחֵשׁ

דְּלוּקַת צְעָדִים שָׁמַעְתִּי אֶת שַׁאֲגוֹת הַשֶּׁמֶשׁ
אֶת קִיטוֹר הָאָרֶץ הִרְגַּשְׁתִּי בְּעָרְפִּי
לֹא הַגַּעְגּוּעַ תָּקַף אוֹתִי לְהַפְנוֹת עֵינַיִם

בְּסַקְרָנוּת שֶׁגּוֹבֶרֶת תָּמִיד עַל הַפַּחַד
נוֹלַד בִּי הַמַּבָּט לְאָחוֹר
כְּשֶׁמַּבִּיטִים לְאָחוֹר לֹא רוֹאִים דָּבָר.
וְעַכְשָׁו אֲנִי רוֹאָה אוֹתְךָ, לוֹט

מִתְנוֹדֵד כְּמוֹ נֹאד יַיִן בְּתוֹךְ הַהֲפֵכָה
בְּעֵמֶק הַשִּׂדִים שֶׁפָּרַח בְּרֹאשְׁךָ הַשָּׁתוּי
מֶלַח עַצְמוֹתַי מַצְמִיא אוֹתְךָ לָעַד.
לָעַד תִּזְכֹּר אֶת הֶעָבָר הַמֵּת
בֵּין הַבַּרְבָּרִים בָּנִינוּ בַּיִת

וְגוֹרָלוֹת בִּשְׁנַיִם: אֲנִי אַתָּה
שְׁתֵּי בְּנוֹתֵינוּ וּשְׁנֵי הַמַּלְאָכִים
זְנוּחָה כָּל כָּךְ זָרָה אַפְּלוּ לְעַצְמִי
בִּטְנִי תָּפְחָה פַּעֲמַיִם מִזַּרְעֲךָ
אַחַר כָּךְ תָּפַחְתִּי מִמֶּלַח הָאֲדָמָה
וְאָז יָדַעְתִּי: חַיַּי הָיוּ לְהָבָה בַּת חֲלוֹף.

LOT'S WIFE: THE LOOK BACKWARD

Here I am a firebrand, moving about as a grain of earth.

Behind me I left a city dripping dawn to its fate.
What happened there I could guess

afire as I stepped I heard the roaring of the sun
the smoke of the land I felt at my neck
it was not longing to turn my eyes that seized me

with a curiosity that always overcomes fear
was born in me the look backward
when looking back one doesn't see a thing.
And now I see you, Lot

wandering like a wine skin in all that's overturned
in the valley of lime that blossomed in your drunk head

184

the salt of my bones making you thirsty forever.
Forever you'll remember the dead past
among barbarians we built our house

and fates in pairs: you and I
our two daughters and the two angels
forsaken so foreign even to myself
my belly swelled twice from your seed
afterward I swelled from the salt of the earth
and then I knew: my life became an ephemeral flame.

Most readers of the original biblical story have the impression that when Lot's wife turns back to look at the destruction of the corrupt city of Sodom she is acting inappropriately and consequently receives the divine punishment of being transformed into a pillar of salt. In Reich's poem, however, Lot's wife portrays herself as morally superior to Lot. It was not, she declares, because she longed to return there that she looked back at Sodom but simply because she was curious to see the destruction. She has continued to feel connected to Sodom not because she approves of its ways but because she feels a large degree of empathy for the doomed Sodomites. Throughout her flight she experiences a measure of the Sodomites' suffering—feeling the heat of the fire at her feet, hearing the roaring of the sun, and feeling the smoke of the land at her neck. There appears to be in her a degree of survivor's guilt as she reflects on leaving Sodom "to its fate."

In the second half of the poem she contrasts her own relationship with Sodom and that of her husband's. As she looks back, she realizes that in fact her husband Lot, not she, had always been too closely tied to Sodom. Drawing on the later image of Lot's daughters getting him drunk after the flight from Sodom (Genesis 19), the poet has Lot's wife describe her vision of him as a drunkard who foolishly saw the barren valley as a place that can blossom. Lot, who the Bible recounts chose to live in the region of Sodom because it was "well watered" (Genesis 13:10), did not understand what his wife understood, that they had settled among barbarians in a land ultimately doomed to destruction.

Their life, she tells the absent Lot, was burdened by the limitations of fate, represented by the constant repetition of pairs of characters during their sojourn in Sodom: she and Lot, their two daughters, and the two angels who came to rescue them. She was so alienated from their life that she felt "foreign even to [her]self." She uses the image of salt, the substance into which she is about to be transformed, to represent the dissatisfying frustration that lay at the heart of their relationship. The salt of her bones made him "thirsty forever," and when she was pregnant, she felt as if she were swelling "from [his] seed," an experience she associates with the later feeling that she was swelling from the destructive "salt of the earth." In a sense, Lot's wife suggests, the process of her being transformed into a pillar of salt began already in the desolate life that they experienced in Sodom. Now that she is about to die by being fully transformed into salt, she regrets how short her life has been, with so few memories of fulfillment. In contrast, she declares, because Lot never understood what was wrong with their settling in Sodom, he will always be foolishly tied to the "dead past" of their life in Sodom that was so lacking in vitality.

Aryeh Sivan begins his poem "*Le'ah haytah*" ("Leah Was")[18] with a play on the name *Le'ah* and the meaning of the word *le'ah* (tired). Leah, the less favored wife of Jacob, appears in the poem as a woman, separated from her husband, ruminating on what has led to the failure of their marriage. As she sits at home in the evening after a hard day as a mother, she is too tired to do anything but "count drops of candle fat." In the process of assessing her situation she tries to come to terms with her past by thinking of it as inevitable:

לֵאָה הָיְתָה

לֵאָה הָיְתָה
לֵאָה. תָּמִיד
הָיְתָה לֵאָה. בָּעֲרָבִים
הָיְתָה יוֹשֶׁבֶת וּמוֹנָה
טִפּוֹת שֶׁל חֵלֶב מִן הַנֵּר.
סְבִיבָהּ קִפְצוּ הַיְלָדִים
וְהִיא לֹא נִזְכְּרָה בִּשְׁמוֹתֵיהֶם.
הֲלֹא כָּל מַה שֶּׁבָּא
צָרִיךְ הָיָה לָבֹא.
כָּל שֶׁצָּרִיךְ הָיָה
בָּא.

LEAH WAS

Leah was
tired. Always
was tired. Evenings
she would sit and count
drops of candle fat.
Around her pranced the children,
but she remembered not their names.
Didn't everything that came
have to come.
Everything that had to
came.

Leah suffers from the image others have of her as a deceitful person who knowingly participated in her father Laban's trick to get Jacob to marry her (Genesis 29). Because others will never believe her, she can only seek to convince herself that she entered into her marriage with Jacob because she really loved him and that somehow he "redeemed" her when he engaged her in sexual relations. She recognizes that her assertion may be only partly true. Indeed, she admits that the complexities of life have left her in a painful solitude. She speaks of these complexities as if they were threads woven tightly together into a knot, reflecting the "lump" in her throat as she experiences unresolved sadness and loneliness:

לֹא יַאֲמִינוּ לָהּ. לֹא
יַאֲמִינוּ לָהּ, שֶׁלֹּא נִסְתָה
לְהַעֲרִים בְּעֶרוֹמָהּ
וּבמוּמָהּ עַל אִישׁ,
וְלֹא מֶרֹב בֶּכִי עֵינֶיהָ רַכּוֹת.
וְרוּחַ לֹא הָיָה בָּהּ
לְהַסְבִּיר, וּלְשֵׁם מָהּ? הַרְבֵּה
הַרְבֵּה יוֹתֵר פָּשׁוּט הָיָה לָהּ
לְשַׁכְנֵעַ אֶת עַצְמָהּ, שֶׁאָהֲבָה
אֶת יַעֲקֹב, וְשֶׁמַּגַּע
בְּשָׂרוֹ גָּאַל אוֹתָהּ
מִמַּשֶּׁהוּ, בְּאֵיזֶה אֹפֶן.

הָיָה בָּזֶה וַדַּאי מִן הָאֱמֶת.
בְּכָל דָּבָר יֵשׁ מַשֶּׁהוּ
מִן הָאֱמֶת, וּמִמֵּילָא

הַכֹּל נִסְבַּךְ וְנֶאֱרַג
עִם הַשָּׁנִים
לְאֶרֶג מִתְעַבֶּה, לִפְקַעַת
בַּגָּרוֹן.

No one will believe her. No one
will believe her, that she never tried
deceiving anyone with her nakedness
and with her blemish,
and it's not from much crying that her eyes are weak.
But she never had the spirit
to explain, what's the point? Much
much simpler it was for her
to convince herself, that she loved
Jacob, and that the touch
of his flesh redeemed her
from something, somehow.
In this there was of course something of the truth.
In everything there's something
of the truth, and anyway

it all got tangled and woven
with the years
into a thickened weave, into a knot
in the throat.

In Amir Gilboa's prose poem *"Sarai"* ("Sarai")[19] the speaker pre-
sents Sarah's view of the period of her marriage to Abraham when
near the end of her life she is about to give birth to Isaac (Genesis 21):

שָׂרַי

דֶּרֶךְ אֲרֻכָּה עָבְרָה. עַל פְּנֵי הָרִים וּבְקָעִים. הָרְרֵי הָרִים
נָטְשָׁה מֵאֲחוֹרֶיהָ וַעֲדַיִן הִיא הוֹלֶכֶת וְהוֹלֶכֶת. הִיא יָצְאָה

עִם עֲלוֹת הַשֶּׁמֶשׁ תִּשְׁעִים שָׁנָה לִפְנֵי כֵן וְשׁוּב לֹא הָיָה כֹּחַ
בְּרַגְלֶיהָ וְעַתָּה כָּרְעָה תַּחְתֶּיהָ. כָּל אוֹתָהּ דֶּרֶךְ אֲרֻכָּה יָדְעָה
שְׂנָאוֹת הַרְבֵּה וְיוֹתֵר מִכָּךְ אֲהָבוֹת. פָּנֶיהָ מִמַּרְאוֹת הַמַּיִם
נִשְׁקְפוּ אֵלֶיהָ יָפִים וּצְעִירִים. קֹדֶם כְּבַת ז' כַּאֲשֶׁר כְּבָר הָיְתָה
בַּת כ' וְאַחַר, בְּמֶשֶׁךְ עֲשָׂרוֹת שָׁנִים, כְּבַת כ'. גַּם בִּקְשׁוּ
לִקְנוֹתָהּ לְאַהֲבָה מִידֵי אַבְרָם, כִּי יְפַת-תֹּאַר הָיְתָה.
בְּדַרְכָּהּ, בְּמֶשֶׁךְ שָׁנִים תִּשְׁעִים, הָרוּ חֶזְיוֹנֵי רוּחָהּ דּוֹרוֹת
שֶׁל נִינִים, נְכָדִים, אָבוֹת וְסָבִים. אַךְ כֻּלָּם נִזְרוּ בְּנִבְכֵי
תְּהוֹמוֹת, בְּשִׁטְפֵי פְּלָגִים, בַּעֲרוּצֵי הָרִים, בִּטְמִיוֹנֵי אָבָק וְעַל
פְּנֵי סְלָעִים. גַּם שָׁלְחָה רוּחָם לְהַלֵּךְ בַּאֲוִירִים. גַּם נִשְׂאוּ
אֶל מִתַּחַת לָרְקִיעִים וְהָיוּ לַעֲנָנִים מַמְטִירִים עַל שָׂדוֹת זָרִים.
גַּם הֶאֱדִימוּ אֶת קַרְנֵי הַשֶּׁמֶשׁ לְחַמֵּם לְבוֹת וְגוּפוֹת זָרִים.
אוּלָם אַף לֹא בֵּן אֶחָד יָלְדָה בִּזְרוֹעוֹתֶיהָ לְאָמְצוֹ אֶל לִבָּהּ.

דֶּרֶךְ אֲרֻכָּה אֲרֻכָּה עָבְרָה עַל פְּנֵי הָרִים וּבְקָעִים. הָרֵי הָרִים
נָטְשָׁה מֵאֲחוֹרֶיהָ וַעֲדַיִן הִיא הוֹלֶכֶת וְהוֹלֶכֶת. הִיא
יָצְאָה עִם עֲלוֹת הַשֶּׁמֶשׁ שָׁנִים תִּשְׁעִים לִפְנֵי כֵן וְשׁוּב לֹא
הָיָה כֹּחַ בְּרַגְלֶיהָ לְהַמְשִׁיךְ וְעַתָּה כָּרְעָה תַּחְתֶּיהָ
לָלֶדֶת.

שָׂרַי בִּזְרוֹעוֹתֶיהָ בֵּן. פָּנָיו נַעֲוִים כִּמְבַקְּשִׁים לִפְרֹץ בִּבְכִי.
עוֹד מְעַט וְשָׂרָה עִמּוֹ. וְיִצְחָק.

SARAI

A long way she went. Over mountains and in valleys. Mountains
upon mountains she left behind her and still she walks and
walks. She embarked at sunrise ninety years earlier and again
her legs had no power and now she sank down. That whole long
way she knew many hatreds but even more than that loves. Her
face reflected to her in the water was pretty and young. At first
she looked seven when she was twenty and afterward, for
decades she looked twenty. They even sought to acquire her for
love from Abram, for she was beautiful. On her way, during
ninety years she conceived in her imagination generations of
great grandchildren, grandchildren, fathers, and grandfathers.
But they all were secluded in deep fountains, in the flow of
streams, in the channels of mountains, in dusty hidden places
and on rocks. She also sent their spirit to move about within the

air. They also were carried under the sky and became clouds raining on strangers' fields. They also reddened the sun's rays to warm the hearts and bodies of strangers. But she did not bear even one son in her arms that she could bring close to her heart.

A long way she went on mountains and in valleys. Mountains upon mountains she left behind her and still she walks and walks. She embarked at sunrise ninety years before and again her legs had no power and now she sank down
to give birth.

Sarai has a son in her arms. His face contorted as if seeking to burst into tears. Soon Sarah will be with him. And Isaac.

The poem portrays Sarah as feeling no personal connection to the divinely ordained purpose of her journey with Abraham. For Abraham the journey to Canaan was for the purpose of preparing the way for his descendants to inherit the land: Sarah, however, spent the journey preoccupied by emotional relations ("she knew many hatreds but even more than that loves"), her outward appearance ("Her face reflected to her in the water was pretty and young"), and her childlessness ("she did not bear even one son in her arms").[20] Her only connection with Abraham that is mentioned is when the speaker relates that she was so beautiful some men tried to acquire her from him. When she fantasizes having a child, she does not think of that child in the ways that Abraham does. Abraham's view of their progeny is presumably colored by God's promise to him to make of them "a great nation" (Genesis 12:2). In contrast, Sarah's wish is simply to have descendants, without other meaning attached to that wish. Her fantasies of these future generations are connected less to history than to nature ("secluded in deep fountains, in the flow of streams, in the channels of mountains, in dusty hidden places, and on rocks"). At the beginning of the poem the speaker portrays Sarai as sinking down (*karʿah taḥteha*), presumably a sign of her weakness and fatigue at the end of a long journey. At the end of the poem, the original image of her sinking down in the weakness of old age is transformed into an expression of strength; she now sinks down (*karʿah taḥteha*) to give birth to Isaac.

As Hillel Barzel points out, Gilboa makes meaningful use of the matriach's two names: her original name Sarai, associated with her barrenness, and the name Sarah, given to her by God in connection with His promise that she will have many descendants (Genesis 17:15–16). Throughout most of the poem, which describes her life before she gives birth to Isaac, she is referred to as Sarai, and only upon giving birth to Isaac is she transformed into Sarah.[21] As Sarah holds Isaac (whose name in Hebrew, *Yitshaq,* is based on the Hebrew root *ts-h-q,* "to laugh") the baby withholds his crying, and she in turn feels that she has joyously triumphed over the anguish of her life. For Sarah, the end of the journey is not the arrival in Canaan, as it had been for Abraham, but rather the birth of her son. For her, the new name signifies not God's promise but her most important experience of bearing a child.

In Dalia Ravikovitch's poem *"Kemo Rahel"* ("Like Rachel")[22] the speaker expresses her desire to die as she imagines Rachel did when she gave birth to Benjamin on the way to Bethlehem (Genesis 35:16–21). Rachel is portrayed in the poem as having lived a life in which she never found full expression for her soul. Her individuality had been overwhelmed by Jacob's great love for her. At this point she desires death because it will free her soul from the intense devotion of her husband Jacob and her only son Joseph. Such a release of the soul is analogous to the new beginning her son Benjamin is about to have in birth:

כְּמוֹ רָחֵל

לָמוּת כְּמוֹ רָחֵל
כְּשֶׁהַנֶּפֶשׁ רוֹעֶדֶת כַּצִּפּוֹר
רוֹצָה לְהִמָּלֵט.
מֵעֵבֶר לָאֹהֶל עָמְדוּ נִבְהָלִים יַעֲקֹב וְיוֹסֵף,
דִּבְּרוּ בָּהּ רְתֵת.
כָּל יְמֵי חַיֶּיהָ מִתְהַפְּכִים בָּהּ.
כַּתִּינוֹק הָרוֹצֶה לְהִוָּלֵד.

כַּמָּה קָשֶׁה.
אַהֲבַת יַעֲקֹב אָכְלָה בָּהּ
בְּכָל פֶּה.
עַכְשָׁו כְּשֶׁהַנֶּפֶשׁ יוֹצֵאת
אֵין לָהּ חֵפֶץ בְּכָל זֶה.

LIKE RACHEL

To die like Rachel
With the soul quivering like a bird
Seeking escape.
Beyond the tent Jacob and Joseph stood stricken,
They spoke of her with awe
All her days tossed about within her
Like a child wanting to be born.

How hard it is.
Jacob's love consumed her
Voraciously.
Now while the soul expires
She has no desire for all that.

When, on hearing the cry of the newborn baby, Jacob comes into her tent, Rachel feels fully detached from him. Her pleasure is in the convergence of her final childbirth and her death, which liberates her from the love of Jacob and Joseph and thereby grants her the peace she never had in life:

לְפֶתַע צָוַח הַתִּינוֹק
וּבָא יַעֲקֹב אֶל הָאֹהֶל
אַךְ רָחֵל אֵינָהּ מַרְגִּישָׁה
עֶדְנָה שׁוֹטֶפֶת אֶת פָּנֶיהָ
וְרֹאשָׁהּ.

Suddenly the baby screamed
And Jacob came to the tent
But Rachel feels nothing
Tenderness floods her face
And her head.

Because no one eulogized Rachel after her death she can finally rest, free of the problematic emotional devotion of her husband and son:

מְנוּחָה גְדוֹלָה יָרְדָה עָלֶיהָ.
נִשְׁמַת אַפָּהּ שׁוּב לֹא תַּרְעִיד נוֹצָה.

הֵנִיחוּ אוֹתָהּ בֵּין אַבְנֵי הָרִים
וְלֹא הִסְפִּידוּהָ.
לָמוּת כְּמוֹ רָחֵל
אֲנִי רוֹצָה.

A great peace came over her.
Her breath of life will never again stir a feather.
They laid her down among the mountain stones
And spoke no eulogy.
To die like Rachel
That is what I want.

It is significant that the speaker chose Rachel as her model because her relationship with Jacob is one of the most romantic relationships portrayed in the Bible: Jacob was so in love with her that he was willing to work fourteen years to gain her father's permission to marry her (Genesis 29). Rachel could have seen her death in childbirth as a cruel event that wrenched her from her husband. For the speaker, however, the Rachel she imagines can make her peace with death by recognizing in it an opportunity to discover the individuality that Jacob's love for her almost completely overwhelmed.

Sexual Intercourse

The poems we have examined so far present a rather dismal view of relations between men and women. Male characters withdraw from sexual relations with female characters, and wives spend most of their marriages emotionally distant from their husbands. Male characters find satisfying relations with other women or seek religious ecstasy, while women sometimes find a substitute relationship with the babies they bear. Only Tamar succeeds in restoring satisfying sexual relations for herself. Some biblical allusion poems, however, do portray sexual relations between a man and woman that are largely fulfilling for the couple. In these poems the male figure is relatively passive and ignorant of at least some aspect of what is going on between the female figure and him, while the female figure is more in control and aware of what is happening than is the male figure.

T. Carmi's poem *"Ḥavvah yadʿah"* ("Eve Knew")[23] presents a new version of the Adam and Eve story that significantly transforms the biblical view of heterosexual relations into one more accurately reflecting that of the contemporary poet. In Genesis 3, which has often been read as an allegory of sexual initiation, the serpent seduces Eve into eating the forbidden fruit of "the tree of knowledge of good and bad," and Eve then gives the fruit to Adam. In response to their defiance, God curses first the serpent and then Adam and Eve, after which He expels the first man and woman from the Garden of Eden. In Carmi's poem Eve is portrayed as a more positive character and the expulsion from Eden is really not all that tragic:

חַוָּה יָדְעָה

חַוָּה יָדְעָה מַה טָמוּן בַּתַּפּוּחַ.
הִיא לֹא נוֹלְדָה אֶתְמוֹל.
מִבֵּין צַלְעוֹתָיו שֶׁל אָדָם
הִיא הִשְׁגִּיחָה בְּמַעֲשֵׂי בְּרֵאשִׁית,
הִקְשִׁיבָה לְרַחַשׁ דְּשָׁאִים וּשְׁרָצִים.

חַוָּה יָדְעָה מַה טָמוּן בַּתַּפּוּחַ.
הַמַּיִם זָעֲמוּ, הַלְּבָנָה הִשְׁחִירָה,
הָאוֹתִיּוֹת זָקְפוּ אֶת קוֹצֵיהֶן,
חַיְתוֹ-שָׂדֶה טָרְפוּ אֶת הַשֵּׁמוֹת,
וְהַקּוֹל אָמַר: כִּי טוֹב.

חַוָּה יָדְעָה מַה טָמוּן בַּתַּפּוּחַ.
כִּי טוֹב, כִּי טוֹב, וְשׁוּב כִּי טוֹב,
זִרְמָה שֶׁל עֲדָנִים,
גַּן לְדֻגְמָה, מַשְׁקֶה, רָוּי,
אֵם לְמוֹפֵת, אַשְׁרֵי כָּל חַי.

חַוָּה יָדְעָה מַה טָמוּן בַּתַּפּוּחַ.
לְאוֹר הַיּוֹם וּבְדֵעָה צְלוּלָה,
גּוּפָהּ הָעֵירֹם מַכְהֶה אוֹר חַמָּה,
הִיא קָרְאָה דְּרוֹר לַתּוֹלַעַת הַגְּדוֹלָה
שֶׁתְּכַרְסֵם אֶת שָׁרְשֵׁי הָעֵצִים.

הַסּוֹף הָיָה טוֹב.
אָדָם, זֵעָתוֹ נִגֶּרֶת כְּנָהָר,
הוֹדָה בְּפָנֶיהָ לְאוֹר הַחֶרֶב
כִּי לֹא נוֹתְרוּ בּוֹ שֵׁמוֹת,
כִּי כֹּחוֹתָיו כָּלוּ מֵרֹב טוֹבָה,

כִּי טוֹב.

EVE KNEW

Eve knew what was hidden in the apple.
She wasn't born yesterday.
From between Adam's ribs
she observed the order of creation,
listening to the grasses and crawling things.

Eve knew what was hidden in the apple.
The waters raged, the moon grew black,
the letters brandished their thorns,
the beasts of the fields devoured their names
and the voice said: It is good.

Eve knew what was hidden in the apple.
It is good! It is good! And again: It is good!
A torrent of goodness:
a model garden, watered, sated,
an exemplary mother. Happy are all living things!

Eve knew what was hidden in the apple,
In the light of day, and with a clear mind,
her naked body darkening the sun,
she released the Big Worm
to gnaw at the roots of trees.

Happy ending:
Adam, his sweat flowing like a river,
confessed by the light of the sword
that he was out of names, that the good
had exhausted his strength

and that it is good.

A number of the images found in the biblical text are preserved in Carmi's poem: Adam, Eve, fruit, trees, the sweat of Adam, and the sword that prevented Adam and Eve from returning to Eden. The poem, however, suggests a very different understanding of sexuality than does the Bible. In the Bible the seduction of Eve by the phallic-like serpent and the consequences of that event may be understood as the portrayal of sexuality as an irresistible pleasure that the ma-turing human is driven to seize, only to find it accompanied by painful responsibilities. In Carmi's poem, however, not the serpent but Eve, is the active force. She already has the knowledge of sexu-ality contained in the forbidden fruit (*Ḥavvah yadʿah*), putting her on a divine level, or at least on a level above that of the biblical Adam, for she knew of sexuality even before Adam sexually "knew" her ("Now the man knew his wife Eve," *vehaʾadam yadaʿ ʾet Ḥavvah ʾishto*, Genesis 4:1). Here sexuality is a good and liberating force instinc-tively known by women who have the power to show men that sen-suality is as important an aspect of life as are the responsibilities to which men are committed. Carmi's version of the Garden of Eden story critiques the understanding of sexuality in the biblical text. He appears to be rejecting this biblical view of sexuality reflected in Genesis 3 by presenting an alternative view in which Eve does not se-duce Adam away from his responsibility to divine authority, but rather reveals to Adam the greatest pleasure human beings can ex-perience.

Carmi's version also challenges society's assumption that women are to accept the role of wife and mother given to them. As Carmi explains in a note to his translator Grace Schulman, "[Eve] may be repeating what she hears, bitterly. . . . This is a model garden, and I'm supposed to be an exemplary mother: oh yes, happy are all living things!"[24] The worm that she releases (derived from the biblical ser-pent) can be seen as the unrestrained spontaneity of natural sensu-ality from which culture since biblical times has sought to limit both women and men by forcing them into the roles of homemaker and breadwinner.

In his poem *"Raḥav"* ("Rahab"),[25] Amir Gilboa conveys the experi-ence of sexual initiation of a young man by means of the story of Rahab sheltering the spies sent by Joshua into the land of Canaan (Joshua 2). In the biblical text there is no explicit reference to any sexual relations between Rahab and the spies. Gilboa's use of this story to write about sexual initiation may have derived from two factors. The book of Joshua identifies Rahab as a *zonah* ("prostitute"), and sometimes a young man's first sexual relations are with a prostitute, who can provide him with the physical experience of sex unencumbered by any emotional involvement. Gilboa's association between sex and spying preceding an invasion may have also derived from a biblical idiom. The Israelite spies and warriors were men, and the Hebrew word for land (*'erets*) is feminine in gender. When Joseph, accusing his brothers of spying in Egypt, declares: "You have come to see the land in its nakedness" (Genesis 42:9), he associates the act of spying with a man uncovering the nakedness of a woman.

Gilboa's poem begins with the description of a scene of boys in a traditional synagogue. One boy, the speaker of the poem, expresses his excitement at seeing his friend Yosi defying an older authority figure by stealing a ritual ram's horn from the holy ark. This challenge to authority is paralleled by the fact that the speaker, Yosi, and another boy named Yaakov are inappropriately playing cards in the synagogue. In the spirit of this youthful rebellion, the speaker encourages Yosi to blow the ram's horn, even though according to traditional practice it is not to be treated as a mere toy. When Yosi does so, Yaakov, perhaps in astonishment, drops his cards. The blowing of the ram's horn and the dropping of the cards are immediately transformed in the speaker's consciousness into the blowing of the rams' horns and the falling of the walls of Jericho in the days of Joshua:

רָחָב

הַבֵּט, הַבֵּט! הִנֵּה יוֹסִי מִתְגַּנֵּב אֶל הַשּׁוֹפָר שֶׁבַּתֵּבָה.
מַה לַזָּקֵן, אֵיכָכָה זֶה יִרְהֶה לְיַד תֵּבָתוֹ וְלֹא יִרְאֶה אֶת יוֹסִי?
יוֹסִי, יוֹסִי, תְּקַע, תְּקַע בַּשּׁוֹפָר!
יַעֲקֹב קְלָפָיו נוֹפְלִים לוֹ מִיָּדָיו
וְחוֹמוֹת יְרִיחוֹ רוֹעֲמוֹת אֱלֵי-אָרֶץ.

RAHAB

Look, look! Yosi is sneaking up to the ram's horn in the ark.
What's with the old man, how can he hesitate by his ark and
    not see Yosi?
Yosi, Yosi, blow, blow the ram's horn!

Yaakov's cards are dropping from his hands
and the walls of Jericho are crashing to the earth.

When the speaker sees a male figure hugging Rahab he cannot
identify him. He gradually discovers that he himself is that man.
Adult authority regulating religious behavior and respect for ritual
has been successfully challenged; the speaker, having reached the
age of maturity, overcomes the stricture against children engaging in
sex. He is like the spies who set out to explore the land of Canaan,
but he finds instead the exquisite pleasure of sexual relations with a
woman. The name *Raḥav* (Rahab), which means "broad, wide," is ap-
propriate for this prostitute, for contact with her has enabled the
speaker to move beyond the narrow confines of childhood. Hillel
Barzel suggests a possible play on the transformation from his ob-
servation of the "thin feminine form" to her identification as Rahab,
the "broad one," who allows him to break through the authoritative
wall of the control of sexuality.[26] The speaker experiences orgasm as
if it were the transformation of the greenish Yarkon River into flowing
gold. This is the gold he has sought in his new land, and he is de-
lighted to have discovered it. Gilboa's association of sexual initiation
with the spies entering the land of Canaan may reflect the fact that
for him and for others of his generation, adolescent rebellion took
the form of leaving home to pursue the Zionist dream:

מִיֶּשֶׁם בַּמְּעַרְבָּל שֶׁחוֹבֵק אֶת דַּקַּת-הַגִּזְרָה
וְהִיא הֲלֹא רָחָב!
רָחָב!
עַל אָזְנָהּ מִי לוֹחֵשׁ?
וְהֵיכָן יָדִי?
הֲרֵי יָדַעְתִּי אֶת יָדִי!
הִנֵּה הֵן!
הִנֵּה הֵן עָלַי רָחָב.
רָחָב!
מִכְרֶה יָצָאתִי לְבַקֵּשׁ
וָאָרֶץ.
וְהִנֵּה הַנָּךְ שֶׁלִּי, רָחָב, רָחָבָתִי שֶׁלִּי, רָחָב!
אֵיכָכָה זֶה הָפַךְ שִׁטְפוֹ שֶׁל הַיַּרְקוֹן כֻּלּוֹ
זָהָב!

198

Who's that in the whirlpool embracing the thin feminine figure
and is she not Rahab!
Rahab!
In her ear who whispers?
And where are my hands?
But I know my hands!
Here they are!
Here they are upon Rahab.
Rahab!
A mine I went to seek
and land.
And here you're truly mine, Rahab, my Rahab, Rahab!
How did the Yarkon's flow now turn completely into
gold!

In her poem *"Ha'elah shel 'Avshalom"* ("Absalom's Oak")[27] Rachel
Chalfi makes use of the image at the end of the story of Absalom's
rebellion against his father King David, when Absalom dies after his
hair is caught in the branches of a tree (II Samuel 18:9–15), to por-
tray the active role of a woman in sexual intercourse. Absalom pro-
vides a fitting image for the portrayal of sexual intercourse because
in the Bible he is portrayed as exceedingly handsome: "No one in all
Israel was so admired for his beauty as Absalom; from the sole of his
foot to the crown of his head he was without blemish" (II Samuel
14:25). The Bible also recounts that he would let his hair grow so
long that when it was cut, "[it] weighed two hundred shekels by the
royal weight" (II Samuel 14:26). This long hair may have added to his
sensual attractiveness. Absalom serves Chalfi's purposes also be-
cause he engaged in sexual relations with his father David's concu-
bines during the period of his rebellion against David's rule (II
Samuel 16:20–23). These images of the long-haired, handsome Absa-
lom who sexually uses his father's concubines in his attempted rise
to power coalesce to form the image of an aggressive, sensual male.
Yet, just as Absalom was ultimately defeated when his hair was
caught in an oak, the Absalom of Chalfi's poem is caught in the oak
(*'elah*, of feminine gender in Hebrew), a representation of his being
overwhelmed by the sensuality of a woman with whom he has sex-
ual intercourse:

הָאֵלָה שֶׁל אַבְשָׁלוֹם

הָאֵלָה אוֹרֶבֶת לְאַבְשָׁלוֹם
שָׁרָשֶׁיהָ מְעֻצָּבִים
לִקְרָאתוֹ
בַּדֶּיהָ רוֹטְטִים פֶּתַח
דַּהֲרָתוֹ
שֶׁלֹא לוֹמַר עֲצַבֶּיהָ פְּתוּחִים
לְלָכְדוֹ
בְּדָיוֹת חֲלוֹמוֹתָיו לֹא הֶעֱלוּ
כָּל כָּךְ הַרְבֵּה עָלְוָה מִתְנַשֶּׁמֶת
כָּל כָּךְ עָלְוָה מְיֻחֶמֶת עָלָיו
מִסְתּוֹר לְעֶרְוַת הָאֵלָה
אַדְווֹת רַעֲדָתוֹ בִּתְלִיָּתוֹ
יְרֻקּוֹת אֲפֵלוֹת
שְׂעָרוֹ הוּא כְּבָר שְׂעַר
הָאֵלָה
סִימְבִּיוֹזָה שֶׁל גֶּבֶר
וְעֵץ מִמִּין נְקֵבָה
שׁוּב הַמִּיתוֹס שֶׁל דְּלִילָה אֲבָל
זוֹרֵם בְּגִידֵי עֵצָה
מַמָּשִׁי הַשָּׂרָף נוֹטֵף
מַמָּשִׁי בַּקַּרְקֶפֶת הַמֻּשֶׁלֶת
לְאַט   בִּבְעָתָהּ
מִפַּעַם בְּעֵצָה טוֹרֶפֶת דַּעְתּוֹ   דַּעְתָּהּ
בְּעֹמֶק הָאֵלוֹת   כַּמָּה
כַּמָּה   הַלּוּלָה
אֲבֵלָה   שָׁלוֹם

ABSALOM'S OAK

The oak lies in wait for Absalom
Her roots shaped
to greet him
her branches trembling open to
his galloping
to say nothing of her nerves open

200

to trap him
the fantasies of his dreams never raised
so much foliage breathing
so much foliage in heat for him
hiding place for the nakedness of the oak
the ripples of his trembling as he's hung
dark greens
his hair is already the hair of
the oak
a symbiosis of male
and a tree of feminine gender
again the myth of Delilah but
flowing in the sinews of a tree
really the serpent dripping
really through its head whose skin has shed
slowly   in horror
beating at a tree making him crazy   and also her
in the valley of the oaks   how much
how much   jubilation
mourning   peace

The female figure in the poem, the tree, undermines the expectation of the male that he will be the active partner in intercourse. She traps and overwhelms him with a sexual desire more powerful than he imagined any woman possessing. As Delilah had done to the long-haired Samson, the tree has robbed Absalom of any power he thought he had and instead has established her equality with him as her foliage and his hair become entangled symbiotically. The male sense of power associated with the ejaculation of semen is matched by the image of the tree's resin: not only the male actively puts forth a life-sustaining substance, but also the female. In the end, the tree's sensuality is too much for Absalom, and so while their sexual encounter ends with both at peace, the tree mourns her overpowering effect on her male lover.

The biblical allusion poems on men and women that we have examined draw on a variety of biblical texts that reflect problematic and satisfying relations between the sexes. Because the Bible does not always provide these poets with images that convey exactly what they want to convey they have at times taken much liberty with the biblical text and changed it to more accurately reflect their own understanding of the central issues that divide and unite the sexes in their time.

Recurring in this poetry is the situation of a wife detached from or at times even hostile to the dreams and commitments of her husband. Aphek's poem *"'Od hu'"* is relatively close to the original biblical story. As in the Bible, in the poem Michal is contemptuous of David's ecstatic self-expression. Aphek, however, moves beyond the biblical account to portray an ongoing erotic tension between Michal and David in which her contempt for his actions drives him to withhold himself sexually from her throughout their marriage. Carmi's poem *"Ḥavvah yad'ah"* draws on the fact that in the Bible Eve assumes an active role when she convinces Adam to defy God's prohibition of eating of the tree of knowledge. In Carmi's version Eve seduces Adam to abandon himself to sensuality in defiance not of God, but of conventional social norms.

Other poems develop stories of wives detached from their husbands' commitments out of biblical stories that do not explicitly refer to such a situation. In Gilboa's *"Sarai"* Sarah's life is portrayed as a purposeless, frustrating series of wanderings that have nothing to do with the divine purpose that the Bible states was the reason for Abraham's journey. In Reich's *"'Eshet Lot: hamabat le'aḥor"* Lot's wife has nothing but contempt for his decision to settle in Sodom and maintain their residence there right up to the moment of its destruction. In Sivan's *"Le'ah haytah"* and in Ravikovitch's *"Kemo Raḥel"* Jacob's two wives Leah and Rachel do not express any interest in the fact that they are partners in Jacob's historical role as the progenitor of the Israelites. In *"'Al ḥayyei hamin shel ha'ish Mosheh"* Sivan portrays the tension between Moses' relationship with God and his relationship with his Ethiopian wife. It is significant that in none of these poems, whether written by a male or a female author, is the female biblical character viewed negatively for not sharing her husband's commitments. At best the husbands' commitments are portrayed as irrelevant to the interests and needs of the wives, and at worst as actually hostile to their well-being.

It is striking how many of these poems, by both male and female authors, deal with the sexual abandonment of women by men. None of the biblical stories on which these poems are based directly portray such abandonment, so each poet has adjusted the story accordingly. In Aphek's *"Sarah haytah"* Sarah suffers deep jealousy when Abraham in effect carries on an affair with Hagar and forgoes relations with her. In Kafri's *"'Eshet Potifar"* the biblical Potiphar's wife is changed from a scheming seductress to a woman seduced and then abandoned by Joseph, who goes on to do quite well for himself while she languishes in humiliating rejection. In Sivan's *"Tamar"* the central issue for Tamar is not her desire to have a child, as it is in the Bible, but rather her loss of sensual experience after the death of her husbands Er and Onan. In Sivan's *"'Al ḥayyei hamin shel ha'ish Mosheh"* Moses' Ethiopian wife's demands that he fulfill his conjugal obligation go unheeded. In Aphek's *"'Od hu'"* David resists all attempts by Michal to seduce him into having sexual relations with him. Both male and female poets have much sympathy for these sexually frustrated female characters whose husbands have withdrawn by dying, getting involved with another woman, or sublimating their sexual desires.

For the most part, in both the poems about wives being detached from their husbands' commitments and those about husbands sexually withdrawing from their wives the female characters are portrayed as possessing less power and influence than the male characters. This trend reflects the concern these poets share with feminist critics of Israeli culture that the culture is not as egalitarian in nature as is sometimes thought. However, like feminist writers who have presented new readings of the Bible with the purpose of creating female heroines who could serve as role models for contemporary women, some of these poets portray women as possessing a great deal of power either to find fulfillment beyond the marital relationship, particularly in their role as mothers, or to take the initiative in engaging a man in sexual relations. Both in Aphek's *"Sarah haytah"* and in Gilboa's *"Sarai"* Sarah is able to transcend the pain of being detached from Abraham when she gives birth to Isaac. In Aphek's poem the birth provides Sarah with the joy and attachment to another human being that had been absent in her marriage. In Gilboa's poem the birth provides Sarah with a sense of fulfillment that the journey to Canaan to which Abraham was so committed could never provide her.

Tamar in Sivan's *"Tamar"* must wait for Judah to reconnect her with sexual experience. In three poems, however, a female character takes charge of sexual relations with a male character: Eve in Carmi's *"Ḥavvah yad'ah,"* Rahab in Gilboa's *"Raḥav,"* and the oak in Chalfi's

"Ha'elah shel 'Avshalom." In each case the man is led by the woman to give up something for the sake of sexual abandonment: Adam leaves his naming of the creatures; the speaker who has sex with Rahab forgoes his childhood innocence; and Absalom sacrifices his autonomous self in the deathlike experience of orgasm.

Male power to set the cultural agenda and initiate sexual relations, these poets are saying, is often exercised to the great detriment of women. In their relative powerlessness, however, women have much to teach men. The dominant male biblical figures of Adam, Joshua (with whom the speaker in *"Rahav"* is associated), and Absalom are forced to abandon that which distances them from women and submit to a female-initiated sensuality. This sensuality, these poets are saying, could help resolve the tensions between the sexes and free them to engage in mutually satisfying relationships.

CHAPTER FIVE

BUT SUCH IS
HEAVEN'S WAY
AND MAYBE
NATURE'S WAY
AS WELL | SECULAR
ISRAELIS
AND RELIGIOUS
FAITH

At the drafting of Israel's Declaration of Independence in 1948, a heated discussion arose over whether the document should express gratitude to God for the establishment of the new Jewish State. As David Ben-Gurion later recalled, when Rabbi Yehuda Maimon proposed that the document acknowledge the "Rock and Redeemer of Israel" a Marxist politician, "who happened to be the son of a rabbi, insisted that God was not responsible for the coming into being of the state and wanted no credit given Him."[1] The drafters of the Declaration finally accepted Ben-Gurion's suggestion that they compromise by accepting "only the words 'Rock of Israel' which every group might interpret according to its own philosophy."[2] The Marxist politician who raised the objection to the reference to God could live with Ben-Gurion's compromise suggestion because he shared with Rabbi Maimon a sense that the establishment of the State of Israel was the product of an abiding force. Although for Rabbi Maimon the force was of divine origin, for the Marxist politician the force was, presumably, the rocklike determinism of historical forces that led to the establishment of the State.

Zionism had already drawn so heavily on religious terminology from the Bible and from rabbinic tradition that it is it not surprising that the drafters of the Declaration of Independence considered using references to God such as "Rock" (*tsur*) and "Redeemer" (*go'el*) of Israel. It is conceivable that had it not been for the objection of this Marxist politician, the other drafters of this document might have gone along with Rabbi Maimon's insistence on a religious interpretation of the historical event: apparently no one objected when Ben-Gurion invited another rabbi, Yehuda Leib Fishman, to recite the *sheheheyanu* blessing, the traditional prayer of thanksgiving, following the signing of the Declaration.[3] Nevertheless, the vehement opposition of the Marxist politician was also true to the secular nature of the Zionist challenge to the biblical and rabbinic world views. This argument at the moment of the birth of the State represents an issue central to Israeli culture and of obvious relevance to a proper understanding of the relationship of Israeli poetry to the Bible: the tension between the secular Israeli world view and the concepts of God in the Bible and later traditional Jewish texts.

So many of the Israeli poems on biblical themes we have explored in this book reflect secular Israeli culture by eliminating God from their versions of biblical stories. Glenda Abramson observes that "this absence of God [in Israeli poetry] is perhaps not surprising in the work of a group of intellectuals whose own literary tradition has been tempered by contact with a clearly nontheological body of Western European and American [secular] writing."[4] Perhaps even more decisive a factor in the absence of God in their poetry is that these poets are the product of secular Zionism, originally established as one of several cultural and political options open to European Jews who had lost their religious faith under the influence of Western secularism in the late nineteenth and early twentieth centuries.

A central thrust of secularism, as Eliezer Schweid notes, was that it "raised the human being beyond human limits as the inheritor of the divine rule that was pushed aside."[5] This directly challenged central biblical concepts developed by rabbinic Judaism. As a secular movement, Zionism rejected the traditional notion of the dependence of the Jew on God and instead advocated more active human effort to fulfill the needs of Jews to sustain themselves physically, to determine their values and life style, and to protect themselves from political forces that caused them suffering. The Jewish people, Zionism claimed, must not wait for the supernatural intervention of God and His Messiah to redeem them from exile; instead, they must take matters into their own hands and establish and maintain a Jewish state by means of all the economic and political skills they can develop. Jews, secular Zionists also believed, are not subject to the authority of the code of Jewish law that the Jewish tradition claimed was sanctioned by God; therefore, personal morality and the laws of society in the new Jewish State must be based on human judgment, not divine authority.

A central feature of the discourse of secular pre-State Zionists and Israelis of the period of the State has been the removal of religious terms and expressions from their religious contexts and their transformation into terms and expressions that reflect a secular world view. Good examples of this process may be found in an address delivered in 1962 by Baruch Kurzweil, a scholar of modern literature who identified as a traditional Jew. In that address he argued that the secular insistence on letting human beings inherit the role that tradition once reserved for God represented a grave spiritual danger for Israeli culture. "The sanctification of modern life," he argues in the address, "gave birth to a pseudo-sanctification of the gods of the nation and the state."[6] Kurzweil heaps scorn on examples of the expression in contemporary Hebrew of this secularization of the Jewish religious tradition, such as the transformation of the biblical verse "the guardian of Israel [i.e., God] neither slumbers nor sleeps" (Psalms 121:4) into the contemporary slogan "the Israel Defense Forces neither slumber nor sleep," and the transformation of the biblical verse "who can tell the mighty acts [gevurot] of the Lord" (Psalms 106:2) into the line in a popular Israeli Hanukkah song, "who can tell the might [gevurat] of Israel." Once, Kurzweil relates in disgust, he even heard someone refer to an educational institution with the words addressed by God to Moses when He revealed Himself in the burning bush: "remove your sandals from your feet, for the place on which you stand is holy ground" (Exodus 3:5). From the viewpoint of secular Israelis these examples represent a creative secularization of traditional Jewish culture to more adequately reflect their world view. For Kurzweil, however, the elevation of human institutions such as the army and the schools to a status replacing that of the divine is nothing less than a modern form of idolatry, for it involves in his words "the raising of a limited, temporary value to the level of the absolute."[7]

Despite the persistent challenges to religious faith in Israeli society, there have been continuing signs of interest on the part of secular Israelis in spiritual matters. This may be attributed to what S. Zalman Abramov refers to as "the crisis of secularism"[8] that emerged after the establishment of the State. For Jewish settlers in the pre-State period their commitment to the Zionist dream could function as a secular national substitute for the spiritual passions of their traditional Jewish parents. "They believed," as Gershon Shaked puts it, "that they were the vanguard of a cultural renaissance. They were the principal proponents of the process of secularization: With their help religious culture could become the basis for a reconstructed secular Jewish culture."[9] As Abramov notes, with the establishment of the State, "a good deal of the original voluntary aspect [of the pre-State period] was lost. Activities previously carried on on a voluntary basis were now largely taken over by the state."[10] In effect, Abramov observes, the citizens of the new State were asked to trade in the spirit of voluntary pioneering for patriotic loyalty to the State. "With all its highly gratifying elements," Abramov argues, "the emergence of an Israeli patriotism could not bridge over the void created by the decline of Zionist ideology."[11]

An example of the emergence of this crisis of secularism, characterized by what Herbert Weiner refers to as "the realization of a vacuum in the spiritual life of [Israel's] residents,"[12] may be found in an interview of Yaakov Dori conducted by Weiner in the 1950s. Dori, then president of the Technion in Haifa, told Weiner of his immigration to Israel as a young boy. As he grew up, he recalls, he was well educated in the Bible but not in other aspects of the Jewish tradition. The efforts he and other Zionists engaged in to establish the State gave their lives sufficient meaning. Once the State was established, however, he began to feel that something was lacking in his life. "There is much yet to be built," he explains, "but everybody knows now that this is it, this is life in the Jewish state, and lo and behold it leaves something unfulfilled and unsatisfied."[13] The citizens of the new State of Israel have begun to realize, Dori states, that "it is evident there are problems in life that cannot be solved by great events or politics."[14] This realization has led him and others to be more open to considering the teachings of religious tradition: "I don't say that religion can solve them either," he admits, "but they are problems that religion at least deals with."[15]

Since the early years of the State there have continued to be signs of interest on the part of secular Israelis in maintaining some connection with the Jewish religious tradition. Many secular Israelis engage in at least a partial observance of the rituals of the Jewish tradition, and a small percentage of the secular population has found spiritual meaning in praying at synagogues sponsored by non-Orthodox Jewish movements of the Diaspora.[16] This concern about maintaining a connection with the Jewish religious tradition received official sanction when in 1994, after cultural and political leaders in Israel became alarmed at the distancing of secular Israeli youth from the sources of the Jewish tradition, the government appointed a commission chaired by Aliza Shenhar to explore how to incorporate more effectively the teaching of Jewish tradition in state-sponsored secular schools.

Two important barriers continue to make it difficult for many secular Israelis to connect with the Jewish tradition and thereby possibly arrive at a measure of religious faith. One is the image of religion presented to the public by the Israeli religious establishment. Since the early years of the State, religious political parties were able to establish Orthodox Judaism as the only form of Judaism with official recognition. This helped Orthodoxy succeed in establishing a cultural assumption in Israel that the only way to be religious was to be Orthodox. On the basis of this assumption, Abramov observes, "it logically followed that secularism was the only ideological alternative to Orthodoxy, there being no religious alternative."[17] This distancing of secular Israelis from religion was reinforced on the level of the Hebrew language as well. As Abramov notes, "the word *religion* in the Western sense has no equivalent in the Hebrew language."[18] The term used for religion, *dat,* means law, thereby, as Abramov observes, equating observance of traditional Jewish law with religiosity.[19]

Over time, Shaked notes, Israeli culture has become increasingly divided between those who embrace Western secularism and those who follow Orthodox Judaism.[20] Secularists have little use for religion, which they see as represented by an Orthodoxy that has the political power to impose aspects of religious law on all Israeli citizens, particularly in the realm of marriage and divorce, which often conflicts with the needs of the individuals affected. Dovish secular Israelis are alienated from religion because of the uncompromising attitude of many religious Israelis to the rights of Palestinians to parts of the Land of Israel.

The second barrier making it difficult for secular Israelis to connect with the Jewish tradition derives from one main difference between the secular and religious world views: the extent to which one can conceive of a God who actively intervenes in history. In recent decades, especially since the Six-Day War, as Nurith Gertz has observed, right-wing secular Israeli nationalists have to an extent embraced the religious notion of divine intervention in contemporary Israeli history. It would appear, Gertz notes, that there is an inherent contradiction between the traditional Jewish religious reliance on divine power and the secular Israeli reliance on the power of the military to protect Israel. This contradiction, Gertz argues, has been resolved by the claim of right-wing Israelis that divine power is asserted by means of the power of the Israeli army. As an example she quotes an Israeli journalist who described Israel's conquest of the Old City of Jerusalem in the Six-Day War: "The Messiah arrived yesterday in Jerusalem, tired, gray, riding on the back of a tank. . . . The Messiah this time was wearing a uniform. A man of the Israel Defense Forces, a Jewish warrior. . . . I saw him."[21]

This belief that contemporary Israeli history is a manifestation of God's providence has appealed to a large segement of religious Israelis, although it has been largely rejected by ultra-Orthodox Jews in Israel, and to right-wing Israelis comfortable with the use of theological concepts. Many secular Israelis, however, have not found it easy to accept such a belief. A story is told that in the period of the aftermath of Israel's conquest of the West Bank in 1967, a participant in a meeting with Prime Minister Levi Eshkol suggested that, just as Israel annexed parts of Palestine it conquered in the War of Independence, Israel should now annex the West Bank. The participant's argument for this annexation was that God Himself had intervened in history to give Israel the opportunity to grow territorially as a result of the 1948 war, and He did so once again in 1967. The man referred to this divine intervention with the expression *'etsba' 'elohim* ("the finger of God"), which Pharaoh's magicians used to express their opinion to Pharaoh that the third plague suffered by Egypt before the Exodus came from God (Exodus 8:15): "What's the difference?"

he declared. "The finger of God moved King Hussein to start a war so that we could return to the land of our forefathers. The finger of God cleared them out of Ramla and Jaffa in '48; maybe, with God's help and a little help from us, the same thing will happen in Nablus, Bethlehem, and Hebron."[22] Eshkol, however, expressed his hesitancy to accept the argument. He was not so sure that Israel's victory was God's doing and that the Jews could assume God would always be on its side. After all, the Jewish people had suffered greatly; it would appear that either God does not intervene in history, or, if He does, He does not always do so for the benefit of the Jews. Filled with such doubts about God's role in history, the notion of undertaking the politically and militarily risky action of annexing the West Bank was too frightening for him to contemplate. "The finger of God? Did you say 'the finger of God?' " Eshkol asked the man. "If so," Eshkol went on to say, "then all the death and destruction throughout our history was the finger of God. Maybe the finger of God really is giving us Hebron now. Maybe. Who knows? *Obber ich hob moire* [a Yiddish expression meaning "I am afraid"]."[23]

Shulamith Hareven, an outspoken dovish opponent of religious and right-wing expansionist ideologies, was asked in an interview what she thought the divine plan for the world was. She responded that as human beings it is really impossible to know the answer to that question. "We do not have a common language with this other Being [God], who is so very different from ourselves that He is, by definition, unfathomable."[24] From Hareven's point of view, neither Judaism nor any other religion can actually discover the divine plan in the way that the Bible and later rabbinic tradition claim. Instead, Hareven insists, the concept of God conceived of by human beings must be seen as an inadequate attempt "to explain all the things they do not understand."[25] As Hareven puts it, "that is precisely the argument I have with all religions. Nothing they say about God, none of the excuses they make for God, can answer the fundamental questions."[26]

As for God's role in bringing about evil or good in human affairs, Hareven calls for eliminating any consideration of such a divine role. The deaths of over sixty million people in World War II, Hareven maintains, were caused by "man, all by himself, not God."[27] If we look to God to repair the evil of the world, Hareven argues, then we denegrate the value of the individual as a contributer to this repair. "In essence," she declares, "every admission of the existence of God means disdain for the individual and makes the individual cower."[28] She rejects therefore all attempts to conceive of God contributing to the improvement of the world. "Repair of the world," she argues, "concerns us. It is not commanded from the heavens, but by us and for us, so that things will be better for all of us. I suggest we not mix God up in this."[29]

Some secular Israeli poets explore religious issues in their poems. For the most part, these poems struggle with the central issue of religious faith: to what extent do our human experiences convince us that we must despair of finding meaningful fulfillment in our existence, and to what extent do they convince us that, as religious people believe, we can find that fulfillment?[30] One of the foremost representatives of this trend in Israeli poetry is Yehuda Amichai, who refers frequently in his poetry to God and religious experience.[31] Speaking as one who rejected his upbringing in a traditionally observant home, Amichai admits to an interviewer that he continues to be preoccupied by the question of meaning and purpose in the cosmos that has preoccupied the Jewish religious tradition since biblical times. "Nothing is purposeless," he states. "There must be some reason for everything, which we don't understand."[32]

Boaz Arpali argues that in Amichai's poetry God represents " 'the objective order' of the world, as it is perceived by the Amichaian human being who observes it, that is, as a large mechanism of processes over which the human being has no influence, and which in their essence oppose his existence, and are even hostile to it."[33] Even if he has ceased to believe in God in the traditional sense and he no longer practices Jewish ritual, Amichai keeps writing about God because, as Arpali suggests, it is a way to represent the basic human drive to make sense of existence. "And truly in the poetry of Amichai," Arpali maintains, "the presence of God . . . perhaps has in it an expression of the poet's refusal to empty the world of the human being of the wish for meaning."[34] In a similar vein, Glenda Abramson observes, "Amichai's God . . . represents the poet's own sense of need for universal order and his personal quest for meaning."[35]

Several biblical allusion poems address the question of the nature of the relationship between human beings and God. The examples I explore in this chapter are by members of both generations of Israeli poets included in this study, and the dates of the publication of the poems range from the late 1950s to the early 1990s. In these poems we find two barriers to the secular poet's willingness to embrace traditional Jewish notions of God, which are parallel to the two barriers to religious faith encountered by secular Israelis in general. One barrier, parallel to the secular Israeli's alienation from the Israeli Orthodox religious establishment, is a discomfort with what the poets consider to be inhumane positions taken by religious figures submitting to the will of God as they understand it. The other barrier, parallel to the skeptical attitude of the secular Israeli to concepts of divine intervention in history, is the crisis of faith set off by the persistence of human suffering, unalleviated by divine power, in both the Holocaust and Israel's wars. As these poets try to come to terms with the biblical faith in a divine being whose powers transcend those of humanity they are driven to reconsider biblical notions of God as Creator of the Universe and God as a Redeemer who intervenes in human history.

The Dangers of God Obsession

The poem "ʾAvraham" ("Abraham"),[36] by Meir Wieseltier, makes use of the Bible's prime example of religious faith, Abraham, to present a secular critique of excessive preoccupation with the divine. Abraham's close relationship with God, even to the extent of his willingness to sacrifice his son Isaac, provides Wieseltier with a setting to raise serious questions about the gap between the religious and secular world views. As a secularist, Wieseltier suspects the religious world view of denying the basic needs of everyday human existence. The speaker of the poem is highly critical of Abraham's rejection of idolatry and his perfect, almost inhuman devotion to God throughout his life:

אַבְרָהָם

הַדָּבָר הַיָּחִיד שֶׁאָהַב אַבְרָהָם בָּעוֹלָם הָיָה אֱלֹהִים.
הוּא לֹא אָהַב אֶת אֱלֹהֵי הָאֲנָשִׁים הָאֲחֵרִים,
שֶׁהָיוּ עֲשׂוּיִים עֵץ אוֹ חֹמֶר וְשֻׁנְצְבְעוּ בְּשָׁשַׁר,

שֶׁיּוֹצְרָם הָיָה בָּא כָּל עֶרֶב אֶל אִשְׁתּוֹ וְסוֹבֵא בָּשָׂר וָיַיִן,
שֶׁנִּמְכְּרוּ בְּשׁוּק הָעִיר כְּבָצָל, לְכָל הַמַּרְבֶּה בִּמְחִיר :
הוּא חָשַׁב לוֹ אֵל מִשֶּׁלּוֹ וְעָשָׂה עַצְמוֹ בְּחִירוֹ.

וּמִכֹּל שֶׁהָיָה בָּעוֹלָם אָהַב רַק אוֹתוֹ-אֱלֹהִים.
הוּא לֹא הִשְׁתַּחֲוָה לֵאלֹהֵי הָאֲחֵרִים ; הוּא אָמַר לָהֶם : אִם תֵּימִינוּ
אַשְׂמְאִיל, אִם תַּשְׂמְאִילוּ אֵימִינָה.
הוּא אָמַר : לֹא יֹאמַר, אָנֹכִי הֶעֱשַׁרְתִּי.

הוּא מֵאֵן לְקַבֵּל דָּבָר מֵאָדָם אוֹ לָתֵת דָּבָר לְמִישֶׁהוּ,
זוּלַת הָאֵל. זֶה, אִלּוּ רַק בָּא לְבַקֵּשׁ
הָיָה מְקַבֵּל. כָּל דָּבָר. אֲפִלּוּ יִצְחָק הַיָּחִיד, הַיּוֹרֵשׁ הָרַךְ
(אַךְ אִם יֵשׁ אֱלֹהִים, יֵשׁ לוֹ גַּם מַלְאָךְ).

הוּא לֹא הֶחֱשִׁיב בָּעוֹלָם אֶפֶס דָּבָר, רַק הָאֵל.
לוֹ לֹא חָטָא מֵעוֹדוֹ, לֹא הָיָה בֵּינֵיהֶם הֶבְדֵּל.
לֹא כְּמוֹ יִצְחָק, שֶׁאָהַב אֶת בְּנוֹ גַּס-הַמֹּחִין, לֹא כְּמוֹ יַעֲקֹב
שֶׁעָבַד בַּעֲבוּר נָשִׁים, שֶׁצָּלַע מִן הַמַּכּוֹת שֶׁהִכָּהוּ הָאֵל בַּלַּיְלָה,
שֶׁרָאָה סֻלָּמוֹת מְמֻלְאָכִים רַק בַּחֲלוֹמוֹת.
לֹא כֵן אַבְרָהָם, שֶׁאָהַב אֶת הָאֵל וְהָאֵל אֲהֵבוֹ.
וְעִמּוֹ הָיָה עוֹשֶׂה אֶת חֶשְׁבּוֹן צַדִּיקֵי הַמָּחוֹז, בְּטֶרֶם יַחֲרִיבוֹ.

ABRAHAM

The only thing in the world that Abraham loved was God.
He didn't love the gods of other people,
made of wood or clay and painted with lacquer,
created by one who would come each evening to his wife and
    consume meat and wine,
that were sold in the town's market like onions to the highest
    bidder:
he thought up his own God and made himself His chosen one.

And of all that was in the world he loved only that God.
He didn't bow to the others' gods; he said to them: if you go
    right
I'll go left, if you go left I'll go right.
He said: No one will say I enriched him.

He refused to take anything from anyone or to give anything
   to anyone,
except God. This one, if He only came to ask
He would get. Anything. Even Isaac the only one, the young
   heir
(but if there's a God, He also has an angel).

He didn't take into account anything in the world, only God.
Against Him he never sinned, between them there was no
   difference.
Not like Isaac, who loved his coarse-minded son, not like
   Jacob
who worked for the sake of women, who limped from the
   blows that God dealt him at night,
who saw angeled ladders only in dreams.
Not Abraham, who loved God and God loved him.
And with him He made an accounting of the righteous of the
   region, before He destroyed it.

Abraham's devotion to God is portrayed here not in the positive light
of Genesis, but rather as motivated largely by a disturbing self-
isolating individualism. In Genesis, when Abraham and his nephew
Lot discuss how to divide the land between them, Abraham in a self-
effacing and generous spirit says to Lot, "If you go north [or: right], I
will go south [or: left]; and if you go south [or: left], I will go north
[or: right]" (Genesis 13:9). In the context of the poem, however, Abra-
ham's words make him come across as an extremely stubborn per-
son who takes a position contrary to that of others just because it is
so important to him to be different. In the Bible Abraham refuses to
accept gifts offered to him by the King of Sodom because he does not
want to be beholden to other people and feels free to take such a po-
sition because of his trust in God's providence (Genesis 14:22-23). In
the poem, this refusal to accept the King of Sodom's gifts is trans-
formed into a position that Abraham takes of being so distant from
people that he does not want to take anything from them or to give
them anything; he wants only to take from and give to God. The
speaker's Abraham is saved from the folly of his willingness to give
everything, including his beloved son Isaac, to God only by the

intervention of an angel of God who prevents Isaac's slaughter (Genesis 22).

The speaker is impatient with the absolute, perfect faith of Abraham, which to the speaker is so much less attractive than the down-to-earth involvements with reality of the later patriarchs Isaac and Jacob. Most disturbing to the speaker, however, is the apparent collusion between Abraham and God in the destruction of Sodom and Gomorra. Abraham's argument with God to save the cities if at least some righteous people can be found in them (Genesis 18:16-33) is seen by the speaker as calculating the sum of the righteous or perhaps as preparing the bill for the righteous who unfairly will pay in the destruction of these cities the same price as do the evil people.

Yehudit Kafri's poem *"Bare'shiyyot"* ("In the Beginnings")[37] critiques Abraham's willingness in the binding of Isaac story to be more loyal to God than to the human bond of love between parents and children:

בְּרֵאשִׁיּוֹת

בְּרֵאשִׁיּוֹת הָעֲמוּמוֹת שֶׁלָּנוּ
מְחַלְחֵל הַסִּפּוּר הַזֶּה:
אָב
בְּנוֹ
וְהַמַּאֲכֶלֶת.
אֵיךְ זֶה קָרָה?
וְאֵיפֹה הָיְתָה שָׂרַי?
אֵיךְ הִיא יָכְלָה לִסְמֹךְ
עַל אֵל כָּל כָּךְ עָרִיץ
שֶׁיָּגֵן בָּרֶגַע הָאַחֲרוֹן?
לָמָה הִיא לֹא צָעֲקָה
עוֹד קֹדֶם,
כְּשֶׁרָק רָתַם אֶת הַחֲמוֹר
וְהֶעֱמִיס אֶת הָעֵצִים:
אַל תִּשְׁלַח יָדְךָ
אֶל הַיֶּלֶד?!
לָמָה הִיא לֹא נֶעֶמְדָה
בְּאֶמְצַע הַדֶּרֶךְ
וְלָחֲשָׁה מִבַּעַד לִשְׂפָתַיִם חֲשׁוּקוֹת:

לֹא תַעֲבֹר בַּדֶּרֶךְ הַזּוֹ
כָּל עוֹד אֲנִי חַיָּה!
לֹא אֶת הַיֶּלֶד הַזֶּה
שֶׁחִכִּינוּ לוֹ מֵאָה שָׁנָה,
לֹא אֶת הַיֶּלֶד
שֶׁבְּנַפְשֵׁנוּ.

In the Beginnings

In our dim beginnings
this story penetrates:
a father
his son
and the slaughtering knife.
How did it happen?
And where was Sarai?
How could she depend
on a God so tyrannical
to protect at the last moment?
Why didn't she shout
even early on,
when he just hitched the donkey
and loaded the wood:
Do not raise your hand
against the boy!?
Why didn't she take a stand
in the middle of the road
and hiss through pursed lips:
You'll not pass this way
as long as I live!
Not this child
for whom we waited a hundred years,
not this child
who's in our soul.

The speaker insists that Sarah, who is curiously absent from the biblical account of the binding of Isaac, should have acted on autonomous human moral instinct to oppose that which Abraham perceived as a divine command. From the speaker's point of view, the God to whom Abraham remained loyal is not to be trusted. True, in the biblical account an angel of God stops Abraham at the last minute from sacrificing his son Isaac. The speaker, however, does not believe that God sends angels to save religious fanatics from their acts of madness. In the speaker's version of the binding of Isaac, therefore, Isaac's only hope is for his mother Sarah to speak the words of the biblical angel, "*al tishlaḥ yadekha*" ("do not raise your hand," Genesis 22:12) before Abraham and Isaac set out on their journey to Mount Moriah. Only Sarah, the speaker believes, can assert that the connection between Isaac's soul and the souls of Abraham and Sarah is of greater value than the connection between Abraham and God.[38]

The God of Creation Reconsidered

Nathan Zach and Dan Pagis address in biblical allusion poems the need to reconsider after the Holocaust what the Bible relates about God's creation of the universe. In different senses both poets may be seen as Holocaust survivors: Zach left Germany in 1935 at the age of five; as a child Pagis actually experienced the Holocaust. The childhood worlds of both poets were destroyed in this period of the triumph of evil. Each poet suggests that after a period so plagued by human suffering it is difficult to accept the biblical accounts of the Creation and the relationship between God and humanity that these accounts imply.[39]

In Zach's poem "*Keshe'elohim 'amar bapa'am hari'shonah*" ("When God First Said")[40] the divine Creator is portrayed as having only a limited interest in the universe He is creating:

כְּשֶׁאֱלֹהִים אָמַר בַּפַּעַם הָרִאשׁוֹנָה

כְּשֶׁאֱלֹהִים אָמַר בַּפַּעַם הָרִאשׁוֹנָה יְהִי אוֹר
הוּא הִתְכַּוֵּן שֶׁלֹּא יִהְיֶה לוֹ חָשׁוּךְ.
הוּא לֹא חָשַׁב בְּאוֹתוֹ רֶגַע עַל הַשָּׁמַיִם
אֲבָל הָעֵצִים כְּבָר הֶחֵלוּ מִתְמַלְּאִים מַיִם
וְצִפֳּרִים קִבְּלוּ אֲוִיר וְגוּף.

אָז נָשְׁבָה הָרוּחַ הָרִאשׁוֹנָה אֶל עֵינֵי אֲדוֹנֵנוּ
וְהוּא רָאָה אוֹתָהּ בְּמוֹ עֵינֵי עֶנֶן כְּבוֹדוֹ
וְחָשַׁב כִּי טוֹב. הוּא לֹא חָשַׁב בְּאוֹתוֹ רֶגַע
עַל בְּנֵי־הָאָדָם, בְּנֵי־אָדָם לָרֹב.
אֲבָל הֵם כְּבָר הִתְחִילוּ לַחְשֹׁב עַל עַצְמָם בְּלִי עָלִים
וּכְבָר הֶחֶלָה מִתְרַקֶּמֶת בְּלִבָּם
מְזִמָּה עַל מַכְאוֹב.
כְּשֶׁאֲדוֹנֵנוּ חָשַׁב בַּתְּחִלָּה עַל הַלַּיְלָה
הוּא לֹא חָשַׁב עַל שֵׁנָה.
כָּךְ, כָּךְ אֶהְיֶה מְאֻשָּׁר, אָמַר בְּלִבּוֹ הָאֱלֹהִים הַטּוֹב.
אֲבָל הֵם כְּבָר הָיוּ לָרֹב.

WHEN GOD FIRST SAID

When God first said Let there by light
He meant it would not be dark for Him.
In that moment He didn't think about the sky,
but the trees already were filling with water,
the birds receiving air and body.
Then the first wind touched God's eyes
and He saw it in all His glory
and thought It is good. He didn't think then
about people, people in their multitude,
but they already were standing apart from the fig leaves,
unraveling in their hearts
a scheme about pain.
When God first thought of night
He didn't think about sleep.
So be it, God said, I will be happy.
But they were multitudes.

The only part of nature created by God in this version is the light created on the first day according to Genesis 1. This light was created by an essentially self-centered divine being whose only purpose was that "it would not be dark for Him." Subsequently, the process of Creation develops spontaneously without any of the control with which God shapes the universe in the Bible. God enjoys the emergence of the universe and says, like God in Genesis 1, "It is good." Such a divine being, however, who has not invested anything of Himself in the Creation, can hardly be expected to be concerned with the fate of the universe. In His enjoyment of this emerging universe, He is blissfully unaware of the initiatives of human beings who are already on the way to ruining the good universe that was created, "unraveling in their hearts / a scheme about pain." In their multitudes they will have plenty of power to overwhelm with evil the universe whose creation was set off by God's call for light, and God will be powerless to stop them because He waited too long to take control.

In two poems, "*Edut*" ("Testimony") and "*Edut 'aheret*" ("Another Testimony")[41] Dan Pagis explores by means of the form of courtroom testimony the ways that the events of the Holocaust radically challenge basic assumptions about the nature of humanity underlying the account of Creation in Genesis 1. In the testimony in the first poem the speaker focuses on the statement in Genesis 1 that God created humanity "in the image of God" (Genesis 1:27). For the speaker, the contrast between the characteristics and fate of the Nazi victimizers and those of their Jewish victims was so great that it is difficult to conceive of both types of human beings as having been created by the same God. The speaker begins by rejecting the commonly held assumption that the Nazis, exceeding the bounds of normal human behavior, had somehow turned themselves into amoral monsters:

עֵדוּת

לֹא לֹא: הֵם בְּהֶחְלֵט
הָיוּ בְּנֵי-אָדָם: מַדִּים, מַגָּפַיִם.
אֵיךְ לְהַסְבִּיר. הֵם נִבְרְאוּ בְּצֶלֶם.

TESTIMONY

No no: of course they
were human: uniforms, boots.
How to explain it. They were created in the image.

Ironically, the speaker is forced to conclude that if the Nazis were human beings then he and his fellow victims belonged to a different category of humanity:

אֲנִי הָיִיתִי צֵל.
לִי הָיָה בּוֹרֵא אַחֵר.

וְהוּא בְּחַסְדוֹ לֹא הִשְׁאִיר בִּי מַה שֶּׁיָּמוּת.
וּבָרַחְתִּי אֵלָיו, עָלִיתִי קַלִּיל, כָּחֹל,
מְפֻיָּס, הָיִיתִי אוֹמֵר: מִתְנַצֵּל:
עָשָׁן אֶל עָשָׁן כֹּל יָכוֹל
שֶׁאֵין לוֹ גּוּף וּדְמוּת.

I was a shadow.
I had a different maker.

And He in His mercy left nothing in me to die.
And I fled to Him, rising so light, blue,
appeased, I'd say: apologetic:
smoke to omnipotent smoke
that has no body or form.

The triumph of the Nazis over the victims suggests that the former were created and protected by a demonic God who gave them power and the capacity for great cruelty. They were the human beings who, according to the Bible, were created "in the image of God" (*betselem 'elohim,* Genesis 1:27). A different God must have created the victim in His image, which the speaker considers to be as substantial as "shade" (*tsel,* a Hebrew word made up of two out of three letters of the Hebrew word for image, *tselem*). The God of those whose bodies were turned into smoke in the crematoria did not help them, presumably because He too is no more powerful or substantial than smoke. Sadly, the victim is so degraded by his experience that he somehow feels the need to apologize to this powerless God who did not save him. In portraying the ineffectual, insubstantial nature of this victim's God, the speaker uses the expression *she'eyn lo guf udemut,* which alludes to the *Yigdal* prayer that poetically presents the belief of the medieval Jewish philosopher Maimonides in an incorporeal God: *'eyn lo demut haguf ve'eyno guf* ("He does not have the image of a body and He is not a body"). Maimonides' lofty notion of a God without a body is transformed by the victim into a notion of a powerless God. He also juxtaposes the medieval Hebrew philosophical term for "omnipotent" with the Hebrew word for "smoke" (*'ashan kol yakhol*); this ironically suggests that the victim knows his God is as omnipotent as the ephemeral smoke into which his body was transformed in the crematorium.

In the second poem it is not the speaker who offers the testimony. The speaker begins the poem by turning to God who, although eternal, appears to share humanity's inability to comprehend the injustices of the Holocaust. According to Deuteronomy, when the local communities in ancient Israel found a legal case too difficult to resolve, they were supposed to turn to the central legal authorities:

> If a case [or: judgment] is too baffling [or: wondrous] for you to decide, be it a controversy over homicide [literally: between blood and blood], civil law [literally: between law and law], or assault—matters of dispute in your courts—you shall promptly repair to the place which the Lord your God has chosen, and appear before the levitical priests, or the magistrate in charge at the time, and present your problem. (Deuteronomy 17:8-9)

Now after the Holocaust God is as confused as humanity. His only recourse, the speaker asserts, is to pay closer attention than He had before to the suffering of the Holocaust victim:

עֵדוּת אַחֶרֶת

אַתָּה הָרִאשׁוֹן וְאַתָּה הַנִּשְׁאָר אַחֲרוֹן,
כִּי יִפָּלֵא מִמְּךָ מִשְׁפָּט בֵּין דִּין לְדִין
בֵּין דָּם לְדָם,
הַקְשֵׁב לְלִבִּי הַקָּשֶׁה בַּדִּין, רְאֵה אֶת עָנְיִי.

ANOTHER TESTIMONY

You are the first, and You remain the last,
If You're not able to judge between plea and plea,
between blood and blood,
listen to my heart, hardened in judgment, see my plight:

One traditional Jewish interpretation of the puzzling use of the plural in God's utterance, "Let us make man" (Genesis 1:26) is that God consulted with the angels before creating humanity. On the basis of this interpretation, the speaker imagines the archangels Michael and Gabriel testifying as eye witnesses who share God's guilt for having created human beings capable of genocide:

מְשֻׁתְּפֵי-הַפְּעֻלָה שֶׁלְּךָ, מִיכָאֵל, גַּבְרִיאֵל,
עוֹמְדִים וּמוֹדִים
שֶׁאָמַרְתָּ: נַעֲשֶׂה אָדָם,
וְהֵם אָמְרוּ אָמֵן.

Michael, Gabriel,
Your angel collaborators,
stand and admit
that You said: Let us make Man,
and they said Amen.

God's Role in History Reconsidered

The Holocaust also raises questions about the biblical view of God as the ruler of the universe who preserves the moral integrity of human affairs by intervening in history to save those who suffer from their oppressors. In "*Kemo ḥol*" ("Like Sand"),[42] Zach questions God's role in history by reflecting in the poem on God's promise to Abraham to make his descendants "as numerous as the stars of heaven and the sands on the seashore" (Genesis 22:17):

כְּמוֹ חוֹל

כְּשֶׁאֱלֹהִים בַּתַּנַ"ךְ רוֹצֶה לְהַבְטִיחַ,
הוּא מַרְאֶה עַל כּוֹכָבִים.
אַבְרָהָם יוֹצֵא מִפֶּתַח אָהֳלוֹ בַּלַּיְלָה
וְרוֹאֶה אוֹהֲבִים.
כְּמוֹ חוֹל עַל שְׂפַת הַיָּם, אוֹמֵר אֱלֹהִים,
וְהָאָדָם מַאֲמִין. אַף כִּי הוּא עַצְמוֹ מֵבִין
שֶׁלּוֹמַר כְּמוֹ חוֹל, הִיא רַק לָשׁוֹן כִּבְיָכוֹל.

וּמֵאָז נִשְׁאֲרוּ הַחוֹל וְהַכּוֹכָבִים שְׁלוּבִים
בְּרֶשֶׁת הַדְּמוּיִים שֶׁל הָאָדָם. וְאוּלַי לֹא כְּדַאי
לְעָרֵב כָּאן אֶת הָאָדָם. לֹא עָלָיו דֻּבַּר אָז שָׁם.

וַהֲרֵי נֶאֱמַר בִּמְפֹרָשׁ כְּמוֹ חוֹל, וּמְמֵילָא מְדֻבָּר
גַּם עַל הַיְכֹלֶת לִסְבֹּל. אוֹ שֶׁמָּא אֶפְשָׁר לַחְשֹׁב שֶׁהַכֹּל
הֻתַּר אָז וְאֵין עוֹד, בְּפֵרוּשׁ אֵין עוֹד, גְּבוּל.

כַּחוֹל עַל שְׂפַת הַיָּם. וַהֲרֵי אֵין שָׁם מִלָּה עַל מַיִם. וּבְפֵרוּשׁ
מְדֻבָּר שָׁם עַל זֶרַע. אֶלָּא שֶׁכָּךְ הוּא מִדֶּרֶךְ הַשָּׁמַיִם
וְאוּלַי גַּם מִדֶּרֶךְ הַטֶּבַע.

LIKE SAND

When God in the Bible makes a promise
he points to the stars.
Abraham leaves his tent at night
and sees lovers.
Like sand on the seashore, God says,
and man believes it. Even though he knows
"like sand" is only a figure of speech.
Since then sand and stars remain tangled
in the web of human metaphor. And maybe it's senseless
to speak here of men. They weren't spoken of just then.

Look, it says explicitly "like sand," and this must mean
the ability to suffer. Or do you think that nothing
was forbidden then and there's no longer—explicitly no
longer—any limit.

Like sand on the seashore. Look, there's not a word there
about water.
And it explicitly says "seed." But such is Heaven's way
and maybe Nature's way as well.

As Chana Kronfeld notes, this poem is largely about God's figurative
language in which He makes His promise of a large progeny to Abra-
ham. Throughout the poem there is a tension between the perspec-
tive of God reflected in divine speech and the way that humanity in-
terprets that speech.[43] God points to the stars of heaven and

Abraham sees human lovers, who will actually bring about the increase in the numbers of human beings. In believing in God's promise human beings realize that whatever language is used to express that promise reflects human experience more than it reflects divine reality, but as a consequence it is unclear to human beings what their role in the scheme of things is because it wasn't humanity that was "spoken of just then." Such a tension between the divine and human perspectives allows for the possibility that the divine perspective is not valid when applied to human experience. God's covenant with Abraham and later with Israel is contradicted by the reality of human suffering, and so perhaps God never really promised Abraham that He would prevent human suffering.

From a human point of view something is missing from the linking of the images of "sand" and "seed," for God never mentions the water necessary to nourish the seed. It is significant that the title Zach chose for the poem modifies the original biblical simile "like sand" from *kaḥol* to *kemo ḥol;* the latter connotes a more mundane image than does the original biblical term. Perhaps, the speaker muses, there is a way to discern a connection between God's biblical language that expresses "heaven's way" and our human perspective of "nature's way." Perhaps our understanding that the increase of our progeny comes from human seed is somehow connected to Heaven's promise to be the cause of that increase. Zach seems to suggest in this poem that the gap between the divine and human perspectives leads human beings to doubt the efficacy of God's supernatural power in the world.[44] This conclusion forces human beings to rely on their understanding of reality and to try by natural means to change the world and hope that in some sense they are helping God to fulfill His will.

In Zach's poetic version of the Daniel story, *"Dani'el begov ha'arayot"* ("Daniel in the Lions' Den")[45] Daniel's descent into the lions' den represents the descent of so many victims in the poet's time into the realm of suffering:

דָּנִיֵּאל בְּגֹב הָאֲרָיוֹת

כְּשֶׁדָּנִיֵּאל יָרַד לְגֹב הָאֲרָיוֹת
הוּא מָצָא שָׁם חֲשֵׁכָה וּצְעָקָה

וּגְוִיּוֹת נִלְפָּתוֹת זוֹ בָּזוֹ. דָּנִיֵּאל הָיָה
נָבִיא, הוּא מוֹפִיעַ בְּסֵפֶר כְּתוּבִים, בִּזְהִירוּת
עָשָׂה אֶת דַּרְכּוֹ, כְּדֵי לֹא לְהַכְאִיב לַאֲחֵרִים, הָאֲרָמִית
לְצִדּוֹ. צַעַד אַחַר צַעַד וְאַחַר
הַקֹּר וְזִכְרוֹן צִדְקָתוֹ. דָּנִיֵּאל בָּכָה.
אֵלִי אֵלִי לָמָה עֲזַבְתָּנִי, לָמָה בְּגֹב הָאֲרָיוֹת
נְתַתָּנִי. וְאֵיךְ אֵצֵא.
אֵיךְ עָשִׂיתָ לִי, אֱלֹהִים, דָּבָר כָּזֶה.

וֵאלֹהִים מַחֲרִישׁ. לֹא אִישׁ הוּא אֱלֹהִים.
לִשְׁמֹעַ. לֹא אִישׁ הוּא אֱלֹהִים
לִתְבֹּעַ אֶת עֶלְבּוֹנָם שֶׁל נְבִיאָיו
בְּעֱנוּתָם.

DANIEL IN THE LIONS' DEN

When Daniel descended to the lions' den
he found there darkness and shouting
and bodies wound around each other, Daniel was
a prophet, he appears in the Book of Writings, carefully
made his way, so as not to hurt the others, Aramaic
by his side. Step following step and following
the cold and the memory of his righteousness. Daniel wept.
My God, my God, why have You forsaken me, why in the lions'
    den
have You placed me. And how will I get out.
How did you, God, do such a thing to me.

But God is silent. God is not a man
to hear. God is not a man
to avenge His prophets' honor
in their suffering.

As he enters this realm of suffering Daniel is careful to maintain his
moral integrity and not cause any more suffering to those around
him. In deep pain, however, he cries out to God the verse from
Psalms, "My God, my God why have You forsaken me?" (Psalms
22:2). God, however, is silent. As the speaker ironically comments,

"God is not a man / to hear. God is not a man / to avenge His prophets' honor." In His transcendent unwillingness to interfere in history, even to save His prophets, God is on a morally *lower* plane than Daniel, who at least was sensitive enough to make his way carefully lest he hurt his fellow human beings.

To the amazement of the speaker Daniel is actually able to transcend his perplexity and despair by accepting his suffering:

אוּלָם רְאוּ זֶה פֶּלֶא, שִׁמְעוּ, דָּנִיֵּאל כְּבָר קָם, שָׁר: הוּא
מַשְׁלִים עִם הֶחָסֵר, אוֹמֵר אֵין דָּבָר, יֶשׁ לוֹ מַה לוֹמַר
עַל הַמַּמְלָכָה וְהוּא כְּבָר אוֹמֵר. לֹא כֻּלָּם
מְבִינִים אֲבָל הַשָּׁעָה דּוֹחֶקֶת.
אַחֲרֵי הַמַּמְלָכָה הַשְּׁלִישִׁית תָּבוֹא
הָרְבִיעִית. מִי מֵבִין? רֶגַע שֶׁקֶט. אַךְ
לֹא אִישׁ הוּא דָּנִיֵּאל כְּיוֹנָה וְהוּא גַם בָּא אַחֲרָיו בַּסֵּפֶר: הוּא
לֹא יִבְרַח, אֲרָיוֹת הֵם צִירָיו וּשְׁלִיחָיו, וּפְסוּקָיו כַּמַּתֶּכֶת,
אִם גַם צְרִיכִים הֵם תַּרְגּוּם. אֲנִי הָאִישׁ, אֲנִי שֶׁבָּאתִי לְכָאן
מִן הַלֹא-כְלוּם. אֲנִי דָּנִיֵּאל מְאֹד
וְרַעְיוֹנוֹתַי יְבַהֲלוּנִי וַאֲמָרַי יִשָּׁמְעוּ
עַד שֶׁיֵּאוֹר הַיּוֹם אוֹ עַד שֶׁבִּמְקוֹם אַחֵר,
זוֹהַר, יִהְיֶה גּוּפִי הַקָּרוּעַ מְלַבְלֵב. אֲנִי דָּנִיֵּאל
מְאֹד. לֹא דָּנִיֵּאל כְּאֵב.

But, look at this wonder, listen, Daniel has already risen, he
    sings: he
makes peace with what is missing, says it's all right, he has
    something to say
about the kingdom and he already says it. Not everyone
understands but the hour is pressing.
After the third kingdom will come
the fourth. Who understands? Quiet a moment. But
Daniel is not a man like Jonah and he also comes after him in
    the Book: he
will not flee, lions are his representatives and messengers,
    and his verses are like metal,
even if they also need translation. I am the man, I who came
    here

from the nothing. I am very much Daniel
and my thoughts will terrify me and my words will be heard
until day breaks or until in another place,
splendorous, my torn body blooms. I Daniel
very much. Not Daniel pain.

Daniel is not only on a higher moral plane than God ("God is not a man to hear"); he is also on a higher moral plane than the prophet Jonah ("Daniel is not a man like Jonah"). He will not flee the scene of suffering but will stand his ground and warn the people of the future emergence of evil ("After the third kingdom will come / the fourth.") He will do so even though it is not clear that anyone understands him, for he speaks in the obscure Aramaic language of most of the book of Daniel. Daniel refuses to be defined by his suffering. He will be "Daniel / very much," declaring to all the vision of suffering that he beholds, but "not Daniel pain."

Thus, by conflating Daniel's role in the biblical story as a predictor of the future and his punishment of being thrown into the lions' den, Zach creates an image of the modern individual, perhaps the poet himself, who is powerless to stop human suffering but who accepts the difficult challenge of not turning away from the suffering and calling on humanity to come to terms with it. Zach's most radical departure from the biblical story of Daniel is that in the poem God does not rescue Daniel from the lions' den:

וּבְאוֹתוֹ הַלַּיְלָה נָדְדָה שְׁנַת הַמֶּלֶךְ
וַיִּזְכֹּר אֶת דָּנִיֵּאל הַנָּתוּן כָּל אוֹתוֹ לַיְלָה
בֵּין הַמְּצָרִים, גֶּבֶר בִּגְבָרִים, בְּתוֹךְ הַבּוֹר
שֶׁבּוֹ הֻשְׁלַךְ לִהְיוֹת טֶרֶף לַכְּפִירִים. וַיִּתְעוֹרֵר
מִשְּׁנָתוֹ הַכְּבֵדָה לִפְנוֹת בֹּקֶר וּבְשַׂעֲרוֹתָיו נְחָשִׁים
וְהָאֶבֶן אֲשֶׁר הֻכְּתָה אֶת הַצֶּלֶם הָיְתָה
לְהַר גָּדוֹל וַתִּמָּלֵא אֶת כָּל הָאָרֶץ
וְאֵין פּוֹתֵר.

And that night sleep deserted the king
and he remembered Daniel caught that whole night
between the narrow straits, a man among men, within the pit
to which he was cast to be prey to the lions. And he awoke

from his heavy sleep at dawn and in his hair were snakes
and the rock that hit the image became
a large mountain and filled the whole world
but there is no one to explain.

God's relationship to Daniel's suffering is referred to with an expression from the book of Esther that refers to King Ahasuerus ("that night sleep deserted the king," Esther 6:1), an expression from the Noah story in Genesis ("God remembered Noah," Genesis 8:1). and the term *bor* (pit), which comes from the first chapter of the Joseph story (Genesis 37:22-28). God is as unaware of reality as Ahasuerus, and, although like God in the Noah story He remembers His faithful servant, in this poem He is powerless to save Daniel, even in the indirect way that He does so by guiding Joseph's fate from the time he was thrown in the pit by his brothers until his ascent to a position of great prominence in Egypt. "The rock that hit the image (*hatselem*)" may be understood to be the suffering that destroyed for all of humanity the dignity of the images of God and humanity. Daniel appears here as the other great dream interpreter of the Bible, Joseph, cast into the pit (*bor*) by his brothers. In the poem no one can interpret Daniel's suffering and give it meaning (*'eyn poter*), as Joseph and Daniel had interpreted royal dreams. Nevertheless, Daniel does not submit to the destructive force of despair. He asserts his will to live despite the fact that the meaningfulness of faith in God is not available to him.

Even more strongly than he does in his poem on Daniel, in the poem "*Lif'amim mitga'gea'* ("Sometimes He Longs For")[46] Zach ironically critiques God's lack of intervention in human affairs. The poem portrays God as nostalgically longing for Job after he has died:

לִפְעָמִים מִתְגַּעְגֵּעַ

לִפְעָמִים מִתְגַּעְגֵּעַ אֱלֹהִים
עַל עַבְדּוֹ הַמָּתוֹק אִיּוֹב. אֲבָל הוּא מֵת.
אִיּוֹב רָחוֹק כָּעֵת מֵאֱלֹהִים
כְּמוֹ מִדְּבָרִים אֲחֵרִים, מַלְאָכִים.
מַה יַּעֲשֶׂה אֱלֹהִים?

הוּא קוֹרֵא — תַּאֲמִינוּ אוֹ לֹא —
בַּתְּהִלִּים. עֲדַיִן אֵינוֹ יוֹדֵעַ עַל־פֶּה,

וְהַדְּבָרִים כָּאן כָּל כָּךְ מַרְגִּיעִים:
כָּל כָּךְ הַרְבֵּה שִׁירִים.
יָם גָּדוֹל וּרְחַב יָדַיִם וְאֵין
מִסְפָּר חַיּוֹת קְטַנּוֹת עִם גְּדוֹלוֹת
וְעֵצִים, הֲמוֹן עֵצִים, וְתָמִיד מַיִם.

'אֵין חֹשֶׁךְ וְאֵין צַלְמָוֶת',
הוּא מְשַׁנֵּן לְעַצְמוֹ בְּקוֹל רָפֶה
וְאַחַר זוֹכֵר דְּבַר-מַה בְּתוֹכֵחָה אוֹהֶבֶת:
אֱלֹהִים כְּבָר בּוֹכֶה,
מְסָרֵב לְהִנָּחֵם, אֵין לוֹ נִחוּמִים
עַל עַבְדּוֹ הַמָּתוֹק אִיּוֹב, הַמָּתוֹק בָּעֲבָדִים,
שֶׁכָּל גַּלְגַּל עַיִן שֶׁלּוֹ הָיָה כְּמוֹ גַּן עֲדָנִים,
לֹא הָיָה כְּעַבְדּוֹ אִיּוֹב, עַד הַיּוֹם הַזֶּה, בְּכָל הַזְּמַנִּים.

SOMETIMES HE LONGS FOR

Sometimes God longs for
his sweet servant Job. But he died.
Now Job is as far from God
as from other things, angels.
What will God do?

He reads—believe it or not—
in Psalms. He still doesn't know them by heart,
but the words are so soothing:
so many songs.
A vast, spacious sea and numberless
small animals alongside large ones
and trees, a lot of trees, and always water.

"No darkness and no shadow of death,"
he drills into himself in a quiet voice
and then recalls a thing or two with loving rebuke:
God is already crying,
refuses to be consoled, he has no consolation
for his sweet servant Job, the sweetest of servants,
each eyeball of his a garden of delight,
there was never anyone like his servant Job, to this day, in all
    ages.

God longs not for Job as he is portrayed throughout the poetic sec-
tion of the biblical book, strenuously demanding that God explain to
him his suffering, but rather for the pious Job suffering in silence in
the introductory prose section of the book. What bothers God so
much is that no one except Job has been willing to put up with suf-
fering without a protest: "there was never anyone like his servant
Job, to this day, in all ages." It is clear that the poet has no sympathy
for God's misery. The ironic image of God finding comfort in the book
of Psalms, which "He still doesn't know . . . by heart" that Jews have
traditionally used to find comfort in God makes clear that in the eyes
of the poet something is terribly wrong. Indeed the expressions in
Psalms 104:25 that so draw God to the text—"a vast, spacious sea
and numberless" and "small animals alongside large ones"—glorify
nature but have nothing to say about the experience of innocent suf-
fering for which the Job figure is a paradigm. God, it seems would like
to ignore what the concluding verse of that psalm ("may sinners dis-
appear from the earth and the wicked be no more [Psalms 104:35]")
says about the world, namely that evil people who cause human suf-
fering continue to mar the world. It is also significant that the well-
known verse in which the psalmist declares his confidence that God
is with him even in the "valley of the shadow of death" (Psalms 23:4)
is transformed in God's reading into "No darkness and no shadow of
death," as if He refuses to recognize the reality of the pain that Job
and so many other human beings have suffered.

How human beings respond to suffering and how they imagine
God causing or alleviating suffering are explored in poems by Dan
Pagis about the biblical characters Saul and Job. In *"Tefillat Sha'ul
ha'aharonah"* ("Saul's Last Prayer")[47] Pagis imagines the first king of
Israel praying to God, presumably shortly before he commits suicide
rather than fall into the hands of the enemies of Israel who have de-
feated him in battle (I Samuel 31):

תְּפִלַּת שָׁאוּל הָאַחֲרוֹנָה

אֱלֹהַי, כִּבְקָר בְּחָרִישׁ
בֵּין כָּל אֲבָנֶיךָ הָיִיתִי אֵיתָן.
בְּעֹל רְעָמֶיךָ הָיִיתִי מַחֲרִישׁ.
וַתְּהִי שְׁתִיקָתִי לִי לְשָׂטָן.

יָגַע אֲנִי. וְאַתָּה אֶת מְעִיל הַמַּלְכוּת
מֵסִיר מִכְּתֵפַי, וּבְתֹם רְגָבֶיךָ טוֹמֵן
אַרְגְּמַן צְבָאֲךָ הַשָּׁחוּט.
הוֹ אֱלֹהַי, הָרָם, הָרוֹדֶה,
הַיּוֹרֵד לְנַפְשִׁי כְּסוּפָה לַשָּׂדֶה,
קְצִירְךָ לְפָנֶיךָ. אָמֵן.

SAUL'S LAST PRAYER

My God, like cattle at the plowing
among all Your stones I was strong.
In the yoke of Your thunder I was silent.
But my silence became my foe.

I'm tired. And You the mantle of royalty
remove from my shoulders, and in the innocence of Your
        furrows You bury
the purple of Your slaughtered army.
O my God, the exalted one, the tyrant,
who descends to my soul like a storm to the field,
Your harvest is before You. Amen.

Saul sees himself as the loyal servant of God, who like the hard-working oxen does his master's bidding. He realizes now that the greatest barrier to his survival is his willingness to suffer all that accompanies this role, never to protest. God's power to set the day of a person's death cannot be challenged by humanity. Saul realizes, however, that humanity still has the power to question the justice of God bringing mortality to human beings. Having been beaten down by the tyrannical and arbitrary power of God, Saul portrays his death ironically as the planting of his dead army and the harvest of his soul. For Saul only in the indirectly ironic tone of this prayer can he express at least in part the anger that he feels toward God for how He has treated him.

In his prose poem "*Derashah*" ("Homily"),[48] Pagis presents a secular sermon that sharply dissents from the original biblical story of Job. In the poem Pagis uses Job's ignorance of the wager between God and Satan (Job 1-2) to represent the incomprehensibility of the

Holocaust to the survivors. The speaker refers to this wager as if it were a competitive sports contest between Job, representing God, and Satan. The speaker's complaint that the contest is unfair refers to the poet's sense that much of the pain of the Holocaust came from the inability of the victims to discern cosmic meaning in their suffering:

דְּרָשָׁה

גּ. כְּבָר מֵרֹאשׁ לֹא הָיוּ הַכֹּחוֹת שְׁקוּלִים: הַשָּׂטָן שַׂר גָּדוֹל בַּמָּרוֹם, וְאִיּוֹב בָּשָׂר וָדָם.
מִלְּבַד זֶה לֹא הָיְתָה הַתַּחֲרוּת הוֹגֶנֶת. אִיּוֹב שֶׁקֻּפַּח אֶת עָשְׁרוֹ וְשָׁכַל אֶת בָּנָיו וּבְנוֹתָי
וְהֻכָּה בִּשְׁחִין לֹא יָדַע כְּלָל שֶׁזּוֹ תַּחֲרוּת.

HOMILY

From the start, the forces were unequal: Satan a grand seigneur in heaven, Job mere flesh and blood. And anyway, the contest was unfair. Job, who had lost all his wealth and had been bereaved of his sons and daughters and stricken with loathsome boils, wasn't even aware that it was a contest.

God's reply out of the whirlwind to Job's insistent pleading (Job 38-41) becomes in Pagis's version a penalty given by the referee of the competition (*shofet* can mean judge in the human or divine sense, as well as referee). In the Bible Job is rewarded for humbly accepting God's reply by having his wealth restored and by having new children (Job 42). Pagis's Job gets a similar reward for ceasing to complain about his suffering. Still unaware of the cosmic significance of the Holocaust, however, he does not even realize that his survival is a kind of victory:

כֵּיוָן שֶׁהִתְלוֹנֵן יוֹתֵר מִדַּי, הִשְׁתִּיק אוֹתוֹ הַשּׁוֹפֵט. וְהִנֵּה, כֵּיוָן שֶׁהוֹדָה וְשָׁתַק, נִצַּו
בְּלֹא שֶׁיֵּדַע, אֶת יְרִיבוֹ. וּבְכֵן הוּשַׁב לוֹ עָשְׁרוֹ וְנִתְּנוּ לוֹ בָּנִים וּבָנוֹת — חֲדָשִׁיַ
כְּמוּבָן — וְנִטַּל מִמֶּנּוּ אֶבְלוֹ עַל הָרִאשׁוֹנִים.

Because he complained too much, the referee silenced him. So, having accepted this decision, in silence, he defeated his opponent without even realizing it. Therefore his wealth was restored, he was given sons and daughters—new ones, of course—and his grief for the first children was taken away.

The compensation of Job's restored wealth and new children (*pitsuy*, a word used in Hebrew to refer to the reparations paid by Germany to Israel and to Holocaust survivors after World War II), may seem obscenely inappropriate, for it can never make up for Job's original suffering. The fact that Job did not understand why he was suffering may be as terrible as the fact that the Holocaust survivors could never understand why they suffered. The speaker, however, finds an even more disturbing fact. Echoing the rabbis' assertion that "Job never existed, but was just a parable" (Baba Batra 15a), the speaker asserts that the most terrible thing about the Holocaust is that it cannot be compared to the Job story. In the real life historical experience of the Holocaust there is no cosmic significance:

יָכֹלְנוּ לַחְשֹׁב שֶׁהַפְּצוּי הַזֶּה הוּא הַנּוֹרָא מִכֹּל; יָכֹלְנוּ לַחְשֹׁב שֶׁהַנּוֹרָא מִכֹּל הוּא חֶסְרוֹן דַּעְתּוֹ שֶׁל אִיּוֹב, שֶׁלֹּא הֵבִין שֶׁנִּצַּח, וְאֶת מִי. אֲבָל הַנּוֹרָא מִכֹּל הוּא בָּזֶה, שֶׁאִיּוֹב לֹא הָיָה וְלֹא נִבְרָא, אֶלָּא מָשָׁל הָיָה.

We might imagine that this retribution was the most terrible thing of all. We might imagine that the most terrible thing was Job's ignorance: not understanding whom he had defeated, or even that he had won. But in fact, the most terrible thing of all is that Job never existed and was just a parable.

Searching for God

I conclude this chapter with the poem "*Midrash Yonah*" ("Midrash Jonah")[49] by Maya Bejerano, which more than any other poem I have included holds out the hope for the contemporary Israeli to find God despite the modern breakdown of faith in the God of

Nature and the God of History. As Pagis did in the title of his poem "Derashah," Bejerano in the title of this poem presents it as a secular homiletical interpretation of the biblical text, in this case the story of Jonah.

The choice of Jonah as a figure who tries to come to terms with the differences between God and humanity represents a reversal of the portrayal of Jonah in the Bible. Indeed, the central theme of the book of Jonah is a theological disagreement between Jonah and God. Jonah defies God by fleeing to Tarshish rather than fulfill the divine commandment to prophesy against the wicked city of Nineveh. After Jonah finally delivers his prophecy to Nineveh, the people repent, and God refrains from punishing them. Jonah then declares to God that he cannot accept God's forgiveness of the people of Nineveh and that he had fled to Tarshish originally because he had suspected that God would eventually forgive them: "O Lord! Isn't this just what I said when I was still in my own country? That is why I fled beforehand to Tarshish. For I know that You are a compassionate and gracious God, slow to anger, abounding in kindness, renouncing punishment" (Jonah 4:2).

In the poem, when he travels to Tarshish Jonah is not fleeing God, but rather bravely seeking a greater understanding of Him:

מִדְרַשׁ יוֹנָה

יוֹנָה
יוֹנָה כַּמָּה אֹמֶץ
אֹמֶץ לָדַעַת הָיָה בְּךָ,
לֹא פָחוֹת וְלֹא יוֹתֵר מֵרַחְבּוֹ וְעָמְקוֹ שֶׁל הַיָּם;
כִּי רַק בּוֹ רָצִיתָ,
נָשֵׂאתָ וְהִטַּלְתָּ אֶל יָם הָאֶפְשָׁרֻיּוֹת הַגּוֹעֵשׁ,
בְּקַשְׁתְּךָ לָבוֹא.
וּכְמִסְפַּר הָאֲנָשִׁים אֱמוּנוֹת יֵשׁ.

וְהַיָּם שָׁתַק מְזֻעְפּוֹ
בְּקַבְּלוֹ אֶת פָּנֶיךָ בְּתוֹכוֹ.
בְּרִיחָתְךָ הַנּוֹעֶזֶת תַּרְשִׁישָׁה נֶהְפֶּכֶת לִצְלִילָה נֶחֱרֶצֶת לִקְרָאתוֹ
צְלִילַת שִׁיאָן נִצְחִי שֶׁל הַכָּרַת הָאֱלֹהִים
תְּנוּעַת בְּרִיחָה — תְּנוּעַת צְלִילָה,
שְׁתֵּי טְעָנוֹת סוֹתְרוֹת

עַל רְצוֹנוֹ שֶׁל אֱלֹהִים וּרְצוֹנוֹ שֶׁל הָאָדָם,
עַל רְצוֹנוֹ הַזֶּהֶה שֶׁל אֱלֹהִים לְמַצָּבוֹ הַחוֹלֵשׁ בַּכֹּל
וְעַל חֻלְשַׁת הַפְּעָרִים שֶׁל הָאָדָם לְעֻמָּתוֹ.

MIDRASH JONAH

Jonah
Jonah how much courage
courage to know was in you,
not less or more than the width and depth of the sea;
for it was just that which you wanted,
carried and cast into the stormy sea of possibilities,
you sought to come.
And there are as many faiths as peoples.

And the sea ceased its raging
as it welcomed you in it.
your daring flight to Tarshish transformed into determined
        diving toward Him—
an eternal record dive of acknowledging God
movement of flight—movement of diving,
two contradictory arguments
about the will of God and the will of humanity,
about the will of God identical to His situation overpowering
        all
and about the frailty of the gaps of humanity over against
        Him.

Jonah's search for divine knowledge requires great courage because
it defies the modern assumption that there are many valid beliefs.
His challenge as he is cast into "the stormy sea of possibilities" is to
find the divine truth that might transcend the relativism of human
opinion. As the sea becomes calm and welcomes him to his search
for divine truth Jonah faces the essence of his quest, which is how to
reconcile the will of humanity with the more powerful will of God
that so often thwarts humanity's desires and purposes. Jonah then
undergoes a transformation of identity that allows him to meet God:

כָּךְ רוֹאִים יוֹנָה אֶת הַמַּבָּע הַקָּם וְהַנִּשָּׂא
בְּעֵינֶיךָ הַפְּתוּחוֹת מוּלוֹ,
עֵינַיִם סוּמוֹת מְלוּחוֹת,
בְּדַרְכָּן לִפְגֹּשׁ אוֹתוֹ,
מְלֵאוֹת דְּמָעוֹת שֶׁל יָם הַהַכָּרָה,
וְהַפְּגִישָׁה הַצְּפוּיָה עִם אֱלֹהִים
נֶעְדֶּרֶת הַמָּקוֹם וְהַזְּמַן — בּוֹלְעִים אוֹתְךָ
מְשַׁבְּשִׁים גְּבוּלוֹת זֶהוּתְךָ.

זְמַן מָה אַתָּה הוֹפֵךְ לְדָג עֲנָקִי,
אֲבָל אֲפִלּוּ חַיָּה כְּמוֹ דָּג
יוֹדַעַת מַשֶּׁהוּ עַל אֱלֹהִים, רַחוּם וְנָקִי
שֶׁנָּכְחוּתוֹ הַמֻּחְלֶטֶת בִּבְטָנָה מְנַצַּחַת
וְקוֹלְךָ נִשָּׂא אֵלָיו בְּפַחַד
מִן הַקָּו הֲכִי נִדָּח וְלֹא צָפוּי,
כִּי בִּלְבָבְךָ נָצַרְתָּ אוֹתוֹ, כָּפוּי
מִן הָעֶמְדָּה הָרְחוֹקָה בְּבֶטֶן חַיָּה
לְקַבֵּל מָרוּתוֹ הַיְחִידָה,
כְּכָל שֶׁהִיא מָרָה וְאַחֶרֶת מִשֶּׁלְּךָ;

מָרוּת הַיָּם,
מָרוּת הַיַּבָּשָׁה וְהָרוּחַ
מָרוּת הַקִּיקָיוֹן
מָרוּת הָאֲמוּנָה
וְאַתָּה לְ-אָנָה תֵּלֵךְ

Thus we see, Jonah, the expression gradually arising
in your eyes open before Him,
blind salty eyes,
on their way to meet Him
full of tears of the sea of acknowledgment,
and the expected meeting with God
lacking place and time—you're being swallowed
the boundaries of your identity are being blurred.

For some time you become a giant fish,
but even a creature like a fish
knows something of God, merciful and blameless

whose absolute presence in its belly triumphs
and your voice is raised to Him in fear
from the remotest and least expected line,
for in your heart you preserved Him, forced
from the distant position in the belly of a creature
to submit to His sole authority,
even as it's bitter and other than yours;

the authority of the sea,
the authority of the dry land and the wind
the authority of the gourd
the authority of faith
and you to—toward—where'll you go

Jonah does not get swallowed by a large fish, but rather becomes a fish. This experience leads to an acceptance of the fact that there are elements beyond human control, in both nature and God, that people must accept. Jonah's transformation into a fish represents well the willingness of the prophet in the poem to submit to the authority of God: as the fish is in full harmony with his watery surroundings, so does Jonah discover a way to bring his will in harmony with the divine will.

The book of Jonah ends with God's rebuke of the prophet for mistakenly clinging to the principle of justice to the exclusion of the principle of mercy (Jonah 4:10-11). Jonah never responds to God's rebuke, and so we do not really know if he has submitted to God's teaching. In a similar fashion, the conclusion of the poem is ambiguous. After the speaker reports that Jonah's daring search for God has resulted in his acceptance of divine authority, she turns to the prophet and asks haltingly where the prophet thinks he will go from here: "and you to—toward—where you'll go (*ve'attah le'anah telekh*)." As clearly and forcefully as the speaker captures the process of a human being searching for and meeting God, she cannot envision what effect such an encounter would have on the life of one who undergoes this experience.

On the whole, these secular poets radically question the validity of biblical faith. In Wieseltier's "*Avraham*" and in Kafri's "*Bare'shiyyot*" Abraham's single-minded devotion to God can be seen as nothing less than a life-denying fanaticism that deserves only condemnation. In the post-Holocaust world Zach and Pagis are impelled to envision God in ways that radically depart from His portrayal in the Bible. In several poems God is portrayed as weak, apathetic, powerless. Zach's God of both Genesis and Job loves to contemplate the beauties of nature, but He is oblivious to the realities of human suffering. Zach's God of the Daniel story is a weak figure powerless to save human beings from suffering. Pagis's God of Genesis and Job, as well as his God of the Saul story, is a more sinister figure than He appears to be in Zach's poetry. For Pagis, the God of Creation may have to be seen as two gods: a strong one who created the human monsters, the Nazis, and a weak one who created the defeated victims of the Nazis. Alternatively, Pagis suggests, God is nothing less than a war criminal who created, with his "collaborators" the angels, the human perpetrators of the evils of the Holocaust.

What is to be the human response to this post-Holocaust perception that God is much weaker and less involved in the world than the Bible claims Him to be? Some human figures emerge in these poems who respond constructively and with dignity to this loss of faith in a divine Creator and Redeemer. One cannot escape the impression that in portraying these heroes of faithlessness, the poets are referring to their own role as writers committed to struggle candidly with the loss of religious faith in their time. In Zach's "*Kemo hol*" as the speaker considers the figure of Abraham, he realizes the need to move beyond the reliance on divine promises and redeem himself by natural means. In Zach's "*Dani'el begov ha'arayot*" Daniel shows up God by acting in a more moral manner and not submitting to the despair he feels when he realizes God will not save him from harm. In Pagis's "*Tefillat Sha'ul ha'aharonah*" Saul, in the guise of a prayer, in effect rebukes God for all the suffering He has caused him.

The most impressive hero of the faithless post-Holocaust world, however, is Bejerano's Jonah in "*Midrash Yonah.*" For Bejerano, although her contemporaries have every reason not to seek God, her Jonah figure represents an impelling drive to bridge the gap between the God who defines reality and the inability of humanity to accept that reality. Bejerano's Jonah jumps into the sea of confusion, the result of the loss of religious faith, and thereby risks his autonomous identity as a thinking, critical being. As he concludes his journey he is prepared to accept what to his contemporaries would have to be seen as the outrageous authority of the God who stands behind reality. Although Bejerano admires this acceptance, she is still too skeptical in her world view to be able to conceive of how one could sustain a life based on such acceptance of the will of God.

SAUL WOULD
FIND RELIEF AND
THE EVIL SPIRIT
WOULD
LEAVE HIM | **BIBLICAL**
ALLUSION POETRY
AND THE
SEARCH FOR
MEANING

Although biblical allusion poetry is not limited to the themes I have explored—the Arab-Israeli conflict, the Holocaust, men and women, and God and humanity—these themes are among the most prevalent in such poetry. They reflect issues associated with the most intense relationships that Israelis experience. How Israelis come to terms with these relationships can have a tremendous effect on how they perceive the nature of their existence. To the extent that such intense relationships make Israelis feel that the world is essentially hostile to their existence, they will feel that they are caught in an absurd void of meaninglessness. To the extent that these relationships make Israelis feel that the world is permeated by the love and acceptance of their existence, they will feel that their lives are meaningful.[1]

Because their neighboring Arab enemies have violently challenged their existence, Israelis have been forced to shed Arab blood and to witness again and again the deaths of their fellow soldiers and civilians. Under these circumstances, it has not been easy for Israelis to see the world as either hospitable or meaningful. Thus, the world has increasingly seemed designed to keep Israelis at the outer limits of anxiety, never knowing if their country will be destroyed some day, or if they will die defending their country.

It is an irony of Israeli history that this increasing sense of vulnerability has made a major contribution to Israeli understanding of the Diaspora experience, including its most tragic period, the Holocaust. Zionist ideology, which promised the Jews they could overcome their role of victim, created a state with an overwhelming number of victims of Arab hostility. As we have seen, not only survivors and their descendants but the vast majority of Jewish Israelis have increasingly felt personally connected to that most hostile of worlds that the Nazis created with the purpose of destroying the Jewish people as a whole. How so many Jewish communities could have been so utterly destroyed in World War II, what Nazi atrocities tell us about humanity and about God, and how the Holocaust might be related to the Arab-Israeli conflict, are all issues that Israelis have struggled with since the end of the war. The lack of clear answers to these questions has intensified the anxiety and sense of meaninglessness experienced by Israelis.

Israeli men and women, like all men and women, deeply wish to experience the acceptance and affirmation that human love can provide. So often, however, in Israeli society, as in the West as a whole, the two sexes have failed to understand each other. The opposite sex has often in fact been perceived more as an enemy than a lover. The sexes have struggled to dominate each other; barriers to erotic fulfillment have at times seemed insurmountable; and the changing role of women in modern society has increased confusion between the sexes.

The Jewish religious tradition, which affirms God's existence, has often appeared oblivious to the human needs of secular Israelis, and so they have concluded that tradition calls on them to choose between what one defines as one's needs and what tradition requires. Western thought has encouraged them to think of human beings as autonomous, free of the need to rely on an outside, caring divine being. In a century plagued by so much untold suffering it has been difficult for secular Israelis to trust in a God who is apparently incapable of defeating evil.

Nurith Gertz notes that many works of Israeli literature reveal a subtext of existential fears not always consciously acknowledged in

Israeli culture: "fear of Holocaust and destruction, . . . the feeling of loneliness in a hostile world, . . . anxiety about history moving in circles with no past and no future."[2] As Leszek Kolakowski observes, we human beings strive to overcome our experience of what appears to be the world's indifference, "and attempts to overcome this indifference constitute the crucial meaning of human struggle with fate, both in its everyday and its extreme form."[3] In general, Kolakowski states, "mythical consciousness . . . is present in every understanding of the world as endowed with values, [and] it is also present in every understanding of history as meaningful."[4] This is certainly the case in Israeli society, whose national myths, as Gertz notes, may be seen as "ideological narratives . . . [whose] purpose . . . [is] to form the society's world view, to give legitimization to its social order, to integrate its members, and to lead them to action."[5]

Kolakowski observes that no culture can escape the paradoxical need for both adherence to myth as a stabilizing source of established values and the opposition to myth for providing too limiting a perspective on life. He notes the danger inherent in members of a culture assuming that the established mythic values, so central to the preservation of "human fellowship, . . . are at any time fixed and completed, that they can relieve one of situational interpretations and situational responsibility for them."[6] To preserve its social usefulness, Kolakowski argues, myths must be "unceasingly suspect."[7]

Roland Barthes also writes of the need to guard against the limitations of myth. Myth, Barthes argues, attempts to convert contingent aspects of history into assertions that are naturally true. While making this claim myth produces a dead and stifling language that "turns [meanings] into speaking corpses" and limits human perspective because of its false claim to represent eternal truths.[8] Barthes looks to poetic language as a force that "resists myth as much as it can."[9]

In turning to the Bible as a source for their own mythopoetic creations, Israeli secular poets demonstrate an appreciation of the value of myth as a conveyer of meaning, while at the same time they demonstrate a need to resist the limitations of mythic thinking based on the Bible. They attempt to meet the cultural challenge put forth by Shulamith Hareven of "not how to negate or kill myth, but how to develop the tools that will let us live well with myth without becoming enslaved to it."[10] In the new versions of biblical texts presented in their biblical allusion poems the poets participate in the Jewish tradition of what Hareven calls "a constant never-ending midrash [which is] one of the strongest and most important ways of overcoming the damage caused by static, sanctified myth."[11] They raise serious questions in their poetry about what Gertz calls "the imaginary view of reality and of history"[12] that is the central means of much of the biblically based ideological narratives that form the basis of Israeli culture.

Israeli biblical allusion poetry, thus, plays both subversive and conservative roles in Israeli culture. It challenges the limited perspectives of the Bible and modern political and cultural myths based on the Bible. It also affirms the importance of the Bible as a source of mythic truths by reworking biblical texts in poems that reflect the modern Israeli's search for meaning.

As they turn to the Bible in their search for meaning, these poets adopt an extremely flexible approach to the biblical text. Like the speaker in Amichai's poem, these poets are virtually unlimited in how far they can go in "confusing" or mixing up a biblical story. God, who is never absent from the Bible for too long, does not often appear in these new poetic versions. Events are sometimes completely reversed: Abraham, not Isaac, is the object of the sacrifice, and Daniel is left in the lions' den. The original heroes of stories are also denigrated, sometimes in favor of alternative heroes: Eve is the being with superior knowledge, not Adam; Lot's wife emerges as much wiser and less corrupt than Lot; Abraham is portrayed as either a lunatic trying to kill his son Isaac or a self-centered religious fanatic turning his back on the rest of humanity; Potiphar's wife is transformed into the innocent victim of Joseph's sexual manipulation; Moses is portrayed as overly ascetic in the insensitive way he imposes celibacy on his Cushite wife; Sisera the Canaanite general is a more attractive figure than Barak the Israelite general.

The anachronisms that abound in this poetry maintain the connection between ancient and modern Israel at the heart of these works. The archangels Michael and Gabriel testify against God in a war crimes tribunal; Eve reflects on what it would be like to live as an exemplary mother in a modern bourgeois home with a well-tended garden; the command to sacrifice Isaac is issued through a loud speaker; Isaac rides to his binding in a steel tank; Isaac and the angel are photographed wearing fancy clothes; Jonah's plunge into the sea is described as if it set a new, unbeatable record for diving; Jeremiah is urged to assassinate King Nebuchadnezzar with a pistol; Job's suffering is a sports match; a contemporary Israeli pilot can fly over and view himself as the man sitting under his vine and his fig tree in biblical times.

The range of possible uses of a biblical story is broad in this poetry. The figure of Abraham represents religious fanatics, men who abandon their wives to carry on affairs, and loving fathers who will not admit that they cannot fully protect their children from harm. The binding of Isaac story conveys the fate of Holocaust victims as well as soldiers who have died in Israel's wars. The story of Absalom provides images to portray bereaved parents during war and men and women in relations of sexual passion.

As these poems establish a link between contemporary experience and the meaningfulness of biblical experience, they keep alive the possibility of discerning meaning in the present. That does not mean, of course, that according to these poets the ways that the Bible transcended anxiety and meaninglessness can always be their way. Yet, even as they recognize the limitations of their attempts to link the ancient past with the present, they reassure their readers that it may be possible to confront that which appears hostile to their existence by knowing that in biblical times such a confrontation yielded the discovery of a larger meaning to human existence.[13]

So many of these biblical allusion poems, however, never seem to fully transcend the void of anxiety and meaninglessness. It is not surprising that such transcendence is generally lacking in those poems that refer to either the Holocaust or the Arab-Israeli conflict. The irrational hatred and violence of war points too strongly to the dominance of the world by hostility and to the failure of human beings to arrive at a more harmonious and meaningful relationship with others. In a century so dominated by war and the threat to Jewish existence, biblical notions of God do not provide much comfort. Indeed, God often seems hostile or at least indifferent to the fate of the Jewish people.

In poems on men and women we find the greatest possibility of harmonious relationships. Many poems on this theme make clear how difficult it is to arrive at such harmony. Some figures however do achieve erotic union in which two individuals are merged, and all misunderstandings, anxieties, and hostilities melt away as they become one flesh. At that moment both feel fully accepted; both feel life is meaningful.

According to the Bible, "whenever the evil spirit of God came upon [King] Saul, David would take the lyre and play it; Saul would find relief and feel better, and the evil spirit would leave him" (I Samuel 16:23). As we saw in the Knesset debate over King David, Jewish tradition also envisions David as singing before God: he is called "the sweet singer of Israel" (ne'im zemirot yisra'el, II Samuel 23:1), whose greatest literary achievement was the poetic book of Psalms that so frequently celebrates the triumph of faith in God over despair.

This study provides a positive answer to the rhetorical question raised by Dor in the title of his poem, "Does David Still Play Before You?" The Israeli authors of biblical allusion poems continue the spirit of David's music and poetry in a manner befitting their times. Israelis afflicted with the "evil spirit" of existential anxiety can turn to these poems for a penetrating and honest exploration of human existence in Israel. These poems may not be as soothing as David's playing was for Saul or as inspiring as David's psalms have been for pious Jews. Nevertheless, by linking the central issues of Israeli existence with Israel's most ancient literary source, these poets play a special role in the ongoing efforts in Israel to understand the meaning of life.

NOTES

Introduction

1. *Ha'arets,* December 15, 1994.
2. Ibid.
3. Ibid.
4. See Avi Ravitzky's analysis of this event in *Hirhurim be'iqvot duaḥ va'adat Shenhar* (Jerusalem: K.Y.H. and Machon Kerem, 1995), 19–20.
5. Phyllis Trible, *God and the Rhetoric of Sexuality* (Philadelphia: Fortress Press, 1978), 5.
6. Ruth Kartun-Blum, " 'Where does this wood in my hand come from?': The Binding of Isaac in Modern Hebrew Poetry," *Prooftexts* 8 (1988): 293.
7. Ibid.
8. Carmela Perri, "On Alluding," *Poetics* 7 (1978): 306.
9. The one exception to this rule is Amir Gilboa, who was born in 1917. As Warren Bargad notes in his monograph on the poet, Gilboa occupies an ambiguous role in the development of modern Hebrew poetry because his poetry bears traces of the poetry of older generations, particularly that of Bialik and Shlonsky, as well as that of younger poets who wrote primarily during the period shortly before and after Israel was established. See Warren Bargad, *To Write the Lips of Sleepers: The Poetry of Amir Gilboa* (Cincinnati: Hebrew Union College Press, 1994).

10. See David C. Jacobson, *Modern Midrash: The Retelling of Traditional Jewish Narratives by Twentieth-Century Hebrew Writers* (Albany: State University of New York Press, 1987), 1–4, in which I argue that modern retold versions of traditional Jewish narratives should be seen as a continuation of the midrashic tradition.

11. Amir Or and Irit Sela, eds., *Heliqon: sidrah ʾantologit leshirah ʿakhshavit* 12 (Tel Aviv: Helicon Society for the Advancement of Poetry in Israel; Bitan Publishers, 1994), 9.

12. Ibid.

13. Ibid.

14. Amos Oz, *The Slopes of Lebanon*, trans. Maurie Goldberg-Bartura (San Diego: Harcourt Brace Jovanovich, 1989), 121. This is a translation of Amos Oz, *Mimordot halevanon: maʾamarim ureshimot* (Tel Aviv: Am Oved, 1987).

15. Ibid.

16. David H. Hirsch and Eli Pfefferkorn, "Meir Wieseltier: An Israeli Poet Reconstructing the Jewish Past," *The Iowa Review* 4, no. 2 (1973): 62.

17. Ibid.

18. Sidra DeKoven Ezrahi, *By Words Alone: The Holocaust in Literature* (Chicago: University of Chicago Press, 1980), 106.

19. Yair Mazor, "Farewell to Arms and Sentimentality: Reflections of Israel's Wars in Yeduda Amichai's Poetry," *World Literature Today* 60, no. 1 (1986): 17.

20. David Montenegro, "Yehuda Amichai: An Interview," *American Poetry Review* 16, no. 6 (1987): 15.

21. Colin Falck, *Myth, Truth, and Literature: Towards a True Post-Modernism* (Cambridge: Cambridge University Press, 1989), 32.

22. Ibid., 118.

23. Ibid., 37.

24. Ibid., 130.

25. Yuri M. Lotman, *Universe of the Mind: A Semiotic Theory of Culture*, trans. Ann Shukman (Bloomington: Indiana University Press, 1990), 129. See also the application of Lotman's semiotic theory to contemporary Israeli poems on the biblical figure Saul in Warren Bargad, "Poems of Saul: A Semiotic Approach," *Prooftexts* 10 (1990): 313–34.

26. Jonathan Culler, *The Pursuit of Signs: Semiotics, Literature, Deconstruction* (Ithaca, N.Y.: Cornell University Press, 1981), 35.

27. Benjamin Harshav, *Language in Time of Revolution* (Berkeley: University of California Press, 1993), 130. In this passage Harshav links the relationship of this earlier twentieth-century Hebrew poetry to the Bible with what the early twentieth-century Russian Formalist critic Victor Shklovsky sees as the central purpose of "poetic speech," which is "to remove the automatism of perception . . . [in order to] create the vision which results from that deautomatized perception." See Shklovsky's essay "Art as Technique" (1917) in *Modern Criticism and Theory*, ed. David Lodge (London: Longman, 1988), 27.

28. Harshav, *Language in Time of Revolution*, 130.

29. Robert Alter, "A Poet of the Holocaust," *Commentary*, November 1973, 60.

30. Julia Kristeva, *Revolution in Poetic Language*, trans. Margaret Waller (New York: Columbia University Press, 1984), 59–60.

31. Michael Riffaterre, "The Interpretant in Literary Semiotics," *American Journal of Semiotics* 3, no. 4 (1985): 44.

32. Ziva Ben-Porat, "The Poetics of Literary Allusion," *PTL* 1 (1976): 107.

33. Ibid., 108.

34. Ibid.

35. Chana Kronfeld, "Allusion: An Israeli Perspective," *Prooftexts* 5 (1985): 147.

36. Ben-Porat, "The Poetics of Literary Allusion," 109.

37. Perri, "On Alluding," 293.

38. Nili Scharf Gold, *Lo' kaberosh: gilgulei 'imazhim vetavniyyot beshirat Yehuda Amichai* (Jerusalem: Schocken, 1994), 98.

39. Robert Alter, *After the Tradition: Essays on Modern Jewish Writing* (New York: E. P. Dutton, 1969), 248.

40. Harshav, *Language in Time of Revolution*, 123.

41. Ibid., 127.

42. Ibid., 169–170.

43. Shulamith Hareven, "*Mar hamavet vehanurah ha'adummah: 'iyyunim belashon hatiqshoret 5608–5748 [1948–1988]*," *Leshonenu* 54, nos. 2–4 (1990): 301.

44. Ibid.

45. Nili Segal, "*'Al 'olamo hapiyyuti shel T. Carmi: sihah 'im hameshorer*," *Bitsaron* 15 (1982): 33.

46. Ibid.

47. Ibid.

48. Zvia Ginor, "*Kaf yadi hi' hanoga'at byrekhi: Aryeh Sivan: 'erets ma'lah*," *Itton 77* 102 (1988): 16.

49. Zvi Luz, *Shirat Nathan Yonathan: monografyah* (Tel Aviv: Sifriat Poalim, 1986), 34.

50. Segal, "*'Al 'olamo hapiyyuti shel T. Carmi*," 33.

Chapter One

1. Myron J. Aronoff, "Myths, Symbols, and Rituals of the Emerging State," in *New Perspectives on Israeli History: The Early Years of the State,* ed. Laurence J. Silberstein (New York: New York University Press, 1991), 175.

2. For an assessment of the ongoing role of the Israeli Declaration of Independence, see Yehoshua Arieli, "The Proclamation of Independence: A Forty-Year Perspective," *The Jerusalem Quarterly* 51 (1989): 48–70.

3. See Nurith Gertz, "Social Myths in Literary and Political Contexts," *Poetics Today* 7, no. 4 (1986): 621–39. See also Nurith Gertz, *Shevuyah bahalomah: mitosim batarbut hayisra'elit* (Tel Aviv: Am Oved, 1995). For a discussion of the association between the biblical account of divine revelation at Sinai and the Sinai Campaign of 1956 in Israeli discourse see Yona Hadari-Ramage, "War and Religiosity: The Sinai Campaign in Public Thought," in *Israel: The First Decade of Independence,* ed.

S. Ilan Troen and Noah Lucas (Albany: State University of New York Press, 1995), 355–73.

4. See Charles S. Liebman and Eliezer Don-Yehiya, *Civil Religion in Israel: Traditional Judaism and Political Culture in the Jewish State* (Berkeley: University of California Press, 1983), 30–31. In this work Liebman and Don-Yehiya provide other examples of the adaptation of religious terminology from biblical and postbiblical sources for use as political terminology in Zionist and Israeli discourse.

5. Moli Brug, *"Ḥagigot ha-3,000, hanissayon hari'shon," Ha'arets,* May 26, 1995.

6. Amos Elon, *The Israelis: Founders and Sons* (1971; rpt., New York: Bantam Books, 1972), 365.

7. Ibid., 367.

8. James S. Diamond, *Homeland or Holy Land?: The "Canaanite" Critique of Israel* (Bloomington: Indiana University Press, 1986), 3. See this work for a detailed study of this movement and its founder and central ideologue, the Hebrew poet Yonatan Ratosh.

9. *Ha'arets,* December 30, 1994.

10. Ibid.

11. Ibid.

12. Ibid.

13. Michael Keren, *Ben-Gurion and the Intellectuals: Power, Knowledge, Charisma* (Dekalb: Northern Illinois University Press, 1983), 100–105.

14. Ibid., 108.

15. Benyamin Uffenheimer notes that Ben-Gurion's theory of the Exodus was not entirely original. It derived, he observes, from theories put forth in the early twentieth century by scholars, including Micha Yosef Berdycewski. See Benyamin Uffenheimer, *"Ben-Gurion vehatanakh"* in *Ben-Gurion vehatanakh: 'am ve'artso,* ed., Mordecai Cogan (Beersheva: Ben-Gurion University Press, 1989), 59.

16. Keren, *Ben-Gurion and the Intellectuals,* 104–5.

17. Ibid., 104.

18. Shulamith Hareven, *Tismonet Dulcinea: mivḥar masot* (Jerusalem: Keter, 1981), 133. See also Hareven's three novellas based on biblical stories: *Sone' hanissim* (Jerusalem: Dvir, 1983), in English translation *The Miracle Hater,* trans. Hillel Halkin (San Francisco: North Point Press, 1988); *Navi'* (Tel Aviv: Dvir, 1988), in English translation, *Prophet,* trans. Hillel Halkin (San Francisco: North Point Press, 1990); and *'Aḥarei hayaldut* (Tel Aviv: Dvir, 1994). The three novellas have been collected and published as a trilogy in both Hebrew and English: *Tsima'on: shelishiyyat hamidbar* (Tel Aviv: Dvir, 1996); *Thirst: The Desert Trilogy,* trans. Hillel Halkin (San Francisco: Mercury House, 1996).

19. Hareven, *Tismonet Dulcinea,* 133.

20. Ibid.

21. A. B. Yehoshua, *Between Right and Right,* trans. Arnold Schwartz (Garden City, N.Y.: Doubleday, 1981), 27. This is a translation of A. B. Yehoshua, *Bezekhut hanormaliyyut: ḥamesh masot beshe'elat hatsiyyonut* (Jerusalem: Schocken, 1980).

22. Ibid.

23. Ibid.

24. Keren, *Ben-Gurion and the Intellectuals,* 107.

25. Liebman and Don-Yehiya, *Civil Religion in Israel,* 112.

26. See the discussions of this phenomenon in Liebman and Don-Yehiya, *Civil Religion in Israel* and in Shalom Lilker, *Kibbutz Judaism: A New Tradition in the Making* (New York: Cornwall Books, 1982), 169–82.

27. *Haggadah shel pesaḥ* (Tel Aviv: Hakibbutz Haartzi, 1965).

28. Eli Landau, ed., *Haggadah: meʿavdut leḥerut* (Givatayim: Nisan Peleg, n.d.).

29. Myron J. Aronoff, *Israeli Visions and Division: Cultural Change and Political Conflict* (New Brunswick, N.J.: Transaction Books, 1989), 10. See also Robert C. Rowland, *The Rhetoric of Menachem Begin: The Myth of Redemption Through Return* (Lanham, Md.: University Press of America, 1985), 3.

30. Amos Oz, *In the Land of Israel,* trans. Maurie Goldberg-Bartura (1983; rpt. New York: Vintage Books, 1984), 70–71. This is a translation of Amos Oz, *Poh vesham beʾerets yisraʾel besetav* 1982 (Tel Aviv: Am Oved, 1983).

31. Ibid., 51.

32. Shulamith Hareven, *Mashiaḥ ʾo keneset: masot umaʾamarim* (Tel Aviv: Dvir; Zmora-Bitan, 1987), 22.

33. Ibid.

34. See Nurith Gertz's discussion of the ideological conflicts between the world view of universalistic, humanistic Israelis on the one hand and religious and right-wing Israelis on the other hand in the late 1970s and 1980s in Gertz, *Shevuyah baḥalomah,* chap. 4.

35. Arie Lova Eliav, *New Heart, New Spirit: Biblical Humanism for Modern Israel,* trans. Sharon Neeman (Philadelphia: Jewish Publication Society, 1988), xvii. This is a translation of Arie Lova Eliav, *Lev ḥadash veruaḥ ḥadashah* (Tel Aviv: Am Oved, 1986).

36. Ibid., xxii.

37. Ibid.

38. In a review of Eliav's book, Amos Oz notes that this reliance on the authority of tradition is based on a longstanding practice of secular Zionists to justify their political and cultural program as a legitimate trend that does not violate biblical sources but rather applies the spirit of the Bible to contemporary issues:

> The struggle between the Zionist revolutionaries and the Orthodox keepers of the commandments was unique in that both sides drew arguments and proofs from the Bible and the holy writings. Zionism did not treat its Orthodox opponents as most revolutions treat their opponents. It did not tell them: "Take your holy writings and go to hell!" It did not proclaim its intent to destroy the old world to its very foundations. Rather, it sought to establish—and indeed, succeeded in establishing—for itself a measure of legitimacy from the standpoint of its opponents. In other words, Zionism based its propositions on "their" texts, "their" sources, "their" sages. It argued that its intent was not to destroy the Jewish heritage, but to give it a new interpretation within the framework of the well-known, familiar, legitimate interpretations shaped and reshaped by Jews throughout the course of time.

See Amos Oz, *The Slopes of Lebanon,* trans. Maurie Goldberg-Bartura (San Diego: Harcourt Brace Jovanovich, 1989), 199. This is a translation of Amos Oz, *Mimordot halevanon: maʾamarim ureshimot* (Tel Aviv: Am Oved, 1987).

39. Yehoshafat Harkabi, *Israel's Fateful Hour,* trans. Lenn Schramm (New York: Harper & Row, 1989), 147. This book is a revised version and translation of Yehoshafat Harkabi, *Hakhraʿot goraliyyot* (Tel Aviv: Am Oved, 1986).

40. Ibid., 192.

41. Ibid.

42. Ibid.

43. Ibid., 187.

44. Ibid.

45. Shulamith Hareven, ʿ*Ivrim beʾazza: sifrut, mediniyyut, ḥevrah* (Tel Aviv: Zemora-Bitan, 1991), 220–21.

46. Ibid., 221.

47. Meir Wieseltier, *Davar ʾoptimi—ʿasiyyat shirim* (Tel Aviv: Siman Keri'a, 1976), 106–7.

48. I have consulted an early edition of the Bible in English translation with the Doré illustrations (*The Holy Bible Containing the Old and New Testaments According to the Authorised Versions With Illustrations by Gustave Doré* [London and New York, n.d.]). Each illustration to which Wieseltier refers appears in that edition. The English titles of the illustrations are: "Death of Saul," "Saul Attempts the Life of David," "David and Goliath," "Samson Slaying a Lion," and "Walls of Jericho Falling Down."

49. Nathan Yonathan, *Shirim* (Merhavia: Sifriat Poalim, 1974), 68–69.

50. Nathan Yonathan, *Shirim leʾorekh haḥof* (1962; rpt., Tel Aviv: Sifriat Poalim, 1990), 70–71.

51. Yehuda Amichai, *Gam haʾegrof hayah paʾam yad petuḥah veʾetsbaʿot* (Jerusalem: Schocken, 1989), 131–32. The translation by Benjamin Harshav and Barbara Harshav is from Yehuda Amichai, *A Life of Poetry, 1948–1994* (New York: HarperCollins, 1994), 459–60.

52. Nili Scharf Gold, "*Vehanedarim loʾ nedarim: Yehuda Amichai: Gam haʾegrof hayah paʿam yad petuḥah veʾetsbaʿot,*" *Siman Qeriʾah* 22 (1991): 368.

53. The playful, down-to-earth quality of the speaker's relationship to the Bible is reinforced by the expression *levalbel ʾet hatanakh* ("to confuse the Bible"), which as Nili Scharf Gold notes, borders on slang. Ibid.

54. Nili Scharf Gold sees in this line an expression of the speaker's desire to challenge current political trends, presumably messianically oriented religious Zionism. By placing this unaltered traditional expression in the context of the "confused" biblical expressions Amichai suggests that this too stems from confusion and that any expectation of the State of Israel leading to the supernatural revelation of a Messiah of the House of David is mistaken and needs to be challenged by secular Israelis as much as the mistaken and misleading verses of the Bible he has already "confused." Ibid., 368–69.

55. Yehuda Amichai, *Hazeman* (Jerusalem: Schocken, 1977). The translation by Benjamin Harshav and Barbara Harshav is from Amichai, *A Life of Poetry,* 276.

56. Moshe Dor, *Sirpad umatekhet* (Ramat Gan: Massada, 1965), 155. The translation by Denis Johnson is from Moshe Dor, *Crossing the River: Selected Poems* (Oakville, Ontario: Mosaic Press, 1989), 25.

57. David H. Hirsch and Eli Pfefferkorn, "Meir Wieseltier: An Israeli Poet Reconstructing the Jewish Past," *Iowa Review* 4, no. 2 (1973): 57.

Chapter Two

1. David Ben-Gurion, *Israel: A Personal History* (New York: Funk & Wagnalls, 1971), 225.

2. Myron J. Aronoff, "Myths, Symbols, and Rituals of the Emerging State," in *New Perspectives on Israeli History: The Early Years of the State,* ed. Laurence J. Silberstein (New York: New York University Press, 1991), 179.

3. Haim M. Y. Gevaryahu, *"Zikhronot meḥug hatanakh beveito shel David Ben-Gurion,"* in *Ben-Gurion vehatanakh: ʿam veʾartso,* ed. Mordecai Cogan (Beersheva: Ben-Gurion University Press, 1989), 73.

4. Ibid. Dan Kurzman quotes Gevaryahu as saying that Ben-Gurion "unconsciously believed he was blessed with a spark from Joshua's soul. This helped give him the will to succeed, a sense of destiny." See Dan Kurzman, *Ben-Gurion: Prophet of Fire* (New York: Simon and Schuster, 1983), 26.

5. Nurith Gertz, *Shevuyah baḥalomah: mitosim batarbut hayisraʾelit* (Tel Aviv: Am Oved, 1995), 66.

6. See the discussion of the story of David and Goliath and its relationship to the myth of the few against the many in Nurith Gertz, "Social Myths in Literary and Political Contexts," *Poetics Today* 7, no. 4 (1986): 621–39.

7. Ibid., 622.

8. For example, Shulamith Hareven recounts the shouts of "Arik king of Israel" by supporters of Sharon protesting an anti-Lebanon War demonstration in 1982. See Shulamith Hareven, *The Vocabulary of Peace: Life, Culture, and Politics in the Middle East* (San Francisco: Mercury House, 1995), 158. Nurith Gertz recounts that supporters of Begin sang "Begin king of Israel," in response to a speech he gave in his campaign for reelection as prime minister in 1982. See Gertz, *Shevuyah baḥalomah,* 71.

9. Gideon Levy, *"ʾEzor hadimdumim,"* *Musaf haʾarets,* December 31, 1993, 20.

10. Ibid.

11. Ibid.

12. Ibid.

13. Shimon Peres and Arye Naor, *The New Middle East* (New York: Henry Holt, 1993), 21.

14. *Haʾarets,* February 27, 1994.

15. This association between Amalek and the enemies of the Jews has been a persistent factor in the rhetoric of religious and secular Jewish Israelis since the early years of the State. Tom Segev observes that the image of Amalek played a

central role in the debate in 1951 in the central committee of the then ruling political party Mapai on whether Israel should negotiate with Germany for reparations payments covering Nazi crimes against European Jews in World War II. Those who opposed the reparations cited the verse, "Remember what Amalek did to you" (Deuteronomy 25:17). As Segev notes, they supported their opposition to the reparations negotiations by claiming that just as God commanded Saul to destroy Amalek and not take any spoils from them and then disapproved of Saul's incomplete revenge on Amalek (I Samuel 15), so should modern Israel not seek payments from or reconciliation with Germany, the country once ruled by the Nazis, the contemporary incarnation of Amalek. See Tom Segev, *The Seventh Million: The Israelis and the Holocaust*, trans. Haim Watzman (New York: Hill and Wang, 1993), 207. This is a translation of Tom Segev, *Hamilyon hashevi'i: hayisra'elim vehasho'ah* (Jerusalem: Keter, 1991).

16. Amos Oz, *The Slopes of Lebanon*, trans. Maurie Goldberg-Bartura (San Diego: Harcourt Brace Jovanovich, 1989), 122. This is a translation of Amos Oz, *Mimordot halevanon: ma'amarim ureshimot* (Tel Aviv: Am Oved, 1987).

17. Yehoshafat Harkabi, *Israel's Fateful Hour*, trans. Lenn Schramm (New York: Harper and Row, 1989), 149. This is a revised version and translation of Yehoshafat Harkabi, *Hakhra'ot goraliyyot* (Tel Aviv: Am Oved, 1986).

18. Ibid.

19. *The Jerusalem Report*, March 24, 1994.

20. *New York Times*, February 28, 1994. Eye-witness accounts of this incident were also reported in *Ha'arets*, February 27, 1994.

21. The casualty figures are those determined by the report of the Israeli Shamgar Commission that investigated the massacre as reported in *Ha'arets*, June 26, 1994.

22. *New York Times*, February 28, 1994.

23. Ibid.

24. Ibid.

25. *Ha'arets*, February 27, 1994.

26. *New York Times*, February 28, 1994.

27. Ibid.

28. Ibid., March 1, 1994.

29. *Ha'arets*, February 27, 1994.

30. Ibid.

31. Ibid.

32. Ibid.

33. *The Jerusalem Report*, March 24, 1994.

34. See Yoseph Milman, "The Sacrifice of Isaac and Its Subversive Variations in Contemporary Hebrew Protest Poetry," *Religion and Literature* 23, no. 2 (1991):61–83. A Hebrew version of this essay may be found in Zvi Levi, ed., *Ha'aqedah vehatokhehah: mitos, temah, vetopos besifrut* (Jerusalem: Magnes Press, 1991), 53–72. See also Yisrael Cohen, *Behevyon hasifrut ha'ivrit: hasifrut ha'ivrit le'or mishnato shel C. G. Jung* (Tel Aviv: Eked, 1981), 51–74.

35. See Dan Miron, *"Al sippurei Moshe Shamir,"* in Dan Miron, *'Arba' panim basifrut ha'ivrit bat yamenu: 'iyyunim bytsirot Alterman, Ratosh, Yizhar, Shamir*

(Jerusalem: Schocken, 1975), 453. The reference is to Shamir's essay *"Oedipus ve'Avraham,"* in Moshe Shamir, *Bequlmos mahir* (Merhavia: Sifriat Poalim, 1960), 329–33.

36. Levy, *"'Ezor hadimdumim,"* 20.

37. Yael Zerubavel, "New Beginning, Old Past: The Collective Memory of Pioneering in Israeli Culture," in *New Perspectives on Israeli History,* ed. Silberstein, 193–215; Yael Zerubavel, "The Politics of Interpretation: Tel Hai in Israel's Collective Memory," *AJS Review* 16 (1991): 133–60; and Yael Zerubavel, *Recovered Roots: Collective Memory and the Making of Israeli National Tradition* (Chicago: University of Chicago Press, 1995), chapter 9.

38. Milman, "The Sacrifice of Isaac and Its Subversive Variations in Contemporary Hebrew Protest Poetry," 68.

39. S. Yizhar, *Yemei tsiqlag* (1958; rpt., Tel Aviv: Am Oved, 1970), 804. Quoted in English translation in Robert Alter, *After the Tradition: Essays on Modern Jewish Writing* (New York: E. P. Dutton, 1969), 221–22.

40. Hanoch Levin, *Mah 'ikhpat latsippor: satirot, ma'arkhonim, pizmonim* (Tel Aviv: Hakibbutz Hameuchad, 1987), 89–91. For a review of the controversy surrounding *Malkat 'ambatyah* (or *Malkat ha'ambatyah,* as it was popularly known), see David Shalit, *"Kemo petsatsat zeman,"* *Musaf ha'arets,* May 12, 1995, 34–40.

41. Yitzhak Laor, *Raq haguf zokher* (Tel Aviv: Adam, 1985), 70. See the interpretation of the poem in Milman, "The Sacrifice of Isaac and Its Subversive Variations in Contemporary Protest Poetry," 79–80.

42. Yehuda Amichai, *Shirim 1948–1962* (1962; rpt., Jerusalem: Shocken, 1977), 119.

43. Noam Flinker, "Saul and David in the Early Poetry of Yehuda Amichai," in *The David Myth in Western Literature,* ed. Raymond-Jean Frontain and Jan Wojcik (West Lafayette, Ind.: Purdue University Press, 1980), 170–78.

44. Ibid., 177.

45. See the interpretation in Glenda Abramson, *The Writing of Yehuda Amichai: A Thematic Approach* (Albany: State University of New York Press, 1989), 46.

46. Ziva Shamir, *"Haytah ruah 'aheret: shirat Amichai: retrospeqtivah,"* *Itton 77* 72–73 (1986): 27.

47. Haim Gouri, *Shoshanat ruhot* (1960; rpt., Tel Aviv: Hakibbutz Hameuchad, 1966), 114. The translation by Ruth Finer Mintz is from Ruth Finer Mintz, ed. and trans., *Modern Hebrew Poetry: A Bilingual Anthology* (Berkeley: University of California Press, 1966), 288, 290.

48. William J. Ubrock, "Sisera's Mother in Judges 5 and in Haim Gouri's '*'Immo,'*" *Hebrew Annual Review* 11 (1987): 428.

49. See Dan Pagis's interpretation of the poem in *The Modern Hebrew Poem Itself,* ed. Stanley Burnshaw, T. Carmi, Ezra Spicehandler (New York: Holt, Rinehart and Winston, 1965), 159.

50. Ubrock, "Sisera's Mother in Judges 5 and in Haim Gouri's '*'Immo,'*" 430.

51. Anadad Eldan, *Levado bazerem hakaved* (Tel Aviv: Hakibbutz Hameuchad, 1971), 76.

52. Haim Gouri, *'Ayumah* (Tel Aviv: Hakibbutz Hameuchad, 1979), 53–54. The translation by Warren Bargad and Stanley F. Chyet is from *Israeli Poetry: A*

Contemporary Anthology, ed. Warren Bargad and Stanley F. Chyet (Bloomington: Indiana University Press, 1986), 77.

53. Moshe Dor, *'Ovrim 'et hanahar* (Tel Aviv: Zmora-Bitan, 1989), 101. The translation by Barbara Goldberg is from Moshe Dor, *Khamsin: Memoirs and Poetry by a Native Israeli* (Colorado Springs: Three Continents Press, 1994), 93.

54. In the translation by Barbara Goldberg the subtitle "A Political Poem" does not appear.

55. Yehudit Kafri, *Koranit* (Tel Aviv: Sifriat Poalim, 1982), 16.

56. Haim Gouri, *Tenu'ah lemaga'* (Tel Aviv: Hakibbutz Hameuchad, 1968), 13. The translation by Warren Bargad and Stanley F. Chyet is from *Israeli Poetry,* ed. Bargad and Chyet, 64–65.

57. Warren Bargad, *"To Write the Lips of Sleepers": The Poetry of Amir Gilboa* (Cincinnati: Hebrew Union College Press, 1994), 258, 324.

58. Gouri, *Tenu'ah lemaga',* 24.

59. Nathan Yonathan, *Shirim ba'arov hayam* (Merhavia: Sifriat Poalim, 1970), 16–17. The translation by Richard Flantz is from Nathan Yonathan, *Stones in the Darkness* (Tel Aviv: Sifriat Poalim, 1975), 10.

60. Zvi Luz, *Shirat Nathan Yonathan: monografyah* (Tel Aviv: Sifriat Poalim, 1986), 70.

61. See references to poems not discussed in this chapter based on the binding of Isaac story written in response to Israeli war experiences in Milman, "The Sacrifice of Isaac and Its Subversive Variations in Contemporary Hebrew Protest Poetry." The use of the binding of Isaac story in twentieth-century Hebrew poetry is discusssed in Yisrael Cohen, *Behevyon hasifrut ha'ivrit: hasifrut ha'ivrit le'or mishnato shel C. G. Jung* (Tel Aviv: Eked, 1981), 51–74; Edna Amir Coffin, "The Binding of Isaac in Modern Israeli Literature" in *Backgrounds for the Bible,* ed. Michael Patrick O'Conner and David Noel Freedman (Winona Lake, Ind.: Eisenbrauns, 1987), 293–308; and Ruth Kartun-Blum, "'Where does this wood in my hand come from?': The Binding of Isaac in Modern Hebrew Poetry," *Prooftexts* 8 (1988): 293–310.

62. Aliza Shenhar, *'Edei halom* (Tel Aviv: Alef, 1970), 12. The translation by Linda Zisquit is from *Voices Within the Ark: The Modern Jewish Poets,* ed. Howard Schwartz and Anthony Rudolf (New York: Avon, 1980), 172.

63. Matti Megged, *Mem: (shem sha'ul)* (Tel Aviv: Sifriat Poalim, 1985), 323–24. See the interpretation of this poem in Jeffrey M. Lubell, "The Life of Biblical Narrative: Jewish Retelling of the 'Binding of Isaac' Into the Twentieth Century," B.A. thesis, Harvard University, 1990, 34–37.

64. Megged, *Mem: (shem sha'ul),* 179.

65. Ibid.

66. Ibid., 323.

67. Ibid., 324.

68. In a translation of this poem Howard Schwartz renders *beten,* the Hebrew word for "belly," as "womb." See Schwartz and Rudolf, eds., *Voices Within the Ark,* 126.

69. For examples of such antiwar poetry of the Lebanon War period, see the collections Yehudit Kafri, ed., *Hatsiyyat gevul: shirim mimilhemet levanon* (Tel Aviv: Sifriat Poalim, 1983); Hanan Hever and Moshe Ron, eds., *Ve'eyn tikhlah lige-*

ravot ulehereg: shirah politit bemilḥemet levanon (Tel Aviv: Hakibbutz Hameuchad, 1983).

70. Yehuda Amichai, *She῾at haḥesed* (Jerusalem: Schocken, 1983), 21–22. The translation by Benjamin Harshav and Barbara Harshav is from Yehuda Amichai, *A Life of Poetry, 1948–1994* (New York: HarperCollins, 1994), 345. See the interpretation of this poem in Milman, "The Sacrifice of Isaac and Its Subversive Variations in Contemporary Hebrew Protest Poetry," 77–79.

71. Yair Mazor, "Farewell to Arms and Sentimentality: Reflections of Israel's Wars in Yehuda Amichai's Poetry," *World Literature Today* 60, no. 1 (1986): 17.

72. Ibid., 16.

73. Ibid., 17.

74. Yitzhak Laor, *Laylah bemalon zar* (Tel Aviv: Hakibbutz Hameuchad, 1992), 58. The translation by Gabriel Levin is from *Modern Hebrew Literature* 11 (Autumn/Winter 1993): 32.

75. Kafri, ed., *Ḥatsiyyat gevul,* 20.

76. Dalia Ravikovitch, *᾽Ahavah ᾽amittit* (Tel Aviv: Hakibbutz Hameuchad, 1986), 67–68. The translation by Chana Bloch and Ariel Bloch is from Dalia Ravikovitch, *The Window: New and Selected Poems* (Riverdale-on-Hudson, N.Y.: Sheep Meadow Press, 1989), 98–99.

Chapter Three

1. Dina Porat, "Attitudes of the Young State of Israel toward the Holocaust and Its Survivors: A Debate over Identity and Values" in *New Perspectives on Israeli History: The Early Years of the State,* ed. Laurence J. Silberstein (New York: New York University Press, 1991), 159.

2. Tom Segev, *The Seventh Million: The Israelis and the Holocaust* (New York: Hill and Wang, 1993), 514. This is a translation of Tom Segev, *Hamilyon hashevi῾i: hayisra᾽elim vehasho᾽ah* (Jerusalem: Keter, 1991).

3. Porat, "Attitudes of the Young State of Israel toward the Holocaust," 166.

4. Arye Carmon, "Holocaust Teaching in Israel," *Shoah: A Journal of Resources on the Holocaust,* 3, nos. 2–3 (1982–1983): 22.

5. Segev, *The Seventh Million,* 180.

6. Ibid., 183.

7. Aharon Appelfeld, *Masot beguf ri᾽shon* (Jerusalem: World Zionist Organization, 1979), 89. Appelfeld portrayed this experience in his novel *Mikhvat ha᾽or* (Tel Aviv: Hakibbutz Hameuchad, 1980). For a more detailed discussion of the issues with which Appelfeld had to deal as a Holocaust survivor writer, see David C. Jacobson, "'Kill Your Ordinary Common Sense and Maybe You'll Begin to Understand': Aharon Appelfeld and the Holocaust," *AJS Review* 13 (1988): 129–52.

8. Porat, "Attitudes of the Young State of Israel toward the Holocaust," 162.

9. Charles S. Liebman and Eliezer Don-Yehiya, *Civil Religion in Israel: Traditional Judaism and Political Culture in the Jewish State* (Berkeley: University of California Press, 1983), 102.

10. Porat, "Attitudes of the Young State of Israel toward the Holocaust," 166.

11. Appelfeld, *Masot beguf ri'shon,* 20.

12. Liebman and Don-Yehiya, *Civil Religion in Israel,* 152.

13. Porat, "Attitudes of the Young State of Israel toward the Holocaust," 168.

14. James E. Young quotes this passsage from the English translation of the law in *State of Israel Yearbook* (Jerusalem, 1954), 250–51. See James E. Young, *The Texture of Memory: Holocaust Memorials and Meaning* (New Haven: Yale University Press, 1993), 246–47. See also Israel Gutman, ed., *Encyclopedia of the Holocaust* (New York: MacMillan Publishers, 1990), 4: 1683.

15. Young, *The Texture of Memory,* 245.

16. Porat, "Attitudes of the Young State of Israel toward the Holocaust," 170.

17. Carmon, "Holocaust Teaching in Israel," 23. See also Amos Elon, *The Israelis: Founders and Sons* (1971; rpt., New York: Bantam Books, 1972), 280, and Alan Mintz, *Hurban: Responses to Catastrophe in Hebrew Literature* (New York: Columbia University Press, 1984), 239–42.

18. Quoted in Jacob Robinson, *And the Crooked Shall Be Made Straight: The Eichmann Trial, the Jewish Catastrophe, and Hannah Arendt's Narrative* (Philadelphia: Jewish Publication Society of America, 1965), 138–39.

19. Ibid., 139.

20. Haim Gouri, *Mul ta' hazekhukhit: mishpat yerushalayim* (Tel Aviv: Hakibbutz Hameuchad, 1962), 284–85. See also the discussion of Gouri's response to the Eichmann Trial in Mintz, *Hurban,* 240–44.

21. Segev, *The Seventh Million,* 297.

22. Ibid., 390–91.

23. Ibid., 395.

24. Liebman and Don-Yehiya, *Civil Religion in Israel,* 152.

25. Segev, *The Seventh Million,* 399.

26. Ibid. For further discussion of the role of the Holocaust in the thinking and political rhetoric of Menachem Begin, see Robert C. Rowland, *The Rhetoric of Menachem Begin: The Myth of Redemption Through Return* (Lanham, Md.: University Press of America, 1985).

27. Segev, *The Seventh Million,* 505.

28. Ibid., 506.

29. References to the documentary are from Nurith Gertz, *Shevuyah bahalomah: mitosim batarbut hayisra'elit* (Tel Aviv: Am Oved, 1995), 145–46.

30. Reuters News Service, January 22, 1995.

31. Israel Information Service, January 23, 1995.

32. Carmon, "Holocaust Teaching in Israel," 22.

33. Segev, *The Seventh Million,* 516.

34. Ibid.

35. David G. Roskies, *Against the Apocalypse: Responses to Catastrophe in Modern Jewish Culture* (Cambridge: Harvard University Press, 1984), 261.

36. In my discussion of the term *sho'ah* I expand on the discussion in Uriel Tal, "Excursus on the Term: Shoah," *Shoah: A Review of Holocaust Studies and Commemorations* 1, no. 4 (1979): 10–11.

37. Benjamin Harshav, *Language in Time of Revolution* (Berkeley: University of California Press, 1993), 11.

38. Shulamith Hareven, *Mashiaḥ ʾo keneset: masot umaʾamarim,* (Tel Aviv: Dvir; Zmora-Bitan, 1987), 176.

39. A. B. Yehoshua, *Between Right and Right,* trans. Arnold Schwartz (Garden City, N.Y.: Doubleday, 1981), 13. This is a translation of A. B. Yehoshua, *Bezekhut hanormaliyyut: ḥamesh masot besheʾelat hatsiyyonut* (Jerusalem: Schocken, 1980).

40. See the discussion of these two poems as well as a third poem by Pagis based on the Cain and Abel story, "*ʾAḥim,*" in David C. Jacobson, *Modern Midrash: The Retelling of Traditional Jewish Narratives by Twentieth-Century Hebrew Writers* (Albany: State University of New York Press, 1987), 145–50.

41. Dan Pagis, *Gilgul* (Ramat Gan: Massada, 1970), 22. The translation by Stephen Mitchell is from Dan Pagis, *Points of Departure,* trans. Stephen Mitchell (Philadelphia: Jewish Publication Society of America, 1981), 23.

42. Dan Pagis, *Moaḥ* (Tel Aviv: Hakibbutz Hameuchad, 1975), 7–8. The translation by Warren Bargad and Stanley F. Chyet is from Warren Bargad and Stanley F. Chyet, eds., and trans., *Israeli Poetry: A Contemporary Anthology* (Bloomington: Indiana University Press, 1986), 114.

43. The reference to the raven teaching Adam and Eve how to bury Abel resembles the rabbinic legend that describes how the fowl and the ritually clean animals buried Abel (*Bereshit Rabbah* 22:18).

44. Mintz, *Ḥurban,* 265.

45. Warren Bargad, *"To Write the Lips of Sleepers": The Poetry of Amir Gilboa* (Cincinnati: Hebrew Union College Press, 1994), 49.

46. Amir Gilboa, *Keḥullim vaʾadummim* (1963; rpt., Tel Aviv: Am Oved, 1971), 213. The translation by Ruth Finer Mintz is from Ruth Finer Mintz, ed. and trans., *Modern Hebrew Poetry: A Bilingual Anthology* (Berkeley: University of California Press, 1966), 256. My interpretation of this poem is drawn, in part, on that of Arieh Sachs in Stanley Burnshaw, T. Carmi, Ezra Spicehandler, eds., *The Modern Hebrew Poem Itself* (New York: Holt Rinehart and Winston, 1965), 136–38. See also my interpretation of the poem in Jacobson, *Modern Midrash,* 137–39.

47. Gilboa, *Keḥullim vaʾadummim,* 217. The translation by Stephen Mitchell is from *Ariel* 33–34 (1973): 6.

48. Warren Bargad notes that eye imagery is frequently found in Gilboa's poetry. See Bargad, *"To Write the Lips of Sleepers,"* 40–42.

49. Ibid., 49.

50. Gilboa, *Keḥullim vaʾadummim,* 344. The translation by Shirley Kaufman is from Howard Schwartz and Anthony Rudolf, eds., *Voices Within the Ark: The Modern Jewish Poets* (New York: Avon, 1980), 82.

51. In his interpretation of the poem, Arieh Sachs points out that "the dedicatory note to the volume [*Keḥullim vaʾadummim*] reads: 'With me are my father and mother Haim and Frieda and my brothers and sisters Bella and Joshua and Brunia, Moses, and Sara and Esther' (slaughtered members of his family who appear in many of the poems and often in terms of their biblical namesakes)." See Burnshaw, Carmi, Spicehandler, eds., *The Modern Hebrew Poem Itself,* 143.

52. Eda Zoritte, *Hahayyim, ha'atsilut: peraqim biyografiyyim ve'iyyunim ba-markivim haqabaliyyim-hahasidiyyim shel shirat Amir Gilboa* (Tel Aviv: Hakibbutz Hameuchad, 1988), 37–42; Bargad, *"To Write the Lips of Sleepers,"* 5.

53. In his interpretation of this poem Arieh Sachs connects the situation in the poem with the first act of Shakespeare's *Hamlet,* in which Hamlet's father's ghost appears to him to reveal to him the fact that he was murdered. See Burnshaw, Carmi, Spicehandler, eds., *The Modern Hebrew Poem Itself,* 144.

54. Ibid., 143.

55. Hillel Barzel, *Amir Gilboa: monografyah* (Tel Aviv: Sifriat Poalim, 1984), 118–19.

56. Bargad, *"To Write the Lips of Sleepers,"* 202.

57. See the interpretation by Arieh Sachs in Burnshaw, Carmi, Spicehandler, eds., *The Modern Hebrew Poem Itself,* 143, 144.

Chapter Four

1. Ilana Pardes, *Countertraditions in the Bible: A Feminist Approach* (Cambridge: Harvard University Press, 1992), 17.

2. Natalie Rein, *Daughters of Rachel: Women in Israel* (New York: Penguin Books, 1980), 101–3; Barbara Swirski, "Israeli Feminism New and Old," in *Calling the Equality Bluff: Women in Israel,* ed. Barbara Swirski and Marilyn P. Safir (New York: Pergamon Press, 1991), 294–301.

3. The figure of Lilith has played such a central role in Jewish feminist thinking that one of the first and most influential English-language Jewish feminist journals is called *Lilith.*

4. Lesley Hazleton, *Israeli Women: The Reality Behind the Myths* (New York: Simon and Schuster, 1977), 115.

5. Ibid., 113.

6. Ibid., 115. Ilana Pardes makes the point that feminist responses to the image of Eve tend to be focused on the text of Genesis 2, in which Eve is created after Adam to cure him of his loneliness, rather than the text of Genesis 1, where the woman is created simultaneously with the man and both are described as being in the image of God. See Pardes, *Countertraditions in the Bible,* 18–33.

7. Shalva Weil, "Women and Language in Israel," in *Women in Israel: Studies of Israeli Society, Vol. VI,* ed. Yael Azmon and Dafna N. Izraeli (New Brunswick, N.J.: Transaction Publishers, 1993), 367.

8. Ibid., 364.

9. Ibid., 365.

10. Ilana Pardes's *Countertraditions in the Bible* is an important example of this trend. In this study Pardes refers to similar efforts by Phyllis Trible and Mieke Bal. For other recent examples of this trend, see Christina Buchmann and Celina Spiegel, eds., *Out of the Garden: Women Writers on the Bible* (New York: Fawcett Columbine,

1994), and Judith A. Kates and Gail Twersky Reimer, eds., *Reading Ruth: Contemporary Women Reclaim a Sacred Story* (New York: Ballantine Books, 1994). For an illuminating discussion of the complexities of the portrayal of men and women in the Bible, see Zvi Jagendorf, " 'In the Morning, Behold It Was Leah': Genesis and the Reversal of Sexual Knowledge," in *Biblical Patterns in Modern Literature,* ed. David H. Hirsch and Nehama Aschkenasy (Chico, Calif.: Scholars Press, 1984), 51–60.

11. Yehudit Kafri, *Mal'an shel qayits* (Tel Aviv: Sifriat Poalim, 1988), 9–10.

12. Aryeh Sivan, *'Erets ma'lah* (Tel Aviv: Hakibbutz Hameuchad, 1988), 18–19. The translation by Aryeh Sivan was submitted by the poet for use in this book.

13. Edna Aphek, *Shirim* (Tel Aviv: Eked, 1981), 11.

14. One rabbinic tradition understands "to her dying day" to mean that Michal did have one child but that she died giving birth to that child as a divine punishment for insulting David.

15. Edna Aphek, *Shirim,* 9.

16. Aryeh Sivan, *Nofel lekha bapanim* (Tel Aviv: Sifriat Poalim, 1976), 54.

17. Asher Reich, *Seder hashirim: mivhar 1965–1984 veshirim hadashim* (Tel Aviv: Sifriat Poalim, 1986), 87. A different earlier version of the poem appears in Asher Reich, *Seder nashim: shnei mahzorei shirim* (Tel Aviv: Ah'shav, 1980), 28.

18. Sivan, *'Erets ma'lah,* 13–14.

19. Amir Gilboa, *Kehullim va'adummim* (1963; rpt., Tel Aviv: Am Oved, 1971), 345.

20. In a subtle way, Gilboa reinforces the portrayal of Sarah as preoccupied with the physical, nature, and childbirth, to the exclusion of Abraham's preoccupation with God by changing an allusion to a rabbinic text. In the midrashic text *Bereshit Rabbah* 58:1 it is stated, "[When Sarah was] twenty, she was as beautiful as she was at seven; when she was one hundred, she was as sinless as she was at twenty." In his allusion to this text, the speaker refers only to Sarah's beauty and eliminates any reference to sin, thereby preserving Sarah's distance from Abraham's covenant with God: "At first she looked seven when she was twenty and afterward, for decades she looked twenty."

21. Hillel Barzel, *Amir Gilboa: monografyah* (Tel Aviv: Sifriat Poalim, 1984), 107.

22. Dalia Ravikovitch, *Tehom qore'* (Tel Aviv: Hakibbutz Hameuchad, 1976), 30–31. The translation by Warren Bargad and Stanley F. Chyet is from Warren Bargad and Stanley F. Chyet, eds. and trans., *Israeli Poetry: A Contemporary Anthology* (Bloomington: Indiana University Press, 1986), 188–89.

23. T. Carmi, *Leyad 'even hato'im* (Jerusalem: Dvir, 1981), 30–31. The translation by Grace Schulman is from T. Carmi, *At the Stone of Losses* (Philadelphia: Jewish Publication Society of America, 1983), 9.

24. Grace Schulman, " 'The Voice Inside': Translating the Poetry of T. Carmi," in *Translating Poetry: The Double Labyrinth,* ed. Daniel Weissbort (Iowa City: University of Iowa Press, 1989), 167–68.

25. Gilboa, *Kehullim va'adummim,* 215.

26. Barzel, *Amir Gilboa,* 119.

27. Rachel Chalfi, *Nefilah hofshit* (Jerusalem: Y. Marcus, 1979), 98.

Chapter Five

1. Herbert Weiner, *The Wild Goats of Ein Gedi: A Journal of Religious Encounters in the Holy Land* (1961; rpt., Cleveland: World Publishing Company, 1963), 223.

2. Ibid.

3. David Ben-Gurion, *Israel: A Personal History* (New York: Funk and Wagnalls, 1971), 81.

4. Glenda Abramson, "Amichai's God," *Prooftexts* 4 (1984): 113.

5. Eliezer Schweid, *Hayehudi haboded vehayahadut* (Tel Aviv: Am Oved, 1974), 21.

6. Baruch Kurzweil, *Bemaʾavaq ʿal ʿerkhei hayahadut* (Jerusalem: Schocken, 1969), 247.

7. Ibid.

8. S. Zalman Abramov, *Perpetual Dilemma: Jewish Religion in the Jewish State* (Rutherford, N.J.: Fairleigh Dickinson University Press, 1976), 321.

9. Gershon Shaked, "The Case for Secularism," in *Voices From Israel: Understanding the Israeli Mind,* " ed. Etan Levine (New York: Cornwall Books, 1986), 133.

10. Abramov, *Perpetual Dilemma,* 330.

11. Ibid., 331.

12. Weiner, *The Wild Goats of Ein Gedi,* 247.

13. Ibid., 248.

14. Ibid.

15. Ibid.

16. Avi Ravitzky notes that in public opinion surveys of Jews in Israel more than 20 percent of the respondents say that they do not listen to the radio on the Sabbath. Although this is a good indication of the percentage of Jewish Israelis who can be defined as Orthodox in observance, it would be a mistake, Ravitzky asserts, to consider the rest of the population secular in the fullest sense of the world. In public opinion surveys, Ravitzky notes, 79 percent of Jewish Israelis say that they fast on Yom Kippur, while 57 percent say that they fully endorse the traditional belief that Moses received the Torah at Mount Sinai. Taking into account that respondents to polls often say what they think they should say, it is significant, as Ravitzky observes, that it is still "politically correct" in Israel even for so-called secular Jews to present positions congruent with traditional Judaism. See Ravitzky's comments in *Hirhurim beʿiqvot vaʾadat Shenhar* (Jerusalem K.Y.H. and Machon Kerem, 1995), 24.

17. Abramov, *Perpetual Dilemma,* 321.

18. Ibid.

19. This point became clear to me in a seminar on Hasidism I attended at the Hebrew University in the early 1970s. In this seminar, when the instructor wanted to characterize something as "religious" in a spiritual sense, she used the term *religiyozi,* presumably because the Hebrew adjective *dati* did not have enough of a spiritual connotation.

20. Shaked, "The Case for Secularism," 139.

21. Nurith Gertz, *Shevuyah bahalomah: mitosim batarbut hayisra'elit* (Tel Aviv: Am Oved, 1995), 109.

22. Amos Oz, *In the Land of Israel,* trans. Maurie Goldberg-Bartura (1983; rpt., New York: Vintage Books, 1984), 72. This is a translation of *Poh vesham be'erets yisra'el besetav 1982* (Tel Aviv: Am Oved, 1983).

23. Ibid., 72–73.

24. Shulamith Hareven, *The Vocabulary of Peace: Life, Culture, and Politics in the Middle East* (San Francisco: Mercury House, 1995), 53. Hareven's remarks, in a 1991 interview for Voice of Israel Radio conducted by Benny Hendel, were published in *Yediot Aharonot,* March 15, 1991, and translated by Marsha Weinstein.

25. Ibid.

26. Ibid.

27. Ibid., 55.

28. Ibid., 57.

29. Ibid.

30. These secular Israeli poets explore religious issues in their poems because they sense that there is, as David Tracy puts it, "a religious dimension in . . . ordinary experience." That dimension, according to Tracy, "is most clearly recognized in such limit experiences as (negatively) anxiety or (positively) fundamental trust in the very worthwhileness of our existence." See David Tracy, "Metaphor and Religion: The Test Case of Christian Texts," in *On Metaphor,* ed. Sheldon Sacks (Chicago: University of Chicago Press, 1979), 92–93. For a discussion of how an earlier secular modern Hebrew poet incorporates such religious concerns in her poetry, see David C. Jacobson, "Religious Experience in the Early Poetry of Yocheved Bat-Miriam," *Hebrew Annual Review* 5 (1981): 47–64.

31. Abramson, "Amichai's God," 111–12. Although, as Abramson notes, Amichai is not fully representative of contemporary Israeli poets owing to his religious upbringing, he is far from unique in his preoccupation with religious themes.

32. David Montenegro, "Yehuda Amichai: An Interview," *American Poetry Review* 16, no. 6 (1987): 20.

33. Boaz Arpali, *"Millim 'shelo' mik'an velo' me'akhshav' : 'al ma'amadam shel 'arakhim beshirat Yehuda Amichai,"* *Hasifrut* 29 (1979): 48.

34. Ibid., 50.

35. Abramson, "Amichai's God," 124.

36. Meir Wieseltier, *Kitsur shenot hashishim: shirim 1959–1972* (Tel Aviv: Siman Keri'a; Hakibbutz Hameuchad, 1984), 78–79. In this collection the poem appears in a section titled "Paris, 1964–65."

37. Yehudit Kafri, *Mal'an shel qayits* (Tel Aviv: Sifriat Poalim, 1988), 7.

38. In an observation on my translation Kafri noted that the final word of the poem, *shebenafshenu,* has an amibiguous meaning that is difficult to capture in English. It could mean that Isaac is in Abraham and Sarah's soul (as I translated it), or it could mean that Abraham's and Sarah's lives are dependent on that of Isaac.

39. See the discussion of this theme in Nathan Zach's poetry in Abramson, "Amichai's God," 113–14.

40. Nathan Zach, *Shirim shonim* (1960; 3d ed. Tel Aviv: Hakibbutz Hameuchad, 1974), 65. The translation by Peter Everwine and Shulamit Yasny-Starkman is from Nathan Zach, *The Static Element: Selected Poems* (New York: Atheneum, 1982), 11.

41. Dan Pagis, *Gilgul* (Ramat Gan: Massada, 1970), 24–25. The translations of these poems by Warren Bargad and Stanley F. Chyet are from Warren Bargad and Stanley F. Chyet, eds. and trans., *Israeli Poetry: A Contemporary Anthology* (Bloomington: Indiana University Press, 1986), 111. See the interpretation of these poems in Alan Mintz, *Hurban: Responses to Catastrophe in Hebrew Literature* (New York: Columbia University Press, 1984), 266–67.

42. Zach, *Shirim shonim,* 84. The translation by Warren Bargad and Stanley F. Chyet is from Bargad and Chyet, eds. and trans., *Israeli Poetry,* 134.

43. Chana Kronfeld, "Allusion: An Israeli Perspective," *Prooftexts* 5 (1985): 157.

44. Kronfeld suggests that in effect Zach is challenging in this poem "the very existence of God." Ibid.

45. Nathan Zach, *Kol hehalav vehadevash* (Tel Aviv: Am Oved, 1966), 48–49.

46. Ibid., 56. The translation by Gabriel Levin is from *The Literary Review* 26, no. 2 (1983): 240–41.

47. Dan Pagis, *She'on hatsel* (Merhavia: Sifriat Poalim, 1959), 18.

48. Dan Pagis, *Millim nirdafot* (Tel Aviv: Hakibbutz Hameuchad, 1982), 73. The translation by Stephen Mitchell is from Dan Pagis, *Points of Departure* (Philadelphia: Jewish Publication Society of America, 1981), 7.

49. Maya Bejerano, *Mizmorei 'Iyyov* (Tel Aviv: Hakibbutz Hameuchad, 1993), 44–45. Most of this collection consists of a lengthy poem on Job, whose title is also the title of the collection. The length of the poem, however, puts it outside the framework of this study.

Conclusion

1. This feeling is related to the religious experience to which I referred in chapter 5, described by David Tracy as "a fundamental trust in the very worth-whileness of our existence." See David Tracy, "Metaphor and Religion: The Test Case of Christian Texts," in *On Metaphor,* ed. Sheldon Sacks (Chicago: University of Chicago Press, 1979), 93.

2. Nurith Gertz, *Shevuyah bahalomah: mitosim batarbut hayisra'elit* (Tel Aviv: Am Oved, 1995), 119.

3. Leszek Kolakowski, *The Presence of Myth,* trans. Adam Czerniawski (Chicago: University of Chicago Press, 1989), 70.

4. Ibid., 29.

5. Gertz, *Shevuyah bahalomah,* 9.

6. Kolakowski, *The Presence of Myth,* 105.

7. Ibid.

8. Roland Barthes, *Mythologies,* trans. Annette Lavers (New York: Hill and Wang, 1972), 133.

9. Ibid. See also the discussion of the relevance of Barthes's approach to myth in the study of Israeli literature in Nurith Gertz, "Social Myths in Literary and Political Texts," *Poetics Today* 7, no. 4 (1986): 621.

10. Shulamith Hareven, *The Vocabulary of Peace: Life, Culture, and Politics in the Middle East* (San Francisco: Mercury House, 1995), 18.

11. Ibid., 26.

12. Gertz, *Shevuyah baḥalomah,* 9.

13. See the discussion of this role of myth in Gertz, "Social Myths in Literary and Political Texts," 621–39.

BIBLIOGRAPHY

Abramov, S. Zalman. *Perpetual Dilemma: Jewish Religion in the Jewish State.* Rutherford, N.J.: Fairleigh Dickinson University Press, 1976.

Abramson, Glenda. "Amichai's God." *Prooftexts* 4 (1984): 111–26.

———. *The Writing of Yehuda Amichai: A Thematic Approach.* Albany: State University of New York Press, 1989.

Alter, Robert. "A Poet of the Holocaust." *Commentary,* November 1973: 57–63.

———. *After the Tradition: Essays on Modern Jewish Writing.* New York: E. P. Dutton, 1969.

Amichai, Yehuda. *Gam ha'egrof hayah pa'am yad petuḥah ve'etsba'ot.* Jerusalem: Schocken, 1989.

———. *Hazeman.* Jerusalem: Schocken, 1977.

———. *A Life of Poetry,* 1948–1994. Trans. Benjamin Harshav and Barbara Harshav. New York: HarperCollins, 1994.

———. *Me'aḥorei kol zeh mistater 'osher gadol.* Jerusalem: Schocken, 1976.

———. *She'at haḥesed.* Jerusalem: Schocken, 1983.

———. *Shirim 1948–1962.* 1962. Rpt. Jerusalem: Shocken, 1977.

Aphek, Edna. *Shirim.* Tel Aviv: Eked, 1981.

Appelfeld, Aharon. *Masot beguf ri'shon.* Jerusalem: World Zionist Organization, 1979.

———. *Mikhvat ha'or.* Tel Aviv: Hakibbutz Hameuchad, 1980.

Arieli, Yehoshua. "The Proclamation of Independence: A Forty-Year Perspective." *The Jerusalem Quarterly* 51 (1989): 48–70.

Aronoff, Myron J. *Israeli Visions and Division: Cultural Change and Political Conflict.* New Brunswick, N.J.: Transaction Books, 1989.

———. "Myths, Symbols, and Rituals of the Emerging State." In *New Perspectives on Israeli History: The Early Years of the State,* ed. Laurence J. Silberstein, 175–92. New York: New York University Press, 1991.

Arpali, Boaz. "*Millim 'shelo' mik'an velo' me'akhshav': 'al ma'amadam shel 'arakhim beshirat Yehuda Amichai.*" *Hasifrut* 29 (1979): 44–57.

Bargad, Warren. "Poems of Saul: A Semiotic Approach." *Prooftexts* 10 (1990): 313–34.

———. "*To Write the Lips of Sleepers*": *The Poetry of Amir Gilboa.* Cincinnati: Hebrew Union College Press, 1994.

Bargad, Warren, and Stanley F. Chyet, eds. and trans. *Israeli Poetry: A Contemporary Anthology.* Bloomington: Indiana University Press, 1986.

Barthes, Roland. *Mythologies.* Trans. Annette Lavers. New York: Hill and Wang, 1972.

Barzel, Hillel. *Amir Gilboa: monografyah.* Tel Aviv: Sifriat Poalim, 1984.

Bejerano, Maya. *Mizmorei 'Iyyov.* Tel Aviv: Hakibbutz Hameuchad, 1993.

Ben-Gurion, David. *Israel: A Personal History.* New York: Funk & Wagnalls, 1971.

Ben-Porat, Ziva. "The Poetics of Literary Allusion." *PTL* 1 (1976): 105–28.

Buchmann, Christina, and Celina Spiegel, eds. *Out of the Garden: Women Writers on the Bible.* New York: Fawcett Columbine, 1994.

Burnshaw, Stanley, T. Carmi, and Ezra Spicehandler, eds. *The Modern Hebrew Poem Itself.* New York: Holt, Rinehart and Winston, 1965.

Carmi, T. *At the Stone of Losses.* Trans. Grace Schulman. Philadelphia: Jewish Publication Society of America, 1983.

———. *Leyad 'even hato'im.* Jerusalem: Dvir, 1981.

Carmon, Arye. "Holocaust Teaching in Israel." *Shoah: A Journal of Resources on the Holocaust,* 3, nos. 2–3 (1982–1983): 22–25.

Chalfi, Rachel. *Nefilah ḥofshit.* Jerusalem: Y. Marcus, 1979.

Coffin, Edna Amir. "The Binding of Isaac in Modern Israeli Literature." In *Backgrounds for the Bible,* ed. Michael Patrick O'Conner and David Noel Freedman, 293–308. Winona Lake, Ind.: Eisenbrauns, 1987.

Cohen, Yisrael. *Beḥevyon hasifrut ha'ivrit: hasifrut ha'ivrit le'or mishnato shel C. G. Jung.* Tel Aviv: Eked, 1981.

Culler, Jonathan. *The Pursuit of Signs: Semiotics, Literature, Deconstruction.* Ithaca, N.Y.: Cornell University Press, 1981.

Diamond, James S. *Homeland or Holy Land?: The "Canaanite" Critique of Israel.* Bloomington: Indiana University Press, 1986.

Dor, Moshe. *Crossing the River: Selected Poems.* Oakville, Ontario: Mosaic Press, 1989.

———. *Khamsin: Memoirs and Poetry by a Native Israeli.* Colorado Springs, Co.: Three Continents Press, 1994.

———. *'Ovrim 'et hanahar.* Tel Aviv: Zmora-Bitan, 1989.

———. *Sirpad umatekhet.* Ramat Gan: Massada, 1965.

Eldan, Anadad. *Levado bazerem hakaved.* Tel Aviv: Hakibbutz Hameuchad, 1971.

Eliav, Arie Lova. *Lev ḥadash veruaḥ ḥadashah.* Tel Aviv: Am Oved, 1986.

———. *New Heart, New Spirit: Biblical Humanism for Modern Israel.* Trans. Sharon Neeman. Philadelphia: Jewish Publication Society, 1988.

Elon, Amos. *The Israelis: Founders and Sons.* 1971. Rpt. New York: Bantam Books. 1972.

Ezrahi, Sidra DeKoven. *By Words Alone: The Holocaust in Literature.* Chicago: University of Chicago Press, 1980.

Falck, Colin. *Myth, Truth, and Literature: Towards a True Post-Modernism.* Cambridge: Cambridge University Press, 1989.

Flinker, Noam. "Saul and David in the Early Poetry of Yehuda Amichai." In *The David Myth in Western Literature,* ed. Raymond-Jean Frontain and Jan Wojcik, 170–207. West Lafayette, Ind.: Purdue University Press, 1980.

Gertz, Nurith. *Shevuyah baḥalomah: mitosim batarbut hayisra'elit.* Tel Aviv: Am Oved, 1995.

———. "Social Myths in Literary and Political Contexts." *Poetics Today* 7, no. 4 (1986): 621–39.

Gevaryahu, Haim M. Y. *"Zikhronot meḥug hatanakh beveito shel David Ben-Gurion."* In *Ben-Gurion vehatankh: ʿam veʾartso,* ed. Mordecai Cogan, 70–74. Beersheva: Ben-Gurion University Press, 1989.

Gilboa, Amir. *Kehullim vaʾadummim.* 1963. Rpt. Tel Aviv: Am Oved, 1971.

Ginor, Zvia. *"Kaf yadi hiʾ hanogaʿat byrekhi: Aryeh Sivan: ʾerets maʾlah."* *Itton 77* 102 (1988): 16–17.

Gold, Nili Scharf. *Loʾ kaberosh: gilgulei ʾimazhim vetavniyyot beshirat Yehuda Amichai.* Jerusalem: Schocken, 1994.

———. *"Vehanedarim loʾ nedarim: Yehuda Amichai: Gam haʿegrof hayah paʿam yad petuḥah veʾetsbaʿot."* *Siman Qriʾah* 22 (1991): 361–78.

Gouri, Haim. *ʾAyumah.* Tel Aviv: Hakibbutz Hameuchad, 1979.

———. *Mul taʾ hazekhukhit: mishpat yerushalayim.* Tel Aviv: Hakibbutz Hameuchad, 1962.

———. *Shoshanat ruḥot.* 1960. Rpt. Tel Aviv: Hakibbutz Hameuchad, 1966.

———. *Tenuʿah lemagaʿ.* Tel Aviv: Hakibbutz Hameuchad, 1968.

Gutman, Israel, ed. *Encyclopedia of the Holocaust.* 4 vols. New York: MacMillan Publishers, 1990.

Hadari-Ramage, Yona. "War and Religiosity: The Sinai Campaign in Public Thought." In *Israel: The First Decade of Independence,* ed. S. Ilan Troen and Noah Lucas, 355–73. Albany: State University of New York Press, 1995.

Haggadah shel pesaḥ. Tel Aviv: Hakibbutz Haartzi, 1965.

Hareven, Shulamith. *ʾAḥarei hayaldut.* Tel Aviv: Dvir, 1994.

———. *ʿIvrim beʿazza: sifrut, mediniyyut, ḥevrah.* Tel Aviv: Zmora-Bitan, 1991.

———. *"Mar hamavet vehanurah haʿadummah: ʿiyyunim belashon hatiqshoret 5608–5748 [1948–1988]."* *Leshonenu* 54, nos. 2–4 (1990): 301–9.

———. *Mashiaḥ ʾo keneset: masot umaʾamarim.* Tel Aviv: Dvir; Zmora-Bitan, 1987.

———. *The Miracle Hater.* Trans. Hillel Halkin. San Francisco: North Point Press, 1988.

———. *Naviʾ.* Tel Aviv: Dvir, 1988.

———. *Prophet.* Trans. Hillel Halkin. San Francisco: North Point Press, 1990.

———. *Sone' hanissim.* Jerusalem: Dvir, 1983.

———. *Thirst: The Desert Trilogy.* Trans. Hillel Halkin. San Francisco: Mercury House, 1996.

———. *Tismonet Dulcinea: mivhar masot.* Jerusalem: Keter, 1981.

———. *Tsima'on: shelishiyyat hamidbar.* Tel Aviv: Dvir, 1996.

———. *The Vocabulary of Peace: Life, Culture, and Politics in the Middle East.* San Francisco: Mercury House, 1995.

Harkabi, Yehoshafat. *Hakhra'ot goraliyyot.* Tel Aviv: Am Oved, 1986.

———. *Israel's Fateful Hour.* Trans. Lenn Schramm. New York: Harper & Row, 1988.

Harshav, Benjamin. *Language in Time of Revolution.* Berkeley: University of California Press, 1993.

Hazleton, Lesley. *Israeli Women: The Reality Behind the Myths.* New York: Simon and Schuster, 1977.

Hever, Hanan, and Moshe Ron, eds. *Ve'eyn tikhlah liqeravot ulehereg: shirah politit bemilhemet levanon.* Tel Aviv: Hakibbutz Hameuchad, 1983.

Hirhurim be'iqvot duah va'adat Shenhar. Jerusalem: K.Y.H. and Machon Kerem, 1995.

Hirsch, David H., and Eli Pfefferkorn. "Meir Wieseltier: An Israeli Poet Reconstructing the Jewish Past." *The Iowa Review* 4, no. 2 (1973): 56–70.

The Holy Bible Containing the Old and New Testaments According to the Authorised Versions With Illustrations by Gustave Doré. London and New York, n.d.

Jacobson, David C. " 'Kill Your Ordinary Common Sense and Maybe You'll Begin to Understand': Aharon Appelfeld and the Holocaust." *AJS Review* 13 (1988): 129–52.

———. *Modern Midrash: The Retelling of Traditional Jewish Narratives by Twentieth-Century Hebrew Writers.* Albany: State University of New York Press, 1987.

———. "Religious Experience in the Early Poetry of Yocheved Bat-Miriam." *Hebrew Annual Review* 5 (1981): 47–64.

Jagendorf, Zvi. " 'In the Morning, Behold, It Was Leah': Genesis and the Reversal of Sexual Knowledge." In *Biblical Patterns in Modern Literature,* ed. David H. Hirsch and Nehama Aschkenasy, 51–60. Chico, Calif.: Scholars Press, 1984.

Kafri, Yehudit, ed. *Hatsiyyat gevul: shirim mimilhemet levanon.* Tel Aviv: Sifriat Poalim, 1983.

———. *Koranit.* Tel Aviv: Sifriat Poalim, 1982.

———. *Mal'an shel qayits.* Tel Aviv: Sifriat Poalim, 1988.

Kartun-Blum, Ruth. " 'Where does this wood in my hand come from?': The Binding of Isaac in Modern Hebrew Poetry." *Prooftexts* 8 (1988): 293–310.

Kates, Judith A., and Gail Twersky Reimer, eds. *Reading Ruth: Contemporary Women Reclaim a Sacred Story.* New York: Ballantine Books, 1994.

Keren, Michael. *Ben-Gurion and the Intellectuals: Power, Knowledge, and Charisma.* Dekalb: Northern Illinois University Press, 1983.

Kolakowski, Leszek. *The Presence of Myth.* Trans. Adam Czerniawski. Chicago: University of Chicago Press, 1989.

Kristeva, Julia. *Revolution in Poetic Language.* Trans. Margaret Waller. New York: Columbia University Press, 1984.

Kronfeld, Chana. "Allusion: An Israeli Perspective." *Prooftexts* 5 (1985): 137–63.

Kurzman, Dan. *Ben-Gurion: Prophet of Fire.* New York: Simon and Schuster, 1983.

Kurzweil, Baruch. *Bema'avaq 'al 'erkhei hayahadut.* Jerusalem: Schocken, 1969.

Landau, Eli ed. *Haggadah: me'avdut leḥerut.* Givatayim: Nisan Peleg, n.d.

Laor, Yitzhak. *Laylah bemalon zar.* Tel Aviv: Hakibbutz Hameuchad, 1992.

———. *Raq haguf zokher.* Tel Aviv: Adam, 1985.

Levin, Hanoch. *Mah 'ikhpat latsippor: satirot, ma'arkhonim, pizmonim.* Tel Aviv: Hakibbutz Hameuchad, 1987.

Liebman, Charles S., and Eliezer Don-Yehiya. *Civil Religion in Israel: Traditional Judaism and Political Culture in the Jewish State.* Berkeley: University of California Press, 1983.

Lilker, Shalom. *Kibbutz Judaism: A New Tradition in the Making.* New York: Cornwall Books, 1982.

Lotman, Yuri M. *Universe of the Mind: A Semiotic Theory of Culture.* Trans. Ann Shukman. Bloomington: Indiana University Press, 1990.

Lubell, Jeffrey M. "The Life of a Biblical Narrative: Jewish Retelling of the 'Binding of Isaac' Into the Twentieth Century." B.A. thesis. Harvard University, 1990.

Luz, Zvi. *Shirat Nathan Yonathan: monografyah.* Tel Aviv: Sifriat Poalim, 1986.

Mazor, Yair. "Farewell to Arms and Sentimentality: Reflections of Israel's Wars in Yehuda Amichai's Poetry." *World Literature Today* 60, no. 1 (1986): 12–17.

Megged, Matti. *Mem: (shem sha'ul).* Tel Aviv: Sifriat Poalim, 1985.

Milman, Yoseph. "The Sacrifice of Isaac and Its Subversive Variations in Contemporary Hebrew Protest Poetry." *Religion and Literature* 23, no. 2 (1991): 61–83.

———. " '*Zakhor 'et 'asher 'asah 'avikha': 'aqedat Yitshaq—yesodot mashma'utah basippur hamiqra'i vegilgulah beshirat hameḥa'ah bat yamenu.*" In *Ha'aqedah vehatokhehah: mitos, temah, vetopos besifrut,* ed. Zvi Levi, 53–72. Jerusalem: Magnes Press, 1991.

Mintz, Alan. *Ḥurban: Responses to Catastrophe in Hebrew Literature.* New York: Columbia University Press, 1984.

Mintz, Ruth Finer, ed. and trans. *Modern Hebrew Poetry: A Bilingual Anthology.* Berkeley: University of California Press, 1966.

Miron, Dan. *'Arba' panim basifrut ha'ivrit bat yamenu: 'iyyunim bytsirot Alterman, Ratosh, Yizhar, Shamir.* Jerusalem: Schocken, 1975.

Montenegro, David. "Yehuda Amichai: An Interview." *American Poetry Review* 16, no. 6 (1987): 15–20.

Or, Amir, and Irit Sela, eds. *Heliqon: sidrah 'antologit leshirah 'akhshavit* 12. Tel Aviv: Helicon Society for the Advancement of Poetry in Israel; Bitan Publishers, 1994.

Oz, Amos. *In the Land of Israel.* Trans. Maurie Goldberg–Bartura. 1983. Rpt. New York: Vintage Books, 1984.

———. *Mimordot halevanon: ma'amarim ureshimot.* Tel Aviv: Am Oved, 1987.

———. *Poh vesham be'erets yisra'el besetav 1982.* Tel Aviv: Am Oved, 1983.

———. *The Slopes of Lebanon.* Trans. Maurie Goldberg-Bartura. San Diego: Harcourt Brace Jovanovich, 1989.

Pagis, Dan. *Gilgul.* Ramat Gan: Massada, 1970.

———. *Millim nirdafot.* Tel Aviv: Hakibbutz Hameuchad, 1982.

———. *Moaḥ.* Tel Aviv: Hakibbutz Hameuchad, 1975.

———. *Points of Departure.* Trans. Stephen Mitchell. Philadelphia: Jewish Publication Society of America. 1981.

———. *Sheʿon hatsel.* Merhavia: Sifriat Poalim, 1959.

Pardes, Ilana. *Countertraditions in the Bible: A Feminist Approach.* Cambridge: Harvard University Press, 1992.

Peres, Shimon, and Arye Naor. *The New Middle East.* New York: Henry Holt, 1993.

Perri, Carmela. "On Alluding." *Poetics* 7 (1978): 289–307.

Porat, Dina. "Attitudes of the Young State of Israel toward the Holocaust and Its Survivors: A Debate over Identity and Values." In *New Perspectives on Israeli History: The Early Years of the State,* ed. Laurence J. Silberstein, 157–74. New York: New York University Press, 1991.

Ravikovitch, Dalia. *ʾAhavah ʾamittit.* Tel Aviv: Hakibbutz Hameuchad, 1986.

———. *Tehom qoreʾ.* Tel Aviv: Hakibbutz Hameuchad, 1976.

———. *The Window: New and Selected Poems.* Trans. Chana Bloch and Ariel Bloch. Riverdale-on-Hudson, N.Y.: Sheep Meadow Press, 1989.

Reich, Asher. *Seder hashirim: mivḥar 1965–1984 veshirim ḥadashim.* Tel Aviv: Sifriat Poalim, 1986.

———. *Seder nashim: shenei maḥzorei shirim.* Tel Aviv: Ah'shav, 1980.

Rein, Natalie. *Daughters of Rachel: Women in Israel.* New York: Penguin Books, 1980.

Riffaterre, Michael. "The Interpretant in Literary Semiotics." *American Journal of Semiotics* 3, no. 4 (1985): 41–55.

Robinson, Jacob. *And the Crooked Shall Be Made Straight: The Eichmann Trial, the Jewish Catastrophe, and Hannah Arendt's Narrative.* Philadelphia: Jewish Publication Society of America, 1965.

Roskies, David G. *Against the Apocalypse: Responses to Catastrophe in Modern Jewish Culture.* Cambridge: Harvard University Press, 1984.

Rowland, Robert C. *The Rhetoric of Menachem Begin: The Myth of Redemption Through Return.* Lanham, Md.: University Press of America, 1985.

Schulman, Grace. " 'The Voice Inside': Translating the Poetry of T. Carmi." In *Translating Poetry: The Double Labyrinth,* ed. Daniel Weissbort, 161–77. Iowa City: University of Iowa Press, 1989.

Schwartz, Howard, and Anthony Rudolf, eds. *Voices Within the Ark: The Modern Jewish Poets.* New York: Avon Books, 1980.

Schweid, Eliezer. *Hayehudi haboded vehayahadut.* Tel Aviv: Am Oved, 1974.

Segal, Nili. " ʿAl ʿolamo hapiyyuti shel T. Carmi: siḥah ʿim hameshorer." *Bitsaron* 15 (1982): 30–34.

Segev, Tom. *Hamilyon hasheviʿi: hayisraʾelim vehashoʾah.* Jerusalem: Keter, 1991.

———. *The Seventh Million: The Israelis and the Holocaust.* Trans. Haim Watzman. New York: Hill and Wang, 1993.

Shaked, Gershon. "The Case for Secularism." In *Voices From Israel: Understanding the Israeli Mind,* ed. Etan Levine, 128–43. New York: Cornwall Books, 1986.

Shamir, Moshe. *Bequlmos mahir.* Merhavia: Sifriat Poalim, 1960.

Shamir, Ziva. "*Haytah ruah 'aheret: shirat Amichai. retrospeqtivah.*" *Itton 77* 72–73 (1986): 27–28.

Shenhar, Aliza. *'Edei halom.* Tel Aviv: Alef, 1970.

Shklovsky, Victor. "Art As Technique." In *Modern Criticism and Theory,* ed. David Lodge, 16–30. London: Longman, 1988.

Sivan, Aryeh. *'Erets ma'lah.* Tel Aviv: Hakibbutz Hameuchad, 1988.

———. *Nofel lekha bapanim.* Tel Aviv: Sifriat Poalim, 1976.

Swirski, Barbara. "Israeli Feminism New and Old." In *Calling the Equality Bluff: Women in Israel,* ed. Barbara Swirski and Marilyn P. Safir, 285–302. New York: Pergamon Press, 1991.

Tal, Uriel. "Excursus on the Term: *Shoah.*" *Shoah: A Review of Holocaust Studies and Commemorations* 1, no. 4 (1979): 10–11.

Tracy, David. "Metaphor and Religion: The Test Case of Christian Texts." In *On Metaphor,* ed. Sheldon Sacks, 89–104. Chicago: University of Chicago Press, 1979.

Trible, Phyllis. *God and the Rhetoric of Sexuality.* Philadelphia: Fortress Press, 1978.

Ubrock, William J. "Sisera's Mother in Judges 5 and in Haim Gouri's '*'Immo.*'" *Hebrew Annual Review* 11 (1987): 423–31.

Uffenheimer, Benyamin. "*Ben-Gurion vehatanakh.*" In *Ben-Gurion vehatankh: 'am ve'artso,* ed. Mordecai Cogan, 54–69. Beersheva: Ben-Gurion University Press, 1989.

Weil, Shalva. "Women and Language in Israel." In *Women in Israel: Studies of Israeli Society, Vol. VI,* ed. Yael Azmon and Dafna N. Izraeli, 363–77. New Brunswick, N.J.: Transaction Publishers, 1993.

Weiner, Herbert, *The Wild Goats of Ein Gedi: A Journal of Religious Encounters in the Holy Land.* 1961. Rpt. Cleveland: World Publishing Company, 1963.

Wieseltier, Meir. *Davar 'optimi—'asiyyat shirim.* Tel Aviv: Siman Keri'a, 1976.

———. *Qitsur shenot hashishim: shirim 1959–1972.* Tel Aviv: Hakibbutz Hameuchad, 1984.

Yehoshua, A. B. *Between Right and Right.* Trans. Arnold Schwartz. Garden City, N.Y.: Doubleday, 1981.

———. *Bezekhut hanormaliyyut: hamesh masot beshe'elat hatsiyyonut.* Jerusalem: Schocken, 1980.

Yizhar, S. *Yemei tsiqlag.* 1958. Rpt. Tel Aviv: Am Oved, 1970.

Yonathan, Nathan. *Shirim.* Merhavia: Sifriat Poalim, 1974.

———. *Shirim ba'arov hayam.* Merhavia: Sifriat Poalim, 1970.

———. *Shirim le'orekh hahof.* 1962. Rpt. Tel Aviv: Sifriat Poalim, 1990.

———. *Stones in the Darkness.* Trans. Richard Flantz. Tel Aviv: Sifriat Poalim, 1975.

Young, James E. *The Texture of Memory: Holocaust Memorials and Meaning.* New Haven: Yale University Press, 1993.

———. *Writing and Rewriting the Holocaust: Narrative and the Consequences of Interpretation.* Bloomington: Indiana University Press, 1988.

Zach, Nathan. *Kol heḥalav vehadevash.* Tel Aviv: Am Oved, 1966.

———. *Shirim shonim.* 1960. 3d ed. Tel Aviv: Hakibbutz Hameuchad, 1974.

———. *The Static Element: Selected Poems.* Trans. Peter Everwine and Shulamit Yasny-Starkman. New York: Atheneum, 1982.

Zerubavel, Yael. "New Beginning, Old Past: The Collective Memory of Pioneering in Israeli Culture." In *New Perspectives on Israeli History: The Early Years of the State,* ed. Laurence J. Silberstein, 193–215. New York: New York University Press, 1991.

———. "The Politics of Interpretation: Tel Hai in Israel's Collective Memory." *AJS Review* 16 (1991): 133–60.

———. *Recovered Roots: Collective Memory and the Making of Israeli National Tradition.* Chicago: University of Chicago Press, 1995.

Zoritte, Eda. *Haḥayyim, haʾatsilut: peraqim biyografiyyim veʿiyyunim bamarkivim haqabaliyyim-haḥasidiyyim shel shirat Amir Gilboa.* Tel Aviv: Hakibbutz Hameuchad, 1988.

INDEX OF NAMES AND SUBJECTS

INDEX OF BIBLICAL PASSAGES